Modern Critical Views

Chinua Achebe
Henry Adams
Aeschylus
S. Y. Agnon
Edward Albee
Raphael Alberti
Louisa May Alcott
A. R. Ammons
Sherwood Anderson
Aristophanes
Matthew Arnold
Antonin Artaud
John Ashbery
Margaret Atwood
W. H. Auden
Jane Austen
Isaac Babel
Sir Francis Bacon
James Baldwin
Honoré de Balzac
John Barth
Donald Barthelme
Charles Baudelaire
Simone de Beauvoir
Samuel Beckett
Saul Bellow
Thomas Berger
John Berryman
The Bible
Elizabeth Bishop
William Blake
Giovanni Boccaccio
Heinrich Böll
Jorge Luis Borges
Elizabeth Bowen
Bertolt Brecht
The Brontës
Charles Brockden Brown
Sterling Brown
Robert Browning
Martin Buber
John Bunyan
Anthony Burgess
Kenneth Burke
Robert Burns
William Burroughs
George Gordon, Lord
  Byron
Pedro Calderón de la Barca
Italo Calvino
Albert Camus
Canadian Poetry: Modern
  and Contemporary
Canadian Poetry through
  E. J. Pratt
Thomas Carlyle
Alejo Carpentier
Lewis Carroll
Willa Cather
Louis-Ferdinand Céline
Miguel de Cervantes

Geoffrey Chaucer
John Cheever
Anton Chekhov
Kate Chopin
Chrétien de Troyes
Agatha Christie
Samuel Taylor Coleridge
Colette
William Congreve & the
  Restoration Dramatists
Joseph Conrad
Contemporary Poets
James Fenimore Cooper
Pierre Corneille
Julio Cortázar
Hart Crane
Stephen Crane
e. e. cummings
Dante
Robertson Davies
Daniel Defoe
Philip K. Dick
Charles Dickens
James Dickey
Emily Dickinson
Denis Diderot
Isak Dinesen
E. L. Doctorow
John Donne & the
  Seventeenth-Century
  Metaphysical Poets
John Dos Passos
Fyodor Dostoevsky
Frederick Douglass
Theodore Dreiser
John Dryden
W. E. B. Du Bois
Lawrence Durrell
George Eliot
T. S. Eliot
Elizabethan Dramatists
Ralph Ellison
Ralph Waldo Emerson
Euripides
William Faulkner
Henry Fielding
F. Scott Fitzgerald
Gustave Flaubert
E. M. Forster
John Fowles
Sigmund Freud
Robert Frost
Northrop Frye
Carlos Fuentes
William Gaddis
André Gide
W. S. Gilbert
Allen Ginsberg
J. W. von Goethe
Nikolai Gogol
William Golding

Oliver Goldsmith
Mary Gordon
Günther Grass
Robert Graves
Graham Greene
Thomas Hardy
Nathaniel Hawthorne
William Hazlitt
H. D.
Seamus Heaney
Lillian Hellman
Ernest Hemingway
Hermann Hesse
Geoffrey Hill
Friedrich Hölderlin
Homer
A. D. Hope
Gerard Manley Hopkins
Horace
A. E. Housman
William Dean Howells
Langston Hughes
Ted Hughes
Victor Hugo
Zora Neale Hurston
Aldous Huxley
Henrik Ibsen
Eugene Ionesco
Washington Irving
Henry James
Dr. Samuel Johnson and
  James Boswell
Ben Jonson
James Joyce
Carl Gustav Jung
Franz Kafka
Yasonari Kawabata
John Keats
Søren Kierkegaard
Rudyard Kipling
Melanie Klein
Heinrich von Kleist
Philip Larkin
D. H. Lawrence
John le Carré
Ursula K. Le Guin
Giacomo Leopardi
Doris Lessing
Sinclair Lewis
Jack London
Frederico García Lorca
Robert Lowell
Malcolm Lowry
Norman Mailer
Bernard Malamud
Stéphane Mallarmé
Thomas Malory
André Malraux
Thomas Mann
Katherine Mansfield
Christopher Marlowe

Modern Critical Views

Modern Critical Views

ANDREW MARVELL

Edited and with an introduction by
Harold Bloom
Sterling Professor of Humanities
Yale University

CHELSEA HOUSE PUBLISHERS
New York ◊ Philadelphia

Printed and bound in the United States of America

10 9 8 7 6 5 4 3 2 1

Library of Congress Cataloging-in-Publication Data
Andrew Marvell.
    (Modern critical views)
    Bibliography: p.
    Includes index.
    1. Marvel, Andrew, 1621-1678—Criticism and
interpretation. I. Bloom, Harold. II. Series.
PR3546.A865 1988   821'.4   87-25697
ISBN 1-55546-320-7

Contents

Editor's Note

This book brings together a representative selection of the best criticism of the poetry of Andrew Marvell that has been published during the last quarter-century, arranged in the chronological order of its publication. I am grateful to John Rogers and Bruce Covey for their erudite aid in editing this volume.

My introduction centers on the enigma of the Mower poems, where European pastoral achieves its apotheosis. John Hollander, poet and scholar, reads "Music's Empire" as a grand instance of "the untuning of the sky," the passage of celestial harmonics into belated poetry. The "Horatian Ode" and the "First Anniversary" are interpreted by Ruth Nevo as contrasting the world's praise of Cromwell's qualities and power with the poet's own vision of "the huge, suprapersonal movement of events to which the hero is servant and instrument."

Geoffrey Hartman provides an intricate exegesis of the astonishingly subtle "The Nymph Complaining for the Death of Her Faun," which he views as bringing the history of pastoral allegory to its close. In a study informed partly by the observations upon visual Mannerism of Arnold Hauser, Louis L. Martz provides an overview of Marvell's poetry that demonstrates its many affinities with Mannerist art.

"The Garden" is interpreted by Donald M. Friedman as a paradoxical vision whose burden "is that man must transcend his natural faculties if he is ever to understand nature correctly and live harmoniously with her." "Upon Appleton House," Marvell's most ambitious poem, is related to visual traditions by Rosalie Colie, and is studied by Isabel G. MacCaffrey as a conscious instance of a poem reflecting upon both the scope and limits of its own imagination. Between Colie and MacCaffrey, David Kalstone charts the place of Marvell in pastoral tradition, with particular reference to Theocritus and to Virgil.

Michael Seidel examines the relation of Marvell's satire "The Last Instructions to a Painter" to Dryden's theories of satire. "To His Coy Mistress," Marvell's most famous poem, is contrasted with his "The Garden" by Cleanth Brooks, one of the most eminent of American formalist critics of T. S. Eliot's school.

Marvell's extraordinary poem on Milton's *Paradise Lost* is illuminated by Kenneth Gross, who sees the poem as yielding to Milton what is Milton's while keeping for Marvell what is truly his own. The satire *The Rehearsal Transpros'd* is analyzed by Warren Chernaik as a quest for form, after which Michael McKeon concludes this volume with an appreciation of Marvell's lifelong labor for a "positive secularization" of society and culture.

Introduction

M arvell is the most enigmatic, unclassifiable, and unaffiliated major poet in the language. It is finally unhelpful to call his poetry Metaphysical, Mannerist, Epicurean, Platonist, or Puritan, though all of those terms somehow are applicable. One of the most original poets in Western tradition, Marvell had no strong precursors, though Spenser may be near his hidden root. His poetry has a clear relation to the schools of Donne and Jonson, but is of neither, unlike that of such contemporaries as Randolph, Carew, and Lovelace. The distance from Milton, his greatest contemporary and the subject of one of his most admirable and admiring poems, is remarkable. His authentic affinities were with quite minor French poets who came after the Pléiade, Théophile de Viau (1590–1626) and Antoine-Girard de Saint-Amant (1594–1661).

Post-Pléiade French pastoralists can be said to have invented Marvell's lyric mode, but there is absolutely nothing Gallic about Marvell's own poetry. Nor are there Marvellian poets after Marvell. T.S. Eliot, though his essay on Marvell has been so influential, is a Tennysonian-Whitmanian elegist of the self, whose actual verse has more in common with that of William Morris than with Marvell.

Eliot's celebrated essay, still being exalted by Frank Kermode and others, is in fact quite bad, being replete with irrelevant assertions as to how much better a poet Marvell is than Shelley, Keats, Wordsworth, Tennyson, Browning, Hardy, and Yeats, all of whom lacked what Eliot "designated tentatively as wit, a tough reasonableness beneath the slight lyric grace." We learn also from Eliot that Marvell surpasses the "L' Allegro" and "Il Penseroso" of Milton, a judgment that might have provoked some amiable skepticism in Marvell himself. Poor William Morris, a poet not very relevant to Marvell's mode, is also dragged in for a drubbing, and Eliot concludes that Browning, whose "A Toccata of Galuppi's" may be the most maturely sophisticated shorter poem in the language, "seems oddly immature, in some way, beside Marvell." Two years after his 1921 essay on Marvell, Eliot changed his mind anyway, in a review of the Nonesuch Press

1

edition of Marvell's *Miscellaneous Poems,* where we learn that Marvell, unlike Chaucer and Pope, is "fantastical," conceit-ridden, and is in any case not as great a poet as Bishop Henry King, author of the "Exequy," but not of much more that engages us now. Though Kermode is Eliot's declared inheritor as a Marvell critic, I find his general emphasis more useful than his precursor's:

> To conclude: Marvell is not a philosophical poet; in his role as poet he engaged his subjects as poetry, bringing to them a mind of great intelligence and intelligently ordered learning. Our knowledge of his religious and political thought helps us only a little more than our knowledge of his personal life (quick temper, preference for solitary drinking) and can be related to the substance of his poetry only very cautiously and generally (the power of a mind engaged but detached, the alertness, leaning on the wind). Negatively, we can learn a lot from other poetry, and from the nature and contemporary use of allegory (habitual intermittency defined by the cult of acuteness or wit, and the resonantly defined detail). Broad categories are misleading; using words such as "puritan," "Platonist," even such as "nature" and "wit," we must constantly discriminate: wit is not seventeenth-century property but an ancient instrument of poetry and of religion, nature an indescribably complex inheritance of assumptions and meanings.

My only dissent here would be to go a bit further; that Marvell was a bad-tempered, hard-drinking lifelong bachelor and controversialist is more helpful knowledge than everything we know of his religion and politics, for the paradoxical reason that such a personality simply does not manifest itself in the poems, except perhaps for the satires. The Mower poems, my subject in this introduction, could have been written by a good-tempered married man who never touched alcohol and had little notion of religious and political quarrels. Yet they are at once absolutely idiosyncratic and personal, and totally universal in scope and emphasis, which is only to say that they are very great, very enigmatic lyric poems rather than philosophical tractates or scholarly investigations.

If Marvell is a poet's poet, then his lyrics and meditations have a particularly refreshing function for us right now, when poetry is studied as everything except poetry, be it politics, societal discontents, gender struggles, historicisms, philosophies, psychologies, semiotics, or what you will. Good critics, when once they still read poems as poems, accurately found in Marvell the culmination of the European pastoral lyric that Theocritus had inaugurated. Thomas G. Rosenmeyer, in his fine book on Theocritus, *The Green Cabinet* (1969), concluded that in the pastoral mode, "the poem as a whole is a trope, rather than any one portion of it." As a principle, this seems truer even of Marvell than of Theocritus and Virgil. Marvell's Mower poems are extended metaphors for a highly individual view of how our fall caused nature's loss of value also, so that the wounding power of sexual love became the wound that sexuality itself ended by being. William Empson interpreted the Mower most grandly:

> In these meadows he feels he has left his mark on a great territory,
> if not on everything, and as a typical figure he has mown all the
> meadows of the world; in either case Nature gives him regal and
> magical honors, and I suppose he is not only the ruler but the
> executioner of the daffodils—the Clown as Death.

In one aspect the pastoral Mower may be the Clown as Death, but in the enigmatic Mower poems this most original of Marvell's tropes cannot be uncovered once and for all. In "The Mower against Gardens," the Mower ends by insisting that "the gods themselves with us do dwell," presumably because we are not altogether fallen anymore than nature is, since "the sweet fields" still "to all dispense / A wild and fragrant innocence." This is very different from the extraordinary triad of "Damon the Mower," "The Mower to the Glow-worms," and "The Mower's Song," all of them reliant upon a great text in Isaiah:

> The voice said, Cry. And he said, What shall I cry? All flesh is grass,
> and all the goodliness thereof is as the flower of the field:
>   The grass withereth, the flower fadeth: because the spirit of the
> LORD bloweth upon it: surely the people is grass.
>   The grass withereth, the flower fadeth: but the word of our God
> shall stand for ever.
>
> (Isa. 40:6–8)

In Walt Whitman, the grass becomes flesh, a metamorphosis in which Marvell preceded Whitman. Damon the Mower, stung by Juliana's scorching beams, attains involuntarily a congruence of inner qualities and outer emblems:

> Sharp like his scythe his sorrow was,   .
> And withered like his hopes the grass.

Marvell's Mower, absurdly enough, is both the ridiculous Polyphemus, the Cyclops of Theocritus, and, I suspect, the Adam Kadmon or unfallen God-Man of Kabbalistic and Hermetic tradition. That is, Damon is Adam, Adam both debased beneath and exalted beyond the Adam of Genesis. Damon is the Clown as Death, if you will, but he is (or was) also the Clown as a more abundant, preexistent life, not so much the Cyclops or Virgil's Corydon as the

Platonic dream of a divine human before the crashing downwards of a catastrophic creation. Marvell's more-than-ironic mode conveys mysteries only through an immensely sophisticated humor, edged by the reality principle of mortality. Ruth Nevo adroitly describes "Damon the Mower" as "a pastoral elegy for the quiet mind disturbed radically by desire unsatisfied," which sensibly leaves undefined whose mind that is, and how cosmological the desire may be. Geoffrey Hartman, sinuously seeking to match the subtle Marvell, finds the theme of the Mower poems in "the labor of hope," with "hope in nature frustrated by love or by the very strength of hope." Hartman's Mower is rather like the afflicted heroine of Wordsworth's "The Ruined Cottage"; what had been cultivated in hope is now destroyed in hope, as the end is hastened. The instrument of that hastening is death's scythe, which dominates the final three exquisite stanzas of this eleven-stanza lyric:

> "How happy might I still have mowed,
> Had not Love here his thistles sowed!
> But now I all the day complain,
> Joining my labour to my pain;
> And with my scythe cut down the grass,
> Yet still my grief is where it was:
> But, when the iron blunter grows,
> Sighing, I whet my scythe and woes."
> While thus he threw his elbow round,
> Depopulating all the ground,
> And, with his whistling scythe, does cut
> Each stroke between the earth and root,
> The edgèd steel by careless chance
> Did into his own ankle glance;
> And there among the grass fell down,
> By his own scythe, the Mower mown.
> "Alas!" said he, "these hurts are slight
> To those that die by love's despite.
> With shepherd's-purse, and clown's-all-heal,
> The blood I staunch, and wound I seal.
> Only for him no cure is found,
> Whom Juliana's eyes do wound.
> 'Tis death alone that this must do:
> For Death thou art a Mower too."

"The Mower mown" might well have been the poem's title, except for its neglect of Damon in his self-apotheosis:

"I am the Mower Damon, known
Through all the meadows I have mown.
On me the morn her dew distills
Before her darling daffodils.
And, if at noon my toil me heat,
The sun himself licks off my sweat.
While, going home, the evening sweet
In cowslip-water bathes my feet."

That does not seem to me the Clown as Death so much as the Clown as
Hermetic Adam, living in a place very much his own, and even more his self,
being at home all the time. We see Damon-Adam fall again in stanzas 9–11, and
so lose his home, possibly forever:

The Mower to the Glowworms

Ye living lamps, by whose dear light
The nightingale does sit so late,
And studying all the summer night,
Her matchless songs does meditate;

Ye country comets, that portend
No war, nor prince's funeral,
Shining unto no higher end
Than to presage the grass's fall;

Ye glowworms, whose officious flame
To wandering mowers shows the way,
That in the night have lost their aim,
And after foolish fires do stray;

Your courteous lights in vain you waste,
Since Juliana here is come,
For she my mind hath so displaced
That I shall never find my home.

This extraordinary lyric, addressed by the fallen Mower to the luminaries
of his severely shrunken world, is surely one of the most mysterious and
beautiful poems in the language. I cannot reread it or recite it to myself without
evoking the beautiful quatrains that Blake added to *The Gates of Paradise* when
he reengraved that little Prophetic Book, addressing the quatrains "To the
Accuser Who is the God of this World." But "The Mower to the Glowworms"
has no Jobean associations, even if it too is a lost traveller's dream under the

hill. "The grass's fall" is the fall of the flesh, and the third stanza might almost have been written by William Blake.

The first stanza of "The Mower's Song" recapitulates the last stanza here, where the Mower's mind is displaced, but the revision is in a finer tone:

> My mind was once the true survey
> Of all these meadows fresh and gay,
> And in the greenness of the grass
> Did see its hopes as in a glass;
> When Juliana came, and she
> What I do to the grass, does to my thoughts and me.

Juliana is the Charmer as Death, and the remainder of the poem centers itself upon the extraordinary revelations of that last line, Marvell's solitary and unique instance of a refrain:

> But these, while I with sorrow pine,
> Grew more luxuriant still and fine,
> That not one blade of grass you spied,
> But had a flower on either side;
> When Juliana came, and she
> What I do to the grass, does to my thoughts and me.

> Unthankful meadows, could you so
> A fellowship so true forgo,
> And in your gaudy May-games meet,
> While I lay trodden under feet?
> When Juliana came, and she
> What I do to the grass, does to my thoughts and me.

> But what you in compassion ought,
> Shall now by my revenge be wrought:
> And flow'rs, and grass, and I and all,
> Will in one common ruin fall.
> For Juliana comes, and she
> What I do to the grass, does to my thoughts and me.

> And thus, ye meadows, which have been
> Companions of my thoughts more green,
> Shall now the heraldry become
> With which I will adorn my tomb;
> For Juliana comes, and she
> What I do to the grass, does to my thoughts and me.

Damon, resenting the flowers, truly resents a green world that will survive his own now irretrievable fall. But his true resentment is also an apocalyptic paradox, since his "revenge" of "one common ruin" is pragmatically a further riot of what Whitman calls the flag of the poet's disposition, out of hopeful green stuff woven. The heraldry of green will make the entire earth the Mower's tomb, but such a heraldry will bury scythe and scyther alike, give death to Death, and perhaps herald the rebirth of Damon as Adam Kadmon, the Primal Man forever not to be mown down.

JOHN HOLLANDER

Marvell's Commonwealth
and "The Empire of the Ear"

Occurrences of *musica speculativa* in the poetry of Andrew Marvell are relatively sparse. With the exception of "Musicks Empire," Marvell's musical references are confined to conventional uses . . . In two of the satires, for example, musical allusions are employed in the ridicule of particular faults and aspirations of the respective victims. In "Clarindon's House-Warming," popular objections to the costly town house of Charles II's Lord Chancellor are used as an occasion for a general vilification of Clarendon. After condemning the barrenness of Clarendon's daughter, wife of the future James II, Marvell harps on the "vanity and folly" which Clarendon himself admitted had characterized his own assumption of the prodigious construction costs.

> And wish'd that his Daughter had had as much grace
> To erect him a pyramid out of her Quarry.
>
> But then recollection how the harper *Amphyon*
> Made *Thebes* dance aloft while he fidled and sung.
>
> He thought (as an Instrument he was most free on)
> To build with the Jews-trump of his own tongue.
> (ll. 15–20)

"Jews-trump" or, more commonly, "jew's harp," was the relatively simple twanging instrument still known to children and rustics. In contrast to Amphion, builder of cities, Clarendon is depicted as having played on a rather opprobrious substitute. But the real point here is that, as Dr. Percy Scholes has pointed

From *The Untuning of the Sky.* © 1961 by John Hollander. Princeton University Press, 1961.

out [in *The Puritans and Music*], the jew's harp was employed during the later seventeenth century as a cheap gimcrack commodity for barter with the American Indian. The "Jews-trump of his own tongue," then, would refer to Clarendon's carelessness about costs and to an implication that his money or his credit was unsound. In these lines, a musical reference is simply part of an invidious mythological comparison, extremely common in all satire, complicated by a further topical joke that refers back to the orignal basis of the comparison as between two builders.

A rather more simple piece of wit, but involving musical lore to a greater degree, occurs in the satire "Fleckno, or an English Priest of Rome." The poet, after having been bored to distraction by his subject's monstrous verses, is subjected to his music-making, when

> the Tyrant, weary to persecute,
> Left off, and try'd t'allure me with his Lute.
>   Now as Instruments, to the same key
> Being tun'd by Art, if the one touched be
> The other opposite as soon replies,
> Mov'd by the Air and hidden Sympathies;
> So while he with his gouty Fingers crawles
> Over the Lute, his murmuring Belly calls,
> Whose hungry Guts to the same streightness twin'd
> In Echo to the trembling Strings repin'd.
>   I, that perceiv'd now what his Musick meant,
> Asked civilly if he had eat this Lent.
>
> (ll. 35–46)

As the gut strings vibrate across the belly of the lute, so rumble the entrails, in sympathetic vibration, of the unfortunate cleric who, for Dryden, "In Prose and Verse was own'd, without disputes / Through all the realms of Non-sense, absolute."

While Marvell may have been prompted by certain musical and/or gastric habits of his target to pinion him in this fashion, the passage is fairly typical of the tradition of Juvenalian, or what Joseph Hall called "biting," satires. In its use of a musical image to represent the feigning or aspirations of one whose actuality is most unmusical, it is suggestive of Donne's lines in his fourth "Satyre," lines 77–78. The fawning sycophant under attack answers the Poet's doubts as to the heuristic value of supposed courtly virtues as "He, like to a high stretcht lute string squeaked, O Sir, / 'Tis sweet to talk of Kings."

If these musical references are little more than accepted satiric devices, a few examples of cosmological hyperbole show rather nicely the course of this musical figure during the later seventeenth century. In his pastoral poems, Marvell conventionally employs the heavenly music as an image of perfection. In "A Dialogue between Thyrsis and Dorinda," a pastoral seduction is conducted as an "Invitation au Voyage." The promised "Elizium" where "tout n'est qu'ordre et beauté" stands to the Arcadian meadow upon which the dialogue occurs as that meadow stands to the world:

> THYRSIS: Oh, ther's neither hope nor fear
> Ther's no Wolf, no Fox, nor Bear.
> No need of Dog to fetch our stray,
> Our Lightfoot we may give away;
> No Oat-pipe's needfull, there thine Ears
> May feast with Musick of the Spheres.
>
> (ll. 21–26)

This "Elizium" resounds to no rustic piping, and the rejection of the syrinx is a little like Polybius' angry denial of the pastoral myths that even in his own time had grown up about his native Arcadia. (It was an ethical realm, he insisted, echoing to no Panic flutes, but where "The children learn to cipher and to sing" in well-regulated academies.) In another poem, "Clorinda and Damon," the wild pastoral piping is itself transformed directly into the *harmonia mundi:*

> Chorus
>
> Of Pan the flowring Pastures sing,
> Caves eccho, and the Fountains ring.
> Sing then while he doth us inspire;
> For all the World is our *Pan's* Quire.

But traditional lore, wrenched from its banal use by a conceit, soon approaches mere overstatement. Thus, Marvell treats the appeal of the Sisters of Nun Appleton to the future Lady Isabel Fairfax so as to employ this sort of figure, although in the context of the poem he probably intends it as a sweet but wanton wile, if not as a blasphemous one:

> Your voice, the sweetest of the Quire
> Shall draw Heav'n nearer, raise us higher.
> ("Upon Appleton House," ll. 161–62)

A more elaborate version of such literally high-flown compliment occurs in "The Fair Singer":

To make a final conquest of all me,
Love did compose so sweet an Enemy,
In whom both Beauties to my death agree,
Joyning themselves in fatal Harmony;
That while she with her Eyes my Heart doth bind,
She with her voice might captivate my Mind.

I could have fled from One but singly fair:
My dis-intangled Soul it self might save,
Breaking the curled trammels of her hair.
But how should I avoid to be her Slave,
Whose subtile Art invisibly can wreath
My Fetters of the very Air I breath?

It had been easie fighting in some plain,
Where Victory might hand in equal choice,
But all resistance against her is vain,
Who has th'advantage both of Eyes and Voice,
And all my Forces needs must be undone,
She having gained both the Wind and Sun.

This is very like Cavalier lyric; we might call it a Metaphysical poem on an Augustan subject. The distinctions between eyes, physical beauty, and the sun, on the one hand, and the voice, intellectual beauty, and the wind, on the other, elegantly support the compliment which raises the lady to the order of the elements themselves. Without the consistent fabric of wit, the elevation would be an unsteady one.

Marvell's most elaborate use of a figure from traditional *musica speculativa* occurs toward the beginning of "The First Anniversary of the Government under O. C." This long musical conceit starts out with the observation that inadequate rulers "No more contribute to the state of Things, / Then wooden Heads unto the Viols strings," an image even more precise than the modern cliché of the figurehead upon the ship of state. Following this, a rather direct cosmological hyperbole leads into an elaborate comparison of Cromwell to Amphion, and a brilliant version of the old notion of the state as a musical concord:

While indefatigable *Cromwell* hyes,
And cuts his way still nearer to the Skyes,
Learning a Musique in the Region clear,
To tune this lower to that higher sphere.

So when *Amphion* did the Lute command.
Which the God gave him, with his gentle hand,
The rougher Stones, unto his Measures hew'd,
Dans'd up in order from the Qarreys rude;
This took a Lower, that an Higher place,
As he the Treble alter'd, or the Base:
No Note he struck, but a new Story lay'd,
And the great Work ascended while he play'd.
    The listning Structures he with Wonder ey'd,
And still new Stopps to various Time apply'd:
Now through the Strings a Martial rage he throws,
And joyning streight the *Theban* Tow'r arose;
Then as he strokes them with a Touch more sweet,
The flocking Marbles in a Palace meet;
But, for he most the graver Notes did try,
Therefore the Temples rear'd their Columns high:
Thus, ere he ceas'd, his sacred Lute creates
Th'harmonious City of the seven Gates.
Such was that wondrous Order and Consent,
When *Cromwell* tun'd the ruling Instrument;
While tedious Statesmen many years did hack,
Framing a Liberty that still went back;
Whose num'rous Gorge could swallow in an hour
That Island, which the Sea cannot devour:
Then our *Amphion* issues out and sings,
And once he struck, and twice, the pow'rful Strings.

(ll. 45–74)

The "ruling Instrument" is the Instrument of Government of 1653 by means of which Cromwell established the Protectorate. Significantly, Marvell has clearly distinguished between the Instrument, or means, and the harmony of the state itself, or end. The heavenly figure in lines 47–48 is supported argumentatively by the reference, in the following couplet, to the traditional imitation of cosmic harmony in practical music. The actual creation of the state is allegorized in the story of Amphion's legendary founding of the city of Thebes in a marvellous way. The changes of pitch sounded upon the governing instrument control the corresponding architectural positions of the dancing masonry, and, by extension, create corresponding degrees in the order of nature. But following this (ll. 57–66), the already ordered structures again arrange themselves, this time with respect to differences of kind and use. These final arrangements, however, are effected not by the varying pitches of the music, but by the respective modes employed. As we have already seen, garbled notions of Greek modality, traditionally handed down, had become by the seventeenth century purely literary, esthetic concepts. Although no particular modes are mentioned by name in this passage, it is quite clear that Marvell's readers might have recognized in "a Martial rage" the Phrygian, in "a touch more sweet" the Hypolydian, and in "the graver Notes," the Dorian mode, their conventional affections being rousing, voluptuous, and stately, respectively. In running through various modes on his instrument, Cromwell-Amphion effects certain changes in the state of the world; I think that another myth can be seen to intrude itself here. Cromwell is being covertly invoked as Timotheus, the fictional musician of the court of Alexander the Great. A famous anecdote about him, retold by John Case in *The Praise of Music* and later employed by Dryden, tells how the fabulous performer, playing Phrygian and Dorian melodies in succession, first urges his monarch to the brink of war and then rapidly calms him again.

The stated comparison throughout this passage, however, treats Cromwell as Amphion, and all the precise elaboration can be seen as the kind of writing that would ordinarily be expected of Marvell, an intricate conceit employing knowledge, lore, and doctrine with the same immediacy as if they were the data of direct sensuous experience. And while the musical ideas here employed are of a completely conventional variety, Marvell's particular use of them in praise of Cromwell raises an interesting problem.

What looked to be a far-reaching critical controversy arose in the recent past over the nature of Marvell's political attitude toward Cromwell as expressed in the "Horatian Ode upon Cromwell's Return from Ireland." Cleanth Brooks, arguing from an ironic reading of the beginning phrase, "The forward Youth," and of

> So restless *Cromwell* could not cease
> In the inglorious Arts of Peace,
> > But through adventurous War
> > Urged his Active Star,
>
> > > (ll. 9–12)

maintained that the received view that Marvell was unambiguously praising Cromwell would simply not do. He went on to insist that these and other ironies demanded a reading which would account for what he calls the "tension" in the poem's language by referring, in some way, to attitudes. Douglas Bush replied that he could see no irony at all in the poem, that the praise intended was direct and bold. In describing Marvell as a "17th century liberal," Professor

Bush seemed to imply that the poet's strong Republican feelings, as evidenced by his loyal and undissenting political service, could easily encompass the actions of a revolutionary leader whom an orthodox royalist would indict with the crime of Brutus. It might be added that while Marvell was willing to imply such a comparison himself ("And *Caesar's* head at last / Did through his Laurels blast"), his use of it in connection with a description of praiseworthy audacity might bespeak an interpretation vastly different from that of a royalist.

It was perhaps unfortunate that the whole controversy died out before any enlightening discussion had occurred of two central problems: namely, the question of how indeed Marvell's attitude toward Cromwell might be determined from his poetry, and the more general question of the relationship of intentions to both poetic and ordinary languages of praise and blame. As far as we are concerned, however, Marvell's treatment of Cromwell need present no crucial problem. We may perceive Marvell's fairly general literary program of describing the Commonwealth in orthodox cosmological and pastoral images, and of invoking its leader as a kind of emperor. And we may, as a consequence, deal with any particular rhetorical difficulty as an irony engendered by two conventionally antithetical modes of discourse, rather than as an irony in the more usual sense, resulting from a conflict of attitude and formal expression. Marvell's pastoral name for England is *Eliza,* and it was the cosmology, at the center of which that earlier reign considered itself, that provided the raw material for so many of his metaphors. If Cromwell's regicide could prove a mortal sin to a royalist, a parliamentarian could retort that

> 'Tis madness to resist or blame
> The force of angry Heavens flame.
> ("Horatian Ode," ll. 25–26)

In Marvell's poetic universe, Cromwell's triumph vaulted over those of his actions that in an earlier Tudor "Elizium" might have been branded as infamies. Cromwell killed a king who "nothing common did or mean" at the scene of his death, and served as the leader of a state who, unlike the king he had replaced, could not perpetuate his leadership through natural inheritance. Similarly, Man, in "The Mower Against Gardens," develops the arts of horticulture and formal gardening and "in the Cherry" does "Nature vex, / To procreate without a sex," at once adulterating and giving order to the "wild and fragrant Innocence" of a pastoral scene. In both cases, however, the ordering by an Intelligence of what was once free and unruly is observed in passing to be *contra naturam.* But our observation must move, along with Marvell's, one step further past these ironies. For Man, the gardener, and Cromwell, the ruler, both govern model universes in which, if innocence is no longer possible, knowledge and the ordering power of imagination are in some sense necessary.

The point is simply that to understand Marvell's political ideology we must try to disentangle such quasi-paradoxes as arise in nearly all the poems (save perhaps for the later satires) by treating them as knots in the thread of the argument in which each occurs, rather than as clusters of conflicting attitudes. And we must realize that the kind of responsibility that Marvell maintained toward his government and toward his constituency in Hull shared his sincerity and even, perhaps, his belief with his commitments to his style. I have raised this point not only in connection with the musical passage in the "First Anniversary" poem, but because of its relevance to the earlier "Musicks Empire." The possible invocation of Cromwell in the final stanza of this apparently simple piece of *laus musicae* might otherwise easily be misinterpreted on the grounds that the poem's subject provides an uncongenial environment for such an allusion. The entire poem had best be quoted:

Musicks Empire

First was the World as one great Cymbal made,
Where Jarring Windes to infant Nature plaid.
All Musick was a solitary sound,
To hollow rocks and murm'ring Fountains bound.

Jubal first made the wilder notes agree;
And *Jubal* tuned Musicks *Jubilee:*
He call'd the *Ecchoes* from their sullen Cell,
And built the Organs City where they dwell.

Each sought a consort in that lovely place;
And Virgin Trebles wed the manly Base.
From whence the progeny of numbers new
Into harmonious Colonies withdrew.

Some to the Lute, some to the Viol went,
And others chose the Cornet eloquent.
These practicing the Wind, and those the Wire,
To sing Mens Triumphs, or in Heavens quire.

Then Musick, the *Mosaique* of the Air,
Did of all these a solemn noise prepare:
With which She gain'd the Empire of the Ear,
Including all between the Earth and Sphear.

> Victorious sounds! yet here your Homage do
> Unto a gentler Conqueror than you;
> Who though He flies the Musick of his praise,
> Would with you Heavens Hallelujahs raise.

The subject here is hardly a traditional praise of music through allusion to *harmonia mundi;* in the first place, music is dealt with throughout as having undergone a kind of historical evolution, parallelling the social history of mankind. In the second place, *musica instrumentalis* is considered historically prior to the celestial harmony, and the normal notion of practical music as the macrocosmic model of the universal music is certainly rearranged, if not actually reversed. Most important of all, however, is that the musical conceit is combined with a political one in a way vastly different from the more traditional treatment in "The First Anniversary of the Government Under O.C." for example, where conventional musical metaphors and myths are revitalized only in the wit.

"Musicks Empire" commences with the random sounds of nature. A physical world "as one great Cymbal made" is the sounding instrument struck by its own disordering elements. The winds themselves are qualified with a standard epithet of discord ("jarring"), but there is no indication that the untamed babble, the "solitary sound" which exhausts the domain of the audible, is in any metaphysical sense inharmonious. "Infant" nature's wildness gives promise of a growth into orderly maturity.

At this point, we are still in possession of an argumentative schema admitting of various interpretive developments; from what we have come to see of the treatment of both practical and speculative music in the writing of the period we might expect the poem to take any one of a number of courses. An elaborate description of harmony as an ordering principle might follow, personified in Orpheus or Amphion, for example, or perhaps some moralized recounting of the fabled Pythagorean "invention" of the intervals. But in the second stanza, Marvell introduces Jubal, "the father of all those who handle the harp and organ" (Gen. 4:21), as his heroic initiator of practical music. It is with Jubal that the metaphorical growth of empire begins. The echoes of the original natural music ("natural" as is the sound of the wind in native forests as compared to the sounds played upon the wood of those same hewn trees, fashioned into lutes—an old figure) are treated, here as throughout the poem, as men. "Sullen" means merely "solitary" here, and we have the sense of two images working at once: men are called from their poor, lonely caves (we are tempted to continue the paraphrase with "solitary, poor, nasty, brutish and short," for this stage of the growth of empire is the very birth of society itself).

On the other hand, there is the distinct implication, in "Cell," of a monastic isolation, and music is here figured as breaking down the walls of monasteries by summoning forth the inhabitants into a world of cities, into the realities of Protestantism and political economy. The organ is almost completely a secular instrument here.

In the "Organs City'" the population of musical sounds is fruitful and multiplies. Starting with the pun on "consort" as sexual mate and instrumental ensemble, the images of stanzas 2–4 depict the gradual overproduction of sounds in the city of towering pipes, resulting in a varied and overflowing music, filling the whole world in search of *Lebensraum.* The "Progeny of numbers new" is undoubtedly all the musical compositions ever invented, here related through a quasi-genetic descent to the primal natural noises. "Harmonious" names both the populations and the political condition of these colonies.

What looks to be a rather conventional catalogue of the instruments in the fourth stanza is turned upside down by the fact that it is the music that seeks out the several instruments. We may see how, in the context between Welsh and English musicians in Drayton's *Poly-Olbion,* various dispositions of different men were satisfied by their choice of instruments when they

> Strooke up at once and sung each to the Instrument;
> (Of sundry sorts that were, as the Musician likes)
> On which the practic'd hand with perfect'st fingring strikes,
> Whereby their height of skill might liveliest be exprest.
> The trembling Lute some touch, some straine the Violl best.
> *(Poly-Olbion,* Song 4, ll. 352–56)

But in "Musicks Empire" the composed sounds themselves choose the instruments by means of which they will applaud the triumphs, the successful advancing marches of human enterprise. The allusion to "Heavens quire" seems almost like a gratuitous tag here, so completely does the idea of mundane expansion dominate the poem.

In the penultimate stanza, the rigor of the conceit appears to relax somewhat. Music, now generally personified, is described as "the Mosaique of the Air." In this remarkable image, however, the multiplicity of the "harmonious Colonies" is recalled by reference to the variegated tesserae of a mosaic which can merge, from any distant viewpoint, into an overwhelming unified figure. It is with a concerted effort of all its diversities in a "solemn" (i.e. religious) noise, corresponding to the assembled mosaic figure, that Music accomplishes her final triumph, gaining "the Empire of the Ear, / Including all between the Earth and Sphear." In the sense of the earlier metaphors, music's heaven is the ultimate civil and territorial acquisition. But in another sense the general personification of Music in this stanza has rendered it as more abstract, and the "Empire of the Ear" is its empirically proper dwelling-place, a heaven of pure audibility.

The word "Mosaique" resonates even further, however. Marvell may or may not have been aware of the common etymological origin of "music" and "mosaic" in the Greek *mousa* ("muse"); perhaps the juxtaposition of the two words in the line was for him the same kind of mock-etymological punning that he had effected earlier in the poem between "Jubal" and "Jubilee." The concealed allusion to Moses he had also employed elsewhere. In the woods about Appleton House, the Poet, "easie Philosopher," divines in the birds and the vegetation all the works of Man:

> Out of these scatter'd *Sibyl's* leaves
> Strange *Prophecies* my Phancy weaves:
> And in one History consumes,
> Like *Mexique Paintings,* all the *Plumes.*
> What *Rome, Greece, Palestine,* ere said
> I in this light *Mosaick* read.
> Thrice happy he who, not mistook,
> Hath read in Natures mystick Book.
> ("Upon Appleton House," ll. 577-84)

Both the ascription of prophecy to fancy and the Hebraic notion of the historical role of *torah,* the Mosaic Law, point to a pun here involving the reading of "light *Mosaick*" as both an adjective-noun and noun-adjective qualification. The notion of music as "the *Mosaique* of the Air," then, might reverberate in a moral and religious dimension as well; it is as a Biblical moral leader that music finally gains the higher reaches of the universe.

In the final stanza, the metaphoric ground again shifts a little as laudatory music attendant upon triumphal processions is recalled. The "Victorious" sounds are at once the flourishes of victory and the actual conquerors of the foregoing parts of the poem. But even they must bend the knee before "a gentler Conqueror," a nobler leader, perhaps the Lord Protector himself. So closely does the growth of music's empire hew to a condensation of human history that it is tempting to suggest that Marvell may have in some way felt the gap between stanzas 4 and 5 to have covered the period 1649–1653, at the end of which time the Protectorate was established. In any case, Cromwell may be said to have brought to "Elizium" the Mosaic leadership historically necessary, a Puritan would undoubtedly have argued, for heaven's consent.

The superimposition of musical lore on a persuasively designed historical frame results, in "Musicks Empire," in a reversal of the usual mythological treatments of *laus musicae*. Earth is filled with sound before Heaven is; the music of the spheres, only obliquely invoked, appears first as a kind of cosmic, triumphal applause. The two conceits on music and human political development interweave so closely that the first five stanzas might be said to address themselves to the subject of "Empire's Music," rather than the other way around. Marvell's historical construction of speculative music is in many ways unique. What Cowley cast into pedantic footnotes appended to a handful of lines of the *Davideis*, Marvell took as the *données* of a compact pseudo-narrative. "Musicks Empire" is, after all, modelled on treatments of the praise of music, . . . but only in the sense that Elizabethan lyrics are, by and large, modelled on *songs*, that Metaphysical lyrics are modelled on *arguments*. The last stanza is an *envoi* to Cromwell, replacing a salute to the Muse; its place there, given the historical narrative that has led to it, is inevitable.

RUTH NEVO

"If these the Times, then this must be the Man"

MARVELL'S "HORATIAN ODE"

The poem is well known and has been much analyzed. Though most critics agree in their recognition of the poem's complexity and irony, there are considerable divergences as to its final bearing. Margoliouth, discussing George Clarke's attribution of "An Elegy on the Death of my Lord Francis Villiers" to Marvell, comes to the conclusion that, if it is his, this "one unequivocally royalist utterance . . . throws into strong relief the transitional character of "An Horatian Ode" where royalist principles and admiration for Cromwell the Great Man exist side by side." Ruth Wallerstein disagrees with Muriel Bradbrook's Hegelian interpretation, on the grounds that such a reading is not consistent with seventeenth-century rhetorical conceptions, and finds in the poem an unresolved conflict of feeling: a turning away, under the stress of anxiety and the hunger for order, from the older loyalties which had been expressed or hinted at in the Lovelace and Hastings poems, and in "Tom May's Death." Cleanth Brooks analyzes the ironies, and finds that Marvell is seeking in a "unified total and complex attitude" to find a meaningful and responsible relationship between the praiseworthy elements of both sides in the conflict. Recently the Hegelian theme has been taken up again by L. D. Lerner, once more with a stress upon ironies. Mr. Lerner finds the explanation and the resolution of these ironies in a near-Marxist acceptance by Marvell of Cromwell as a "revolutionary force, destroying the order of things but ultimately produced by that order." "The previous state of society," contends Mr. Lerner, "has thrown up a force

From *The Dial of Virtue: A Study of Poems on Affairs of State in the Seventeenth Century.* © 1963 by Princeton University Press.

that disrupts, not gradually, but suddenly; . . . the contrast ancient
Rights/greater Spirits is satisfactorily Marxist, so is the recognition that justice
rests on power. All that is missing is the recognition of an ultimately economic
source of the apparently military power."

Though there are indeed illuminating parallels to be drawn between
Marvell's Cromwell, who "does both act and know," and the Plekhanovian hero,
whose "free" power to initiate events is inherent in his recognition of, and obedience to, historical necessity, it is none the less as unhistorical to attribute any
kind of formal Marxist categories to a seventeenth-century mind as it is
misleading to apply such categories to the interpretation of a seventeenth-
century poem. Nor do the alternative readings, "transition," "unresolved conflict," "inclusive attitude," quite seem to fit the case, suggestive and acute as the
comment accompanying them is. Placed in its proper context—that of contemporary panegyric and the contemporary preoccupation with the problem of
history and the hero—the "Horatian Ode," the first of the Cromwellian poems,
will be seen to be both more simple and more central, and also, perhaps more
satisfactory, than is often acknowledged.

The poem, then, in the last analysis, is a most scrupulous record of a profound mind comprehending to the full the fact of social revolution. It is
Cromwell who has precipitated in that mind, formerly reserved and fastidious
towards the popular upsurge and turmoil in the depths of its society, the conviction of a purposeful and providential direction in events. And thus the salient
feature of the panegyric, from its opening in an analysis of the "now"—the particular moment of history with which he deals, to its end in an invocation of
the future—is an overwhelming sense of the significance of the historical
moment.

The poem turns upon this sense of history and of man's (Cromwell's or
citizen's) right relation to it. The sense is that of a moment in time which is
portentous, big with the future, crucial—hence, for "forward" spirits " 'Tis time
to leave the Books in dust," as Cromwell left his Bergamot; hence the rich ambiguity of "restless" in

> So restless *Cromwel* could not cease
> In the inglorious Arts of Peace
>
> (l. 9)

where the restlessness, both in the sense of "ever-seeking" and in the sense of
"indefatigable," is made a necessary consequence of the times; and hence the
all-but-awed insistence upon the magnitude, significance, and audacity of
Cromwell's master-role: Cromwell who

> Could by industrious Valour climbe
> To ruine the great Work of Time,
> And cast the Kingdome old
> Into another Mold.
>
> (l. 33)

The point is made again and more explicitly in "The First Anniversary," 1655:

> And well he therefore does, and well has guest,
> Who in his Age has always forward prest:
> And knowing not where Heavens choice may light,
> Girds yet his Sword, and ready stands to fight.
>
> (l. 145)

In the "Anniversary," too, the apocalyptic relation of the hero to time is clarified in terms parallel to "the great Work of Time" and the casting into "another Mold":

> Like the vain Curlings of the Watry maze,
> Which in smooth streams a sinking Weight does raise;
> So man, declining always, disappears
> In the weak Circles of increasing Years;
> And his short Tumults of themselves Compose,
> While flowing Time above his Head does close.
> *Cromwell* alone with greater Vigour runs,
> (Sun-like) the Stages of succeeding Suns:
> And still the Day which he doth next restore,
> Is the just Wonder of the Day before.
> Cromwell alone doth with new Lustre spring,
> And shines the Jewel of the yearly Ring.
> 'Tis he the force of scatter'd Time contracts,
> And in one Year the work of Ages acts.
>
> (l. 1)

What we have here indeed is Marvell's version of the doctrine "Crownes are for Hero's." In "An Horatian Ode":

> Though Justice against Fate complain,
> And plead the antient Rights in vain:
> But those do hold or break
> As Men are strong or weak.

> Nature that hateth emptiness,
> Allows of penetration less:
>   And therefore must make room
>   Where greater Spirits come.
>
>   (l. 37)

Moreover, the virtues which distinguish the Cromwell of the first part, at least, of the Ode are familiar to us as *virtu:* valor, industry, resolution, subtle wisdom, or cunning, austere self-discipline. But nevertheless it is *Marvell's* version; it is important to see how deeply the conception of the conquering hero is informed and modified by the definitions of a specific historical context.

The description of Caesar in Tom May's translation, 1627, of Lucan's *Pharsalia* illuminates this point particularly, since verbal resemblances make it clear that Marvell had the passage in mind when he composed the Ode. Lucan's description is of the classic conquering hero of epic quality, arbitrary action, and simple motivation:

> But restlesse valour, and in warre a shame
> Not to be Conquerour; fierce, not curb'd at all,
> Ready to fight, where hope, or anger call
> His forward Sword; confident of successe,
> And bold the favour of the gods to presse:
> Orethrowing all that his ambition stay,
> And loves that ruine should enforce his way;
> As lightning by the winde forc'd from a cloude
> Breakes through the wounded aire with thunder loud,
> Disturbes the Day, the people terrifyes,
> And by a light oblique dazels our eyes,
> Not *Joves* own Temple spares it; when no force,
> No barre can hinder his prevailing course,
> Great waste, as foorth it sallyes and retires,
> It makes and gathers his dispersed fires.

Marvell's version is subtly modified, through the fork'd lightning image with its progression from merely natural force to divine instrument, and through the active star image which fuses the two traditional sources of mutations in history—Virtue and Fortune—in one controlling and transcendent act. The poem is thus neither simply a paean to republican Providence nor to the individual heroic role, which Marvell will not let us forget. The idea which emerges is of a providentially directed human agency.

> So restless *Cromwel* could not cease
> In the inglorious Arts of Peace,
>> But through adventrous War
>> Urged his active Star.
> And, like the three-fork'd lightning, first
> Breaking the Clouds where it was nurst,
>> Did thorough his own Side
>> His fiery way divide
>
>> .   .   .   .   .   .
>
> Then burning through the Air he went,
> And Pallaces and Temples rent:
>> And *Caesars* head at last
>> Did through his Laurels blast.
> 'Tis Madness to resist or blame
> The force of angry Heavens flame:
> And, if we would speak true,
> Much to the Man is due.
>
>> (l. 9)

The final couplet is the more effective for the tone of consideration, the unemphatic but insistent precision. The remark forms the transition from the forked lightning passage to the account of Cromwell's progress from private garden to triumphant power. Alone among republican pieces the Ode keeps in perfect balance the decisively heroic nature of the agent and the transcendent nature of his agency. Ripeness is all; it is the ripeness of the hero and his times, or, to put it more clearly, the hero's knowledge of the meaning and direction of emergent history, which turns a random, classical *virtù* into a messianic election.

> So much one Man can do,
> That does both act and know.
>> (l. 75)

It is the knowing, the knowing of ends, which gives to Marvell's version of "Crownes are for Hero's" its seriousness and its morality—as opposed to the abdication of morality in a pure might-is-right doctrine. He bows before the inevitable ruinous, rending power; there is no room in Nature for the Ancient Rights and the Greater Spirits simultaneously; but the source of the power is not presented as the arbitrary cruelty of a natural law, but as a divinely sanctioned necessity. And this idea—that it is a final cause, a millennial task, to which this greater spirit climbs—is prepared for through the placing of

Cromwell's activities in a perspective of historical change. One of the most significant points in the poem is the transition from the execution of the King to Cromwell's triumph. It is the point at which the poem turns from recounting the immediate past to an assessment of the present and a prophecy for the future, and the transition is marked by the near repetition of a phrase:

> He nothing common did or mean
> Upon that memorable Scene:
>
> (l. 57)

> This was that memorable Hour
> Which first assur'd the forced Pow'r.
>
> (l. 65)

Nothing could bring out more strongly Marvell's sense of the historically dynamic in Cromwell's career than this exchange of the static, spatial "scene," for the dynamic, temporal "hour."

The two passages are significant in another way as well. They bring to a point of maximum clarity the great central tug-of-war in the poem, source of all the implications, ambiguities, and reservations, in fact, which inform Marvell's account of the great man of his age. For, that the election and the task, the rearing of God's trophies upon crowned Fortune's neck, as Milton was two years later to put it [in his "Sonnet to Cromwell"], is a demanding undertaking, for which a high price has to be paid, no one was better qualified than Marvell to perceive; no one discussed in these pages was more conscious of the high cost of the "clymacterick" in history, because no one was more aware, or more sensitive, a product of the civilization that was about to be replaced. What is interesting is the degree of his consciousness of this high cost, the profoundly deterministic terms in which he casts his analysis, and the prophetic republican nature of his resolution.

It was Cowley who, in the preface to his poems wrote: "a warlike, various, and a tragical age is best to *write of,* but worst to *write in.* . . . There is nothing that requires so much serenity and chearfulness of *Spirit;* it must not be either overwhelmed with the cares of *Life,* or overcast with the *Clouds of Melancholy* and *Sorrow,* or shaken and disturbed with the storms of injurious *Fortune;* it must, like the *Halcyon,* have *fair weather* to breed in. The *Soul* must be filled with bright and delightful *Idaea's,* when it undertakes to communicate delight to others, . . . So that 'tis almost as hard a thing to be a *Poet* in despight of *Fortune,* as it is in despight of *Nature.*"

It is with a sense almost of an antiphonal contrast that, with such a passage in mind, we re-read the opening of the Ode:

> The forward Youth that would appear
> Must now forsake his *Muses* dear,
> Nor in the Shadows sing
> His Numbers languishing.
> 'Tis time to leave the Books in dust,
> And oyl th'unused Armours rust:
> Removing from the Wall
> The Corselet of the Hall.
>
> (l. 1)

The shadow of regret that lies upon these lines is counterbalanced both by "languishing" with its suggestion of indolence, and by "the Hall," evoking memories of a martial way of life which has been nevertheless a source of liberal culture. This regret, this nostalgia for a more gracious and individualistic past which he shares with Cowley, has a natural history in Marvell's own previous analysis of their "warlike, various, and tragical age." "Our times," he writes to Lovelace,

> are much degenerate from those
> Which your sweet Muse which your fair Fortune chose,
> And as complexions alter with the Climes,
> Our wits have drawne th'infection of our times.
> That candid Age no other way could tell
> To be ingenious, but by speaking well.
> · · · · · · · · · · · ·
> These vertues now are banisht out of Towne,
> Our Civill Wars have lost the Civicke crowne.
>
> · · · · · · · · · · · · · ·
> The Ayre's already tainted with the swarms
> Of Insects which against you rise in arms.
> Word-peckers, Paper-rats, Book-scorpions,
> Of wit corrupted, the unfashion'd Sons.
> The barbed Censurers begin to looke
> Like the grim consistory on thy Booke;
> And on each line cast a reforming eye,
> Severer then the yong Presbytery.
>
> (l. 1)

And again, in "Upon the Death of the Lord Hastings," he sums up, in one witty image, all the distaste and contempt felt by the inheritor of a high and liberal civility for the confining austerities of revolutionary Puritanism:

> He had but at this Measure still increast,
> And on the *Tree of Life* once made a Feast,
> As that of *Knowledge;* what Loves had he given
> To Earth, and then what Jealousies to Heaven!
> But 't is a *Maxime* of that State, That none,
> Lest he become like Them, taste more then one.
> Therefore the *Democratick* Stars did rise,
> And all that Worth from hence did *Ostracize.*
>
> (l. 19)

The opposition felt by both Marvell and Cowley reflects the major social and political conflict of the time—that for which the closing of the by now predominantly courtly theatres by a Puritan parliament may serve as a convenient symbol. Marvell's terms generalize the issue and define the antagonistic values: the Muses, standing for the cultivation of the arts and graces of civilization, free individualistic "wit" and aesthetic values; against the "unfashion'd Sons" of the illiberal, ideological, "democratic" new age.

The "unfashion'd Sons" appear in the Ode. They are the armed bands who clap their bloody hands; they bear the same relation to the scene they witness as an audience at a theatre; and like an audience they are partly responsible, by virtue of their demand and their participation, for the grim spectacle they watch—the spectacle of a king's exit from history. The Muses too, are present—in the formal but instinctive nobility with which the Royal Actor makes his abdication:

> *He* nothing common did or mean
> Upon that memorable Scene:
> > But with his keener Eye
> > The Axes edge did try:
> Nor call'd the *Gods* with vulgar spight
> To vindicate his helpless Right,
> > But bow'd his comely Head,
> > Down as upon a Bed.
>
> (l. 57)

Thus Cromwell's irresistible lightning flashes across a world which is ordered by the traditional, perennial attitudes of aristocracy towards the common multitude; and it is the particular virtue of the "Horatian Ode" that Marvell can present with such scrupulous and concrete objectivity, with such simultaneity, the conflicting sets of values which could issue in a view either of providential hero or of upstart usurper. The result is that the figures of Charles and Cromwell in the Ode are no longer set one against the other as rightful king and ambitious usurper, or as disabled king and mighty hero. They become more universal antagonists: the impotent grace of an ancient and noble civilization, on the one hand, against the ruthless idealism and sacrifice of a social revolutionary force on the other.

If the first part of the poem presents the dialectical relation between "nothing common or mean" and "forced Power," it is the latter part that presents the acceptance, the resolution, and the prophecy, though these have been prepared for from the beginning. For it is the conception of the "forward Youth" in the very first line which has enabled Marvell's thought to transcend the opposition between the Muses and the unfashion'd Sons. The forward youth, in effect, is he who is aware of history as consequent not upon the "virtues and vices, successes and mistakes" of its ruling figures, but upon the movement of great inner forces:

> And well he therefore does, and well has guest,
> Who in his Age has always forward prest:
> And knowing not where Heavens choice may light,
> Girds yet his Sword, and ready stands to fight.
> ("The First Anniversary," l. 145)

It is through the mediation of such a conception that the modern republican idea can come to birth at all. It is only when the plebeian rabble becomes the "Publick" that it can be taken seriously enough to become the bearer of a new order. It is because this has happened in the Ode that the lines

> He to the *Commons Feet* presents
> A *Kingdome,* for his first years rents.
> And, what he may, forbears
> His Fame to make it theirs:
>
> And has his Sword and Spoyls ungirt,
> To lay them at the *Publick's* skirt
> (l. 85)

are not utterly ridiculous, as they might easily be in the older view. Marvell has reinterpreted his "Civicke crowne." It is no longer, as it were, the bloom upon the face of privilege, but the mark of one of whom the following can be said:

> Nor yet grown stiffer with Command,
> But still in the *Republick's* hand:

> How fit he is to sway
> That can so well obey.
>   (l. 82)

The turning point of the poem is the acceptance of a bleeding head at the base of the new structure:

> So when they did design
> The *Capitols* first Line,
> A bleeding Head where they begun,
> Did fright the Architects to run;
>   And yet in that the *State*
>   Foresaw it's happy Fate.
>   (l. 67)

It will be clear from this reading that I do not find "Foresaw it's happy Fate" ironic; nor do I think it historically likely that it should be so, in 1650, no matter how prescient the author. What applies to this line applies also to the "Nor yet" and to the "But still" in the lines quoted above: reservation, or rather a wise knowledge of fallibility, of the possible transformation of republican virtue into ambitious self-regarding *virtú*. Thus, as the "lightning" series forms the main operative image in the first part, so the "falcon" image conveys in the latter part the taming, disciplining, and controlling of the great power of leadership through obedience to an idea and a mission greater than itself. Milton too insisted upon the "sifting and winnowing" of motive and action to be undergone by the republican hero in the performance of his appointed task. Marvell treats the bridling of power emblematically:

> So when the Falcon high
> Falls heavy from the Sky,
> She, having kill'd, no more does search,
> But on the next green Bow to pearch;
>   Where, when he first does lure,
>   The Falckner has her sure.
>   (l. 91)

And now the exhortation, which has been found puzzling, falls perfectly into place, as a solemn and prophetic admonition to the chief executive of revolution:

> But thou the Wars and Fortunes Son
> March indefatigably on;
>   And for the last effect

> Still keep thy Sword erect:
> Besides the force it has to fright
> The Spirits of the shady Night,
> The same *Arts* that did *gain*
> A *Pow'r* must it *maintain*.
>
> (l. 113)

An erect sword forms the shape of a cross; the ambiguity of the lines is of the same kind as that of "Urged his active Star": an identification in one comprehensive act of the mind, of the heroic power and its controlling destiny. The meaning of the last quatrain, which has been found difficult, would seem to lie in the relation between the charismatic power of the cross, and the creative power of the sword-cross in the hands of the revolutionary hero. A parallel relation, this time between mundane origin and transcendental end, is implied in "Thou the Wars and Fortunes Son" as against "for the last effect." There is a very rich ambiguity in the word "Arts," glancing as it does both at the Muses and at Machiavellian "policy," while its meaning in context is the state-craft of a dedicated virtue. This is the "wish'd conjuncture" of "high Grace with highest Pow'r," power constantly chastened by awareness of the final cause, the mysterious work, the latest and blest day.

"THE FIRST ANNIVERSARY"— A REPUBLICAN MANIFESTO

The best gloss upon the "Horatian Ode" is Marvell's own later "First Anniversary":

> Hence oft I think, if in some happy Hour
> High Grace should meet in one with highest Pow'r,
> And then a seasonable People still
> Should bend to his, as he to Heavens will,
> What we might hope, what wonderful Effect
> From such a wish'd Conjuncture might reflect.
> Sure, the mysterious Work, where none withstand,
> Would forthwith finish under such a Hand:
> Fore-shortned Time its useless Course would stay,
> And soon precipitate the latest Day.
> But a thick Cloud about that Morning lyes,
> And intercepts the Beams of Mortal eyes,
> That 'tis the most which we determine can,
> If these the Times, then this must be the Man.
>
> (l. 131)

The "Times" however, were none the less troubling, nor did they cease to be so as time went on. The deep conflict between the Muses and the forward spirit is resumed by Marvell in his Nun Appleton poems in the period between the Ode and the "First Anniversary." Their theme is the opposition between the personal virtues of retreat and the public virtues of the active life. Fairfax chose retirement. Cromwell resigned his privacy so dear to yield to rule. Marvell's "Garden" and the forest stanzas of "Upon Appleton House" are sufficient indication that he felt the full pressure and burden of the choice between public and private, active and contemplative life, and he makes the point explicit in the "Anniversary":

> For all delight of Life thou then didst lose,
> When to Command, thou didst thy self Depose.
>
> (l. 221)

Moreover the "Chammish issue" passage shows how deeply condemnatory Marvell was of the "rage of Sects"—the extreme frenzy of "democracy":

> Accursed Locusts, whom your King does spit
> Out of the Center of th'unbottom'd Pit;
> You who the Scripture and the Laws deface
> With the same liberty as Points and Lace;
> Oh Race most hypocritically strict!
> Bent to reduce us to the ancient Pict;
> Well may you act the *Adam* and the *Eve;*
> Ay, and the Serpent too that did deceive.
>
> (l. 311)

The "First Anniversary" marks, not so much a subsequent stage in Marvell's thought, as an amplification of the republican idea stated in the Ode. In the form of praise for the hero who has deposed himself, renounced "delight of life," it is an extended examination of the operation and the effect of republican leadership and of a "sober liberty." In it he returns, it is significant to notice, to the heroic couplet which Waller had established for panegyric, and in which Denham had written *Cooper's Hill,* a royalist panegyric bearing comparison with Marvell's in its judicious treatment and philosophically generalizing level. A further settling of Marvell's mind is thus indicated, after the highly individual, indeed unique, measure of the Ode, whose shorter lines contribute to an effect of excitement held in firm control by the rhymes.

The emotional and symbolic center of the poem is the image of the order-creating constitution—(the "ruling Instrument")—which, in the hands of this Amphion of state, becomes the means whereby the minds of men, that stubbornest of all matter, are built into the forms of concord:

> Such was that wondrous Order and Consent,
> When *Cromwell* tun'd the ruling Instrument;
> While tedious Statesmen many years did hack,
> Framing a Liberty that still went back;
> Whose num'rous Gorge could swallow in an hour
> That Island, which the Sea cannot devour:
> Then our *Amphion* issues out and sings,
> And once he struck, and twice, the pow'rful Strings.
> The Commonwealth then first together came,
> And each one enter'd in the willing Frame;
>
> . . . .
>
> The Common-wealth does through their Centers all
> Draw the Circumf'rence of the publique Wall;
> The crossest Spirits here do take their part,
> Fast'ning the Contignation which they thwart;
> And they, whose Nature leads them to divide,
> Uphold, this one, and that the other Side;
> But the most Equal still sustein the Height,
> And they as Pillars keep the Work upright;
> While the resistance of opposed Minds,
> The Fabrick as with Arches stronger binds,
> Which on the Basis of a Senate free,
> Knit by the Roofs Protecting weight agree.
>
> (l. 67)

In this central conception, the musical and architectural harmonies fuse in an image of parliamentary *concordia discors,* which gives both perspective and a proper limitation to passages which would otherwise overbalance the poem in the direction of adulation or Carlylean hero-worship:

> When for his Foot he thus a place had found,
> He hurles e'r since the World about him round;
> And in his sev'ral Aspects, like a Star,
> Here shines in Peace, and thither shoots a War.
>
> (l. 99)
>
> Thou Cromwell falling
>
> . . . .

> all about was heard a Panique groan,
> As if that Natures self were overthrown.
> It seem'd the Earth did from the Center tear;
> It seem'd the Sun was faln out of the Sphere:
> Justice obstructed lay, and Reason fool'd;
> Courage disheartn'd, and Religion cool'd.
>
> (l. 201)

Indeed it must be Marvell's vividly grateful sense of Cromwellian order subduing the chaos of the sects which makes him reanimate the ancient cosmic sun-king imagery at the very moment when he is insisting that to be Cromwell

> was a greater thing,
> Then ought below, or yet above a King.
>
> (l. 225)

For, in contradistinction to the simple doctrine of "Crownes are for hero's," he insists that

> He seems a King by long Succession born,
> And yet the same to be a King does scorn.
> Abroad a King he seems, and something more,
> At Home a Subject on the equal Floor.
>
> (l. 387)

For kings, in their regal state, strong only against their subjects, building no temples in their days, consulting no prophecies but those which augur their personal fate, are unlike the forward spirits in their relation to history. The kings

> Thus (Image-like) an useless time they tell,
> And with vain Scepter, strike the hourly Bell;
> Nor more contribute to the state of Things,
> Then wooden Heads unto the Viols strings.
>
> (l. 41)

It is the forward spirits, through their foresight and guiding power, who "contribute to the state of things" and are enabled to "contract the work of ages in a year."

The substitution of the hero, the master of time, for such kingly puppets of time forms one of the main themes of the poem. It is conveyed, with a kind of poetic justice, through traditional, if reanimated, sun imagery, in the long sunset-sunrise passage (ll. 325–42), for example. Once again we have an amplification of the "Crowns are for hero's" doctrine; but the old coins crown-king-sun have been given a different value.

The rest of the poem is concerned with the nature of the leader's mastery of time, which consists of so realizing the direction of the historic present as to determine the future. His own inalienable power of judgment and choice imposes his will on events, while he conforms to the will of the "higher Force," which expresses itself in the movement of history. The "Charioteer" and "Captain" metaphors convey the idea of the Protector's decisive powers of judgment, guidance, and control, and this is recapitulated in a second image from the art of building:

> But walk still middle betwixt War and Peace;
> Choosing each Stone, and poysing every weight,
> Trying the Measures of the Bredth and Height;
> Here pulling down, and there erecting New,
> Founding a firm State by Proportions true.
>
> (l. 244)

The same dual faculty is revealed in the lines on freedom and tyranny:

> 'Tis not a Freedome, that where All commmand;
> Nor Tyranny, where One does them withstand;
> But who of both the Bounders knows to lay
> Him as their Father must the State obey.
>
> (l. 279)

It is worth noticing, however, that praise of Cromwell's specifically personal qualities, as well as his intimidating military power, is placed as dramatic speech in the mouths of the astonished princes of the world. That is the aspect of the hero that strikes the public eye, captures the popular imagination. The poet, in his own voice, insists upon the huge, suprapersonal movement of events to which the hero is servant and instrument:

> What since he did, an higher Force him push'd
> Still from behind, and it before him rush'd,
> Though undiscern'd among the tumult blind,
> Who think those high Decrees by Man design'd.
>
> (l. 239)

The true inward nature of the heroic role is presented in a final brilliant metaphor of intelligent mission:

> And as the *Angel* of our Commonweal,
> Troubling the Waters, yearly mak'st them Heal.
>
> (l. 401)

Except for the elegy on Cromwell's death, which, significantly enough, deals almost entirely with the private and domestic aspects of the Protector's death, Marvell's last Cromwellian panegyric was written in 1657 on Blake's victory over the Spaniards. And that poem too reaches a climax with the idea of conscious mission as opposed to blind Fortune:

> Fate these two Fleets, between both Worlds had brought,
> Who fight, as if for both those Worlds they fought.
> Thousands of wayes, Thousands of men there dye
>
> . . . .
>
> Far different Motives yet engag'd them thus,
> Necessity did them, but Choice did us.
> A choice which did the highest worth express,
> And was attended by as high success.
> For your resistless Genius there did Raign,
> By which we Laurels reapt ev'n on the Mayn.
> So prosperous Stars, though absent to the sence,
> Bless those they shine for, by their Influence.
>
> (l. 125)

GEOFFREY HARTMAN

"The Nymph Complaining for the Death of Her Faun": A Brief Allegory

T he allegories so far proposed have crushed the lightness of nymph and fawn, the high poetic spirits of Marvell's poem. Why allegorize at all? The only good reason is that the poem itself teases us into thinking that nymph and fawn are also something else. This teasing should be respected: either there is some allegory here, or the poem is deceptively suggestive. Is the nymph the human soul; the fawn a gift of grace, or some aspect of Christ or Church? Such thoughts are especially encouraged by images reminiscent of the Song of Songs.

The fawn is not unlike the young hart of the Song of Songs or its fawns that feed among the lilies, while the nymph's garden is a kind of *hortus conclusus* with which fawn and Shulammite are linked. Such allusions, it is true, freely used in the love poetry of the time, do not of themselves establish the presence of allegory. Yet when imagery from the Song of Songs is used in comparable contexts—either directly, as in Crashaw, to celebrated divine love in passionate terms, or allusively, as in Vaughan, to illustrate the quest for evidences of election—it reposes on well-established allegorical tradition. Marvell may have chosen this tradition for its very bivalence, but a reader cannot miss the sacramental and even christological note emerging first in lines 13–24 ("There is not such another in / The World, to offer for their Sin"), crowding around the imagery from Song of Songs (ll. 71–93), and sustained to the end of the poem, whose coda is a series of conceits on weeping that remind us strongly of Crashaw—a Crashaw scaled down to sharp diminutives.

From *Essays in Criticism* 18, no. 2 (April 1968). © 1968 by Geoffrey H. Hartman.

If a literal interpretation could account for these features, I would prefer it. Only one nonallegorical approach, however, has been at all successful. According to Leo Spitzer the poem describes a young girl's desire for an impossible purity. He thinks the poem is an oblique psychological portrait. "The description of her pet reflects on her own character by indirect characterization, the increasing idealization of the fawn allowing inferences about the maiden who so idealizes it." It is certainly true that there is something childlike, deliciously naïve, and deeply human in the nymph, which breaks through the mythological setting as later in Romantic and Victorian poetry. Yet beside the fact that it would be hard to find, at this time, a single prosopopoeia or "complaint," which is primarily psychological portraiture, Spitzer's view is open to a fundamental objection. It substitutes psychological for mythological categories, assuming that the latter are the poet's means of implying the former. His literalism, therefore, does not take the letter of the poem seriously enough: it refuses to explore the possibility that the nymph is a nymph—not simply a young girl, but a mythic being in a privileged relation to the wood-world of the poem, the world of fawns and nature. Yet Marvell insists clearly enough on the presence of this mythical level. While his troopers and their violence come from a contemporary world, almost everything else is set in a world of myth. The impinging, quick but fatal, of one level on the other should not be obscured by a translation into the psychological.

A second approach, which also claims to be literal, is allegorical despite itself. Romance and pastoral may show the beginnings of passion in an innocent mind, the obliquities of a young girl prey to her first love. The theme derives perhaps from Longus's *Daphnis and Chloe* and contains that special admixture of naïveté in the subjects and sophistication in the author which is to be found here as elsewhere in Marvell. A strong suspicion is raised that the fawn's wound is the girl's, that the poem describes a sexual or at least an initiatory wounding. Yet what the reader may interpret in sexual terms, the nymph's consciousness views in terms of creaturely calamity. By some naive and natural balm of vision, of which allegory is the organized form, she keeps within the confines of a pastoral view of things. She is a nymph rather than a girl precisely because her soul is not yet humanized, her love not yet divided into profane and sacred. The fawn mirrors that undifferentiated love which allows her to pass gradually, and without mystery, from man to beast, from Sylvio to the deer. Her extreme grief, moreover, is so gentle ("ungentle men!") that she still seems to live in the last rays of a world where no sharp distinctions between good and evil obtain. She is too whole for the rage of good against evil, or any understanding of the rage of evil itself. She does not, even now, fall into duality, but abandons the whole (this impossible world) for another whole (the world beyond).

The threshold of mature consciousness is not reached—and cannot be reached without a dying of the nymph into a girl or woman.

This ontological interpretation of the poem is, I believe, new. To put it in its simplest form, it respects mythology's insistence that states of soul are correlated with states of being. But it implies a disjunction between the points of view of innocence and of experience, of nymph on the one hand and reader or poet on the other. The poem's playful and artificial flavor, however, betrays a degree of conspiracy between nymph and poet. Naïveté of mood expressed in jeweled conceits is, after all, Marvell's most distinctive trait as author. Instead of arguing that the nymph sees one thing and the poet, who looks at the action from the point of view of experience, sees another, we must suppose a greater unity between the poet and his persona. But once we do this, the nymph begins to appear as a Muse in little, a figure created by the poet to mourn a lost power, perhaps that of poetry itself. The supposition gathers strength if we think of Marvell's poem not in the tradition of complaint or prosopopoeia but in the more comprehensive one of pastoral elegy. The use of pastoral to lament the death of poets was one of its strongest Renaissance developments, and although the lament is usually spoken by an author in *propria persona* and for an individual, Spenser makes the Muses mourn "their own mishaps" (*Epithalamion*, l. 7). It is Marvell's special characteristic to reduce everything to a microcosmic or little-world scale and to view the nymph as a Muse in miniature.

Indeed, the nymph's tragedy, caught in amber, would have reminded a contemporary reader of another tradition cognate with pastoral elegy but now almost extinct. I suspect that the meaning of Marvell's poem became problematic as the tradition lost its natural or commonplace vigor. The medallion, gemlike, or miniature effects found in Marvell can be traced to the epigrams of the Greek Anthology, a considerable portion of which are either verses made for pictures or else little pictures themselves. Those acquainted with the poetry of the Pléiade will remember the impact of the Anacreonta and the Greek Anthology (mediated by the neo-Latin poets) on Ronsard, Du Bellay, and Belleau, who began to develop an alternate tradition to the high style of the great ode which had been their main object of imitation. Not odes but odelettes, not epics and large elegies but little descriptive domestic or rural poems called *Petites inventions, Bocages, Jeux Rustiques, Pierres Précieuses, Idylles*, now became the delectation of their Muse. A strange riot of diminutives and diminutive forms begins. The word *idyll*, in fact, was commonly etymologized as a diminutive of *eidos*, a little picture. The idyll, says Vauquelin de la Fresnaie in his *Foresteries* (1555), "ne signifie et ne represente que diverses petites images et graveures en la semblance de celles qu'on grave aux lapis, aux gemmes et calcedoines pour servir quelques fois de cachet. Les miennes en la sorte, pleines d'amour enfantines, ne sont qu'imagetes et petites tabletes de fantaisies d'Amour." The fortunes of this mode of the minor are difficult to follow; it is always merging with so much else—with emblem poetry for example, or with sonnets and their "little rooms," or with various kinds of pictorialism. Its range is so great, its value so variable, that we can go from Belleau's *petite invention* "Le Ver Luisant" (1552) to Marvell's "The Mower to the Glow-Worms" (about a century later), or from a whimsical epitaph on some faithful pet to Ben Jonson's great verses on Elizabeth L. H. ("Wouldst thou hear what man can say / In a little? Reader, stay"), and again from these to Henry King's moving trifle "Upon a Braid of Hair in a Heart" ("In this small Character is sent / My Loves eternal Monument"). The very range of the tradition, however, may be a result of the fact that the recurrent and operative topos of much-in-little constitutes a poetics as well as a theme: it is a defense of poetry's *ignobile otium,* the trivial yet mystical or contemplative nature of art.

Now Marvell's poem is not only an idyll in this sense, but an idyll of idylls. It is a little picture of the spirit of the genre—an apotheosis of the diminutive powers of poetry. Not only is the fawn a spritely embodiment of much-in-little, not only does the whole poem end with a metamorphosis into art, a votive image of nymph and fawn, but, as if to sum up the genre in one monument to itself, "The Nymph's Complaint" brings together the major types of the Greek epigram: dedicatory, sepulchral, ecphrastic, and amatory. An inspired syncretism produces something very like a collage (although, as in reading Homer, one must be taught to recognize the individual bits or formulae), a collage with two important and successful aims. The first is to fuse semipagan forms of sentiment into a recongizably contemporary genre, that of Spenserian pastoral allegory. What Spenser has done is here done again, but in a much less liberal and inventive, a much more deliberate and self-conscious, way. It is an openly synthetic reconstruction, a reassembly of Spenser's already diminished freedoms. Marvell's poetry has something of the embalmer's art, and his diminutive form points to an ideal it would preserve from total dissolution. The poet's second and correlative aim is to translate these various forms of the idyll (pictorial, votive, sepulchral, amatory) into a situation which is the living content of his poem, as if nature and artifice were interchangeable— and this interchange is itself a generative topic of some of the Greek Anthology epigrams, as of the Renaissance "speaking pictures" inspired by them. Though art, in other words, accepts itself as a tour de force, becoming deliberately diminished and artifactual in its aims, it will not give up a magical ambition to rival or supplant nature. The diminished form simply purifies art's power and concentrates its resemblance to hieroglyph, icon, or charm.

In Marvell, therefore, as in every authentic artist, technique is ethos: the form he has chosen—a playful shadow of greater forms, an artful rivalry of naïver forms—is at once a lament and an acceptance of his situation as poet. To understand that situation in its historical context, the vast continued design of Spenserian allegory shrinking and becoming a brief allegory, will help to interpret this "furthest and most mysterious development of English pastoral poetry" [as Frank Kermode calls it in *English Pastoral Poetry*]. The following interpretation can be extended from its specific allegory to the general problem of the status of Spenserian allegory in Marvell's age. A consideration, therefore, of that brief epic "Appleton House" must also concern itself with the problematic status of the epic in Marvell's age. To this double task of finding a specific allegory and of clarifying the status of Spenserian allegory I now turn.

Those who have tried to discover a sustained allegory in "The Nymph" have made a curious error. This error explains not only the failure of their attempt but also why this kind of interpretation is discredited. Instead of basing their allegories on the action, they have immediately sought to decipher the individual agents: nymph, fawn, Sylvio. But in Spenserian allegory it is the action which identifies the agents rather than vice versa. This by no means excludes more static devices: Spenser's figures can have suggestive names, like Sylvio in Marvell, even if the meaning of a figure is disclosed mainly by an intricate pattern of relationships extended (and even scattered like clues) through canto or book. This type of structure was called by Spenser and others continued allegory, and the mistake of applying to Marvell's poem methods of decoding more appropriate to noncontinued allegories comes from the fact that we have so very few lyrical pieces in this mode: Marvell is almost *sui generis* in his short-form use of the dark conceit. The short allegories of Herbert and Vaughan are not really dark, but rather vivified emblems.

Let us begin, therefore, with a description of the action: of what happens in "The Nymph." The nymph traces in retrospect her subtly changing relationship to the fawn. The fawn is first a love gift, then a consolation, and finally a creature loved for its own sake and even gathering to itself the nymph's love for all creatures. The fawn, indeed, becomes so important that, when it is killed, no creaturely consolation seems possible, and the nymph hastens to die.

So highly stylized an action evokes a specific idea of the progress of the soul. The direct object of love is replaced by an indirect one, a live token, which is in turn replaced by a still more indirect one, an icon (ll. 111ff.). And while the token comforts, the icon comforts only, if at all, as a symbol of the impossibility of being comforted: "I shall weep though I be stone." A love that has turned from temporal fulfillment to temporal consolation becomes a disconsolateness which is love still, but removed from this world.

The pattern is general and human enough not to require a special historical locus. It has such a locus, however, in the Christian idea of the soul's progress and the part consolation plays in this. The Christian soul is weaned from worldliness by privations that contain a comfort. That comfort is usually thought of in other-worldly terms, but Marvell's position is rather complex. Though there is an apotheosis of the fawn, analogous to the Assumption of Astrea or other stellar figures (as Crashaw says, "heav'n must go home"), the fawn might have substituted for Sylvio. As Sylvio's surrogate it entices the nymph with a love that remains this-worldly, though chaste or wider than sexual. The fawn's mode of being is, in fact, so peculiarly mixed with nature's that the possibility of a nature-involved consolation seems to die with its ascent out of this world.

The theme of consolation, which points our poem in the direction of allegory, can be traced back to a specific and authoritative analogue. This is the scriptural story of the Comforter in John 14:16, 26, and 16:7ff. Christ promises the Comforter (Paraclete) to his disciples when they do not suspect or do not understand that he must leave them. For them Christ is part of the approaching and expected apocalypse. But Christ, in preparing them for his absence, for temporality, tells them of the Comforter, who is to be his surrogate and a spirit dwelling with them in his absence, more intimately even than He. (The Paraclete, Donne comments in a sermon, as well as a mediator and advocate, is "in a more intire, and a more internall, and a more viscerall sense, A Comforter.") It is almost expedient that Christ should depart, so that this closer companion, also named "Spirit of Truth" (viz. "troth") and "Holy Ghost," should come to abide with men.

Three kinds of congruence between this analogue and the poem may be considered: the propriety of showing the Comforter as a fawn, the similarities of theme, and similarities bearing on the action as a whole. Concerning the issue of propriety, I can only say that the third Person is traditionally a dove, and that the Church Fathers often associate the third Person with charity, or pure creature-feeling, rather than with power (the first Person) or wisdom (the second Person). To the nymph the fawn is simply a creature that loves her, and she reciprocates its love. When she says, "I cannot be / Unkind, t'a Beast that loveth me," Marvell renders her attitude succinctly, that it would be "un-kind" (unnatural, uncreaturely) to be "unkind." To see the fawn as an allegorical emblem for the Comforter at least respects the fact that the poem deals with the possibility of consolation. The fawn might have been, for a Protestant, a playful yet not unfitting image of the humble Spirit that prefers "th' upright heart and pure." The change from dove to fawn could have been imposed by the very mode of allegory, since the dove is, strictly speaking, not an allegory but a symbol of the third Person. Marvell, moreover, as his poem "On Mr. Milton's *Paradise Lost*" shows, is wary of the direct treatment of religious subjects. The classical image of Lesbia mourning her sparrow, or the archetypal images of child with bird and virgin with unicorn, may also have served to bring the subject to its deeply veiled and affective form. The change from dove to fawn is, however, strong and unusual enough to compel explanation or put the allegory in doubt.

A second, still insufficient congruence is that of theme. Keeping the story of the Comforter in mind, we note that the fawn is a memento given at a time when the nymph suspects nothing, and with a hint (not understood by her) that it will take Sylvio's place:

> Unconstant *Sylvio,* when yet
> I had not found him counterfeit,
> One morning (I remember well)
> Ty'd in this silver Chain and Bell,
> Gave it to me: nay and I know
> What he said then; I'me sure I do.
> Said He, look how your Huntsman here
> Hath taught a Faun to hunt his *Dear.*
>
> (ll. 25–32)

Here the fawn is clearly identified as Sylvio's surrogate. One huntsman will be replaced by another. The fawn, moreover, is to Sylvio as the Comforter is to Christ, insofar as the latter appears "unconstant" compared to this more faithful household spirit. Without her lover the soul must find a way to redeem the time (cf. ll. 37ff.), and it is helped to do so by a subtle comforter who gradually wins her heart.

But against the fawn's wooing—at once a respect of time and nature—is set the irruptive disrespect of the troopers. For these troopers we find no immediate clue in the scripture story, though they could be carried over from another part of scripture. It is also not obvious why Sylvio must be shown as huntsman as well as lover. Adding our previous query, why dove is changed to fawn, the divergencies yield a pattern. They point to the imaginative realm of the spiritual chase. The story of the Comforter is conflated with this most common of Christian and Romance motifs, whose imagery harmonizes with that of Song of Songs. The conflation, which helps to engender a richly detailed allegory, expresses with extraordinary neatness a spiritual chase that kills the spirit—the spirit being the Comforter, the residual and restitutive providence working patiently through church or nature until the Second Coming.

The theme of the chase enters the poem from the beginning. The troopers' pursuit of the fawn is sharply if elliptically distinguished from the way the fawn hunts the nymph, an action which occupies by contrast the major part of the poem. The fawn is subtle: it both entices the nymph and teaches her the futility of chase. It intimates that the Spirit must seek and woo the soul, rather than vice versa:

> Among the beds of Lillyes, I
> Have sought it oft, where it should lye;
> Yet could not, till it self would rise,
> Find it, although before mine Eyes.
>
> (ll. 77–80)

The "wanton" troopers, however—the adjective *wanton* recalling Shakespeare's "As flies to wanton boys, so are we to the gods"—engage on a willful, crude, and untimely act. Their activism paradoxically forfeits what they perhaps wished to gain.

> Though they should wash their guilty hands
> In this warm life blood, which doth part
> From thine, and wound me to the Heart,
> Yet could they not be clean: their Stain
> Is dy'd in such a Purple Grain.
> There is not such another in
> The World, to offer for their Sin.
>
> (ll. 18–24)

The blood they shed, unlike Christ's, has not purifying virtue because the fawn's migration to Elisium means the migration of the Comforter, our remaining source of *temporal* hope. The fawn's departure may be compared to the Ascension of the young girl's soul in Donne's *Anniversaries*. With it goes the world's "balm," the comfortable hope binding a soul to its station here below. The nymph's very haste to die reveals that she too has relinquished the hope of nature being allied to grace.

I would recall, at this point, that the theme of the spiritual chase and that of the Comforter are closely related. The idea of a Comforter enters the Gospels when Christ foresees a conflict between apocalyptic expectation and secular time. What attitude should his disciples take toward things temporal during his "desertion" and before the end of days? The end may be near, yet there remains a space of time not redeemed by the divine presence. One can hardly blame the expectant soul for showing impatience—it has waited sixteen centuries. Its dilemma, at once moral and political, a dilemma Protestantism sharpened, is

whether to accept the temporizing character of the church. It is not difficult
to see the troopers as the spirit of activism wishing to speed redemption or
ruin—in short, to force the issue—by an act directed in a sense against time
itself. The poem, of course, does not allow us to say more about their deed
than that it is epochal, like the slaying of the albatross in "The Ancient Mariner."
But to say this is enough: when their act is compared to the respect for time
and nature shown by their victim, we are apprised of two opposite attitudes
toward temporality.

It is interesting that the chase after the spirit affects even the nymph.
Though her wish to die has, like everything in the poem, a psychological
justness, she too is *hastening the end*. The excess of love speeding her toward
death:

> O do not run too fast: for I
> Will but bespeak thy Grave, and dye
> > (ll. 109f.)

perhaps resembles, on another plane, the haste of the troopers. It is not unusual
in Marvell's world:

> Thus, though we cannot make our Sun
> Stand still, yet we will make him run.
> > ("To His Coy Mistress")

> And Flow'rs, and Grass, and I and all,
> Will in one common Ruine fall.
> > ("The Mower's Song")

Such a chase out of or beyond nature stands directly against the fawn's example, its slow metamorphosis. The fawn prefigured a redemption with nature,
not from it. The comfort it gave was that even the smallest thing in nature is
worthy of love. Thus there are two similar violations depicted in Marvell's poem.
Like wantonness, great spiritual love removes the soul from the sphere of
redemptive patience.

Marvell goes very far in depicting the fawn as an exemplar of the loving
patience which effects the redemption of nature with man, of all in all. Because
of the fawn, nymph and garden merge. With the strong images of Song of Songs
in the background ("I am the rose of Sharon, and the lily of the vallies"), the
nymph comes close to being identified with the garden in which the fawn grazes;
and when the fawn prints roses on her lips it suggests her metamorphosis, one
parallel to its own. The pun in the strangely emphasized lines:

> Said He, look how your Huntsman here
> Hath taught a Faun to hunt his *Dear*
>
> (ll. 31–32)

marks this ultimate blending in a playfully prophetic way. The nymph, hunted by the fawn, approaches fawn nature. The distinction of kind is dissolved, and the statue the nymph imagines at the poem's end also draws her and the fawn into a single, if artificial, body—into an "artifice of eternity."

With this we have an allegory that respects the poem. The fawn, in its widest significance, wooing the soul to hope in a love redemption inclusive of nature, is a *Panunculus,* a little Pan; it foreshadows the reintegration or restitution of all things (see Rom. 8:32 and Acts 3:21). Thus the pastoral trappings (Sylvio, nymph, fawn) are not patina. The poet needs a world in which metamorphosis is possible—where a nymph is a nymph, able to assume both a human and an elemental shape, while her pet is equally amphibious. This is the world of Pan, the reconciler of man and nature—in Marvell's conception, the reconciler of all things, even of Pagan and Christian. For in the poem hardly a sentiment or phrase must be taken as Christian. The poet is himself a Pan who has created through the accepted magic of poetry a middle-world pointing to the ultimate reconciliation of Pagan and Christian. His consciousness, like the nymph's love, stands ideally beyond the division into sacred and profane.

Ideally, for there remains the opening and crucial event, the blood fact which thrusts us into the midst of, and itself on, this happy world. I want to comment finally, on its brevity. It stands against everything the pastoral stands for by a brutal shorthand. As such it threatens not only the realm of the nymph but also that of *musing* generally. The event is the intrusion of a historical into a pastoral world. Perhaps even more: is not history here set fatally against poetry? The problematic situation of the poet begins to emerge.

Before Marvell, the opposition between history and poetry is more conciliable. A poet, following Virgil's example, begins with pastoral or "oaten reeds" and graduates to epic or "trumpets sterne." Not that pastoral is completely aloof from history, from politics in the largest sense. The pressure of the greater world is there for those who can recognize it. Virgil always sings of "arms and the man," even in his pastoral world which is no less precarious or competitive than the world of the *Georgics* or of the *Aeneid.* There are things, crucial things, to be gained or lost in all the worlds. But with Spenser the realm of the pastoral expands so much that we never reach epic as such. *The Faerie Queene* is pastoral which has swallowed both epic and romance. Whatever the reason for this, it is clear from the shape of Spenser's career—which begins with a translation of those strange emblem sonnets in Van der Noot's *Theater for Worldings*—that the opposition now is less between pastoral and epic than between pastoral and acopalypse. Van der Noot's *Theater*, a kind of visionary peep show, sets up a pastoral image (a stately ship, a fair hind, a pure spring of water) only to show its destruction—the ship sunk, the hind hunted to death, the spring defiled. This medieval, or now Calvinistic, exercise can but lead to a passionate cry to be delivered from the body of this death, or to a justifying and compensatory revelation—we are duly given both. Although Spenser's part in the *Theater for Worldings* may have been marginal, his mature poetry develops as an attempt to overcome this crude kind of hiatus or vacillation between levels of truth. His allegories are a marvellous blend of pastoral, historical, and apocalyptic—an imaginative, fluid, and shifty continuum. *The Faerie Queene* is a maze that cannot be threaded except by a kind of relay technique: one interpretation being suspended in favor of another just as, on the level of plot, an action may be suspended in mid-career. Spenser pays a price, however, for this essentially humble emphasis on the depth and deviousness of the progress from pastoral innocence to ultimate truth. His poetry is patently a conceit, a magnanimous yet artificial construct. It suggests that only as *poesis* can poetry mediate between pastoral appearances, historical darkness, and apocalyptic revelation.

Poetry's mediating virtue is still, for Marvell, the great and necessary virtue, but no longer a sufficient one. The new, perhaps desperate faith of his age in the *sortes* of history—its desire for a clean break and a clear commencement of the kingdom of God on earth—militates against an ethic of compromise which poets had learned from their long endeavor to reconcile classical forms and Christian sentiments. The opening of Marvell's "Horatian Ode,"

> The forward Youth that would appear
> Must now forsake his *Muses* dear

drives a wedge between acting and musing as clearly as "The Nymph's Complaint." It does so even as violently as that poem, because Cromwell,

> like the three fork'd Lightning, first
> Breaking the Clouds where it was nurst,
> Did thorough his own Side
> His fiery way divide.

Cromwell's first act is that "bloody" stroke which in Marvell's poetry threatens so often the pastoral consciousness and expresses the necessity for civilization to proceed by and through schism. There is the stroke that separates church from church, and now sect from sect; the stroke that separates province from province; and the stroke that separates the head (the king) from the body. What can poetry do in this situation? It gathers to itself at the opposite pole the vision of lost and original unity, yet cannot be more (because separated by history from history) than a perennial monument of tears. Marvell's poem ends with an image of itself, an evocation of exquisitely fashioned grief.

The irremediable disjoining of—in particular—profane and sacred, or history and providence, is expressed most directly by the "Horatian Ode." Cromwell's rejection of the slowly grinding divine mills, his espousal of an actively urged salvation, violates, like the Troopers, a nature identified as providential time. A "bleeding Head" is once again and ironically the prerequisite for the body politic's wholeness. Marvell acknowledges this wound inflicted on the "great Work of Time." Yet he lives at the heart of the dilemma and refuses to hasten the end. He does not, like the nymph, forsake hope in temporal salvation because of a single unnatural act. There is no doubt, however, that Cromwell's mode of redemption is hazardous. The new order is forced to unify by the sword, by division, by a rape of time.

At this point the obvious classical analogue to Marvell's story of nymph and fawn becomes relevant. I refer to the slaying of Sylvia's stag in the seventh book of the *Aeneid*. Here also there is a wanton intrusion of history-bearers into a pastoral world. Marvell shares the Virgilian regret for a transcended world closer to nature's rhythm. But that world is indistinguishable now from the state of mind that can evoke it, a state of mind which has no future and enshrines itself in idylls and precious relics. For despite Spenser's great example, the forsaking of the Muses has continued. Having ravaged many a blissful bower, the Renaissance hero will not spare the bower of poetry itself. In "The Nymph" Spenserian allegory laments itself in the pagan form of the brief elegy. The death of nymph and fawn denotes too deep a schism in human affairs for pastoral allegory to assuage.

LOUIS L. MARTZ

Andrew Marvell: The Mind's Happiness

Thomas Carew and George Herbert were almost exact contemporaries, members of the generation immediately following the great masters, Donne and Jonson; and both Carew and Herbert were, in their own ways, courtly poets, gathering up in their collected poems all the grace and wit of the world of song that made this era of English culture the greatest era of English music. Both were, in their own ways, courtiers: one, the courtier of the Queen of Love and Beauty, the earthly Venus; and the other, the courtier of Heavenly Love, addressing to his Lord the art that the Cavalier world addressed to Mortal Love. Both sang their songs in what they felt to be a realm of true security: Carew within the elegant Court of Charles I, and Herbert within the "perfect lineaments" of "The British Church":

> A fine aspect in fit aray,
> Neither too mean, nor yet too gay,
> > Shows who is best.
> Outlandish looks may not compare:
> For all they either painted are,
> > Or else undrest.
>
> . . . .
> But, dearest Mother, what those misse,
> The mean, thy praise and glorie is,
> > And long may be.
> Blessed be God, whose love it was
> To double-moat thee with his grace,
> > And none but thee.

From *The Wit of Love.* © 1969 by the University of Notre Dame Press.

Richard Crashaw and Andrew Marvell, in the next generation, knew very little of such security, since both lived through the era of those Civil Wars which shattered the established institutions of Church and State. For a time, during the 1630s, they shared a brief security in place and thought, at Cambridge University, where Marvell was a student at Trinity, and Crashaw, older by about nine years, lived down the road a bit as a fellow of Peterhouse. In 1637 their poems (in Latin and Greek) appeared together in a volume published at Cambridge honoring the birth of the Princess Anne. At this time both poets seem to have shared High Church tendencies: Marvell seems for a short time to have been converted to the Roman Catholic faith, as Crashaw was to be a few years later. But during the Civil Wars their ways utterly diverged. Crashaw, ousted from his post at Peterhouse because of his loyalty to King and Church, went abroad, embraced the Roman faith, and died at the shrine of Loreto in the same year that saw his King's death, in 1649. Marvell, after a period of mixed loyalties, mirrored in the ambiguities of his famous "Horatian Ode," at last gave his full support to the cause of the Commonwealth and, in particular, to Oliver Cromwell. Both the personal and the poetical careers of Crashaw and of Marvell may be taken to symbolize two utterly different ways of resolving the fierce dilemmas of the day.

In this hiatus, a period when a new world of religious and political thought was in the process of violent formation, Marvell looks back upon the remains of courtly culture with attraction and regret, as we may see from the poem that he wrote "To His Noble Friend Mr. Richard Lovelace, upon His Poems"—a poem prefaced to Lovelace's volume of Cavalier poetry published in 1649:

> Our times are much degenerate from those
> Which your sweet Muse which your fair Fortune chose,
> And as complexions alter with the Climes,
> Our wits have drawne th'infection of our times.
> That candid Age no other way could tell
> To be ingenious, but by speaking well.
> Who best could prayse, had then the greatest prayse,
> Twas more esteemd to give, then weare the Bayes:
> Modest ambition studi'd only then,
> To honour not her selfe, but worthy men.
> These vertues now are banisht out of Towne,
> Our Civill Wars have lost the Civicke crowne.
> He highest builds, who with most Art destroys,
> And against others Fame his owne employs.

> I see the envious Caterpillar sit
> On the faire blossome of each growing wit.

It is appropriate that Marvell should thus pay tribute to this poet, whose songs to Lucasta and to Althea represent the very essence of the Cavalier devotion to the Lady and to the King, expressed with all the art of courtly elegance. I say it is appropriate, because Marvell's poetry in many ways derives from the Mannerist art that we have seen in Carew and his fellow Cavaliers. Marvell has a love song, "The Match," addressed to a girl named Celia, praising her as Nature's treasury of "*Orientest* Colours," "Essences most pure," and "sweetest Perfumes." He has another song addressed to a fair Lady singing—one of Carew's favorite themes. He has of course that famous poem "To His Coy Mistress," following in the tradition represented by Carew's poem in the same meter: "To A. L. Perswasions to love." And he has three graceful pastoral dialogues where nymph and shepherd converse in singing repartee, as in two elegant songs by Carew. In many ways Marvell and Carew show the same inheritance of the European love-lyric, modified by an infusion of Donne's argumentative wit, and by Jonson's art of terse craftsmanship.

Yet at the same time Marvell inherits the tradition of the religious love-lyric brought to perfection by Herbert, and in his poem "The Coronet" we find him "Dismantling all the fragrant Towers" which he has used to adorn his shepherdess's head, in an effort to recreate the flowers of secular poetry as a tribute to his Savior. But he finds the serpent old entwined within his garland of devotion, for motives of fame and self-interest have made the attempted tribute impure; and so he prays:

> But thou who only could'st the Serpent tame,
> Either his slipp'ry knots at once untie,
> And disintangle all his winding Snare:
> Or shatter too with him my curious frame:
> And let these wither, so that he may die,
> Though set with Skill and chosen out with Care.
> That they, while Thou on both their Spoils dost tread,
> May crown thy Feet, that could not crown thy Head.

It is, for the most part, a powerful effort in the devotional mode of Herbert, and yet in the last few lines the gnarled and intricate evolution of thought, with a tortured vagueness in the pronouns, creates an effect quite different from the characteristic serenity of Herbert's endings. We need to remember such conclusions in Herbert as these:

Love is that liquour sweet and most divine,
Which my God feels as bloud; but I, as wine.

But while I bustled, I might heare a friend
Whisper, *How wide is all this long pretence!*
There is in love a sweetnesse readie penn'd:
Copie out onely that, and save expense.

But grones are quick, and full of wings,
And all their motions upward be;
And ever as they mount, like larks they sing;
The note is sad, yet musick for a King.

But as I rav'd and grew more fierce and wilde
At every word,
Me thoughts I heard one calling, *Child!*
And I reply'd, *My Lord.*

You must sit down, sayes Love, and taste my meat:
So I did sit and eat.

Far from achieving the goal of humility that Herbert implies in those endings, Marvell ends with an intricate flourish of wit that shows the pride of an indomitable intellect, saying in effect, "I pray all this in order that my poems, while you, God, tread both on Satan and on my poetry, may crown your feet, since they could not succeed in crowning your head." It is all too clever, and yet the whole ending functions in the poem to show that Marvell's Mannerist pride in his exquisite contrivance, his "curious frame," is still a part of his being.

So in Marvell the art of the Cavalier and the religious problems of the time converge in an uneasy alliance: set with skill, and chosen out with care, his poems contemplate, from various angles, the deepest issues of the age. We can feel these issues breaking through the fragile Mannerist artifact in one of his pastoral dialogues, entitled "Clorinda and Damon," where the pagan world of "Gather ye rosebuds" meets with the Christian sense of mortality and sin. Clorinda, the shepherdess, invites Damon to come to her grassy meadow "Where *Flora* blazons all her pride." "The Grass I aim to feast thy Sheep," she explains, "The Flow'rs I for thy Temples keep." But Damon refuses, saying "Grass withers; and the Flow'rs too fade." But Clorinda insists upon her *carpe diem* theme, and so their interplay continues:

C. Seize the short Joyes then, ere they vade.
   Seest thou that unfrequented Cave?
D. That den?   C. Loves Shrine.   D. But Virtue's Grave.
C. In whose cool bosome we may lye
   Safe from the Sun.   D. not Heaven's Eye.
C. Near this, a Fountaines liquid Bell
   Tinkles within the concave Shell.
D. Might a Soul bath there and be clean,
   Or slake its Drought?   C. What is't you mean?

Clearly Damon has at last shattered Clorinda's complacency and has indeed shattered the pastoral scene with the fearful religious question. And Damon then goes on to explain how all is now changed for him, alluding to Christ under the conventional name of Pan, as in Milton's "Nativity Ode":

D. These once had been enticing things,
   Clorinda, Pastures, Caves, and Springs.
C. And what late change?   D. The other day
   Pan met me.   C. What did great *Pan* say?
D. Words that transcend poor Shepherds skill,
   But He ere since my Songs does fill:
   And his Name swells my slender Oate.
C. Sweet must *Pan* sound in *Damons* Note.
D. *Clorinda's* voice might make it sweet.
C. Who would not in *Pan's* Praises meet?

CHORUS

Of *Pan* the flowry Pastures sing,
Caves eccho, and the Fountains ring.
Sing then while he doth us inspire;
For all the World is our *Pan's* Quire.

It is a happy reconciliation, but does Clorinda know what Damon means by Pan? Or does Damon know what Clorinda means by Pan? Is not this happy Chorus perhaps a mixed marriage of voices singing different gods? They are too much in love, it seems, to inquire exactly what each of them means by Pan. Here, within the poem's fragile artifice, the clash between Christian and Pagan threatens for a moment the destruction of both the Mannerist and the pastoral world; but the conflict is gaily and humorously healed.

A more dangerous threat is perhaps suggested in the "Dialogue between Thyrsis and Dorinda," where the shepherd Thyrsis describes his pastoral

Elizium in such attractive terms that the naive nymph Dorinda suddenly falls sick of longing for it and suggests that they commit suicide in order to achieve such beauty in the after-life:

> *Dorinda.* Ah me, ah me. *(Thyrsis.) Dorinda,* why do'st Cry?

> *Dorinda.* I'm sick, I'm sick, and fain would dye:
>   Convince me now, that this is true;
>   By bidding, with mee, all adieu.

> *Thrysis.* I cannot live, without thee, I
>   Will for thee, much more with thee dye.

> *Chorus.* Then let us give *Carillo* charge o'th Sheep,
>   And thou and I'le pick poppies and them steep
>   In wine, and drink on't even till we weep,
>   So shall we smoothly pass away in sleep.

Is Marvell suggesting that there may be a certain danger in the tendency of some religious sects to emphasize the joys of the future life? It would be going too far to say this: one might better say only that Marvell's curiously detached mind is here using the pastoral artifice to contemplate, at a considerable distance, a possible religious issue. This indeed might be said of all five of the poems of conflict that Marvell has cast into the dialogue form, poems that range from the purely spiritual to the purely carnal: from the spiritual victory of the Resolved Soul to the physical victory of the girl Thestylis, as she entices Ametas into her hay-mow, with the words:

> What you cannot constant hope
> Must be taken as you may.

And Ametas answers:

> Then let's both lay by our Rope,
> And go kiss within the Hay.

Even when the pastoral guard is dropped and the religious issues are joined head-on, one senses the curious detachment of Marvell's wit—curious in our meaning of the word and also in Marvell's own meaning of "exquisite," "elegant." Consider the poem that opens Marvell's collected poems of 1681, "A Dialogue between the Resolved Soul, and Created Pleasure," where Marvell deals with a central topic of the age, "the spiritual combat." The poem opens traditionally enough, with a familiar self-address, echoing the words of St. Paul in the Epistle to the Ephesians:

> Courage my Soul, now learn to wield
> The weight of thine immortal Shield.
> Close on thy Head thy Helmet bright.
> Ballance thy Sword against the Fight.

But as we read on we may wonder exactly what is happening, for the temptations of Pleasure seem so absurdly overdrawn:

> On these downy Pillows lye,
> Whose soft Plumes will thither fly:
> On these Roses strow'd so plain
> Lest one Leaf thy Side should strain.

And the Soul's answers seem so clipped and pat and almost smug:

> My gentler Rest is on a Thought,
> Conscious of doing what I ought.
>
> . . . .
>
> A Soul that knowes not to presume
> Is Heaven's and its own perfume.

So the whole poem comes to suggest an undercurrent of playful wit, reinforced and brought into the open by the Soul's pun on the word *Chordage* in answer to the temptation by the pleasure of music:

> Cease Tempter. None can chain a mind
> Whom this sweet Chordage cannot bind.

Is the poem a serious exercise in self-analysis, or is it rather a graceful exercise of lyric wit in the Jonsonian mode of terse craftsmanship?

So it is too with "A Dialogue between the Soul and Body," where Marvell seems to enjoy developing the ingenious play of wit by which Soul and Body, each speaking in monologue rather than dialogue, blindly denounce each other for causing each other's torment. Then the poet at the close cleverly suggests a resolution to the dilemma by adding four lines to the Body's stanza:

> What but a Soul could have the wit
> To build me up for Sin so fit?
> So Architects do square and hew,
> Green Trees that in the Forest grew.

So Marvell suggests to us, perhaps, that there is some purpose in this conflict that the two antagonists do not grasp—that there is a higher architecture in which both Soul and Body are made according to the Architect's design.

This range of subject is characteristic of Marvell's lyric poetry, which ranges from the total celebration of the Soul in "On a Drop of Dew," to the total celebration of the claims of physical passion in "To His Coy Mistress." I say *total*. And yet both poems are written with their own kind of curious detachment. The poem "On a Drop of Dew" is a perfectly executed spiritual exercise. It presents first a clear visual image or similitude (a composition of place): the drop of dew lying on the purple flower; then the understanding proceeds to apply this image to the plight of the human Soul; and finally the power of the will draws forth a firm spiritual meaning. Thus the middle of the poem develops an Augustinian theme:

> So the Soul, that Drop, that Ray
> Of the clear Fountain of Eternal Day,
> Could it within the humane flow'r be seen,
>   Remembring still its former height,
>   Shuns the sweat leaves and blossoms green;
>   And, recollecting its own Light,
> Does, in its pure and circling thoughts, express
> The greater Heaven in an Heaven less.

The word *recollecting* means not only "remembering," and "collecting together," or "concentrating the attention," but it also suggests the spiritual state of "recollection," in which the Soul is absorbed in religious contemplation, leading to the state of "illumination." It would seem that Marvell is tending toward an intense insight, reminiscent of the poetry of Henry Vaughan. But then the poem breaks away into a strange and unexpected dance: a neat series of lines paced with a Cavalier elegance:

> In how coy a Figure wound,
> Every way it turns away:
> So the World excluding round,
> Yet receiving in the Day.
> Dark beneath, but bright above:
> Here disdaining, there in Love,
> How loose and easie hence to go:
> How girt and ready to ascend.
> Moving but on a point below,
> It all about does upwards bend.
> Such did the Manna's sacred Dew destil;
> White, and intire, though congeal'd and chill.
> Congeal'd on Earth: but does, dissolving, run
> Into the Glories of th' Almighty Sun.

It is perfect spiritual exercise—yes—but may one say that it is almost too perfect, too coolly contrived to create a deep religious feeling? The fact that Marvell also wrote a companion poem to this in Latin, using the same themes and images, may suggest the highly tentative, detached, and experimental nature of the approach to religious experience that Marvell is dealing with here. The Latin poem and the English poem work together to create the impression that this poet is contemplating here the possibility of engaging in religious contemplation, but has not re-created the experience of contemplation itself.

This poem, in its ebbing and flowing lines, suggests a cool and miniature version of one of Crashaw's passionate Odes or abundant Hymns, and indeed in one phrase, "its own Tear," the poem echoes a phrase used in Crashaw's poem to Mary Magdalene entitled "The Teare." One may fairly grasp the curiously detached and guarded quality of Marvell's religious poems by contrasting the Baroque exuberance of Crashaw's poems on the tears of the Magdalene with the cool and logical precision of Marvell's contribution to this literature of penitence—his poem "Eyes and Tears." Two stanzas from Crashaw's "The Weeper" will serve to make the point, if set against the opening and closing stanzas of Marvell's poem:

> O cheekes! Beds of chast loves,
>   By your own showers seasonably dash't,
>   Eyes! nests of milkie Doves
>   In your owne wells decently washt.
> O wit of love that thus could place,
> Fountaine and Garden in one face!
>
> . . . .
>
>   'Twas his well pointed dart
>   That dig'd these wells, and drest this Vine,
>   And taught that wounded heart,
>   The way into those weeping Eyne,
> Vaine loves avant! Bold hands forbeare,
> The Lamb hath dipt his white foote here.
>
> (sts. 15, 18)

Now contrast these exuberant stanzas by Crashaw with the lucid, logical couplets of Marvell:

> How wisely Nature did decree,
> With the same Eyes to weep and see!
> That, having view'd the object vain,
> They might be ready to complain.

> And, since the Self-deluding Sight,
> In a false Angle takes each hight;
> These Tears which better measure all,
> Like wat'ry Lines and Plummets fall.
>
> . . . .
>
> Ope then mine Eyes your double Sluice,
> And practise so your noblest Use.
> For others too can see, or sleep;
> But only humane Eyes can weep.
>
> Now like two Clouds dissolving, drop,
> And at each Tear in distance stop:
> Now like two Fountains trickle down:
> Now like two floods o'return and drown.
>
> Thus let your Streams o'reflow your Springs,
> Till Eyes and Tears be the same things:
> And each the other's difference bears;
> These weeping Eyes, those seeing Tears.
>
> > (ll. 1–8, 45–56)

One may wonder whether this is a religious poem, or whether it is better called a witty Mannerist exercise on a religious theme, mingling cleverly the argued wit of Donne, the Baroque paradoxes of Crashaw, and the neat trim craftsmanship of Jonson. However this may be, the strict rational discipline of the poem seems ill suited to the far-flung nature of the imagery here, with the result that the images have an effect of being coolly contrived, not growing out of some inevitable problem or passion, as in the better poems of Donne or Crashaw.

We can see somewhat the same effect in Marvell's poem "The Definition of Love," where Marvell seems determined to outdo Donne in the ingenuity of his metaphysical conceits. It is Marvell's most Donne-like poem, and yet the effect of these terse, clipped, neat stanzas is ultimately quite unlike Donne.

> My Love is of a birth as rare
> As 'tis for object strange and high:
> It was begotten by despair
> Upon Impossibility.
>
> Magnanimous Despair alone
> Could show me so divine a thing,
> Where feeble Hope could ne'r have flown
> But vainly flapt its Tinsel Wing.

> And yet I quickly might arrive
> Where my extended Soul is fixt,
> But Fate does Iron wedges drive,
> And alwaies crouds it self betwixt.
>
> For Fate with jealous Eye does see
> Two perfect Loves; nor lets them close:
> Their union would her ruine be,
> And her Tyrannick pow'r depose.
>
> And therefore her Decrees of Steel
> Us as the distant Poles have plac'd,
> (Though Loves whole World on us doth wheel)
> Not by themselves to be embrac'd.
>
> (ll. 1–20)

It has surely a measure of Donne's passionate reasoning in his pursuit of Love's philosophy, but the reasoning here is so coolly and deliberately done that the passion is carefully tamped down, and never threatens to escape as it so often does in Donne's anguish. So Marvell's "Definition" firmly ends:

> As Lines so Loves *oblique* may well
> Themselves in every Angle greet:
> But ours so truly *Paralel,*
> Though infinite can never meet.
>
> Therefore the Love which us doth bind,
> But Fate so enviously debarrs,
> Is the Conjunction of the Mind,
> And Opposition of the Stars.
>
> (ll. 25–32)

We remember how in Donne's "Valediction: Forbidding Mourning," the geometrical conceit at the close had served as an expression of the strain and anguish that besets the parting of two true lovers, to whom separation is as a death. But here, although one admires the geometrical neatness of this conclusion, there is little sense of an underlying passion. Here again Marvell seems to be contemplating the feeling of what it might be like to be in love instead of creating the dramatic state of Love's actuality.

Even the famous "To His Coy Mistress" has, in its own way, a quality of detachment about it, for all its apparent urgency. We may feel this quality with particular force if we compare the poem with Robert Herrick's "Corinna's Going A-Maying." In Herrick's poem human love is represented as a part of the

fruitful process of nature: love blooms and dies as nature dies, and the emphasis
falls upon the beauty of the natural process. Herrick's poem is in tune with
nature, but Marvell's poem is at war with nature; the speaker's wit seems to
resent the shortness of life, which Herrick's poem sadly accepts. The speaker's
tone toward his reserved and respectable young Lady shifts within each of the
poem's three sections moving from sly, humorous banter, to sardonic threats,
and finally to something like a fierce desperation. The poem opens with mock
politeness:

> Had we but World enough, and Time,
> This coyness Lady were no crime.
> We would sit down, and think which way
> To walk, and pass our long Loves Day.
> Thou by the *Indian Ganges* side
> Should'st Rubies find: I by the Tide
> Of *Humber* would complain.

For, Lady, he says, "you deserve this State," this pomp, this ceremony, "Nor
would I love at lower rate," that is, lower estimation. But, he continues, we have
very little time:

> And yonder all before us lye
> Desarts of vast Eternity.

And after a gruesome reminder of what the worms will do to her he ends with
a sardonic tone of excessive politeness:

> The Grave's a fine and private place,
> But none I think do there embrace.

And then he swings quickly into his conclusion with inevitable logic:

> Now therefore, while the youthful hew
> Sits on thy skin like morning glew.

(I keep the reading of the first edition instead of using the common emenda-
tion "dew," because it seems likely that "glew" is simply a variant spelling of
the word "glow," and that what the poet is saying here is that the youthful color
sitting on her skin is like the morning-glow of sunrise.)

> And while thy willing Soul transpires
> At every pore with instant Fires,
> Now let us sport us while we may;
> And now, like am'rous birds of prey,

> Rather at once our Time devour,
> Than languish in his slow-chapt pow'r.
> Let us roll all our Strength, and all
> Our sweetness, up into one Ball:
> And tear our Pleasures with rough strife,
> Thorough the Iron gates of Life.
> Thus, though we cannot make our Sun
> Stand still, yet we will make him run.

"We cannot make our Sun / Stand still," like Joshua or like Zeus when he seduced Alcmene and produced Heracles, but we can at least eat up our time with devouring strife. But what kind of pleasure is this? Marvell has consumed all the natural beauty out of the experience of human love. Is he suggesting that perhaps the rosebud-philosophy is self-destructive, corrosive, and ultimately empty? Is this a love poem at all? Is it not rather a poem about man's fear of Time?

I hope my emphasis on Marvell's detachment, his concern for style, his coolly crafted art, has not served to suggest that I think Marvell's poems are themselves rather empty. This is the problem that one often faces in dealing with Mannerist art. Is the manner mere imitation, lacking any depth or real significance, or is the manner a way of guarding the mind's uncertainty in its quest for ultimate values? Does the elegance of style stand as a mask before some inner tension? Or does it serve as a defense against the revelation of some intimate, impossible ideal? In asking this question I am moving away from the earlier and simpler account of Mannerism that I used [elsewhere] in discussing the poetry of Carew. I am moving away from John Shearman's emphasis on *style* as the prime criterion, and moving on into the deeper and more inclusive account of Mannerism set forth in the splendid study of Arnold Hauser (*Mannerism: The Crisis of the Renaissance and the Origin of Modern Art*). The greatness of Hauser's conception of Mannerism lies in the fact that he can include the spiritual, the intellectual, the playful, the poignant and the elegant all within one compelling account of a great artistic movement, for which, I am convinced, Andrew Marvell stands as a prime English representative. For Marvell has the qualities that Hauser finds at the heart of Mannerism. "A certain piquancy, a predilection for the subtle, the strange, the over-strained, the abstruse and yet stimulating, the pungent, the bold, and the challenging, are characteristic of mannerist art in all its phases," says Hauser. And he adds, "It is often this piquancy—a playful or compulsive deviation from the normal, an affected, frisky quality, or a tormented grimace—that first betrays the mannerist nature of a work. The virtuosity that is always displayed contributes greatly to the piquancy." But underneath this playfulness or piquancy Hauser finds a quality that seems to me to lie at the very center of Marvell's vision: an intellectualized view of existence that makes it possible to maintain all the conflicting elements of life within a flexible yet highly regulated vision:

> The conflict expressed the conflict of life itself and the ambivalence of all human attitudes; in short, it expresses the dialectical principle that underlies the whole of the mannerist outlook. This is based, not merely on the conflicting nature of occasional experience, but on the permanent ambiguity of all things, great and small, and on the impossibility of attaining certainty about anything. All the products of the mind must therefore show that we live in a world of irreducible tensions and mutually exclusive and yet inter-connected opposites. For nothing in this world exists absolutely, the opposite of every reality is also real and true. Everything is ex-pressed in extremes opposed to other extremes, and it is only by this paradoxical pairing of opposites that meaningful statement is pos-sible. This paradoxical approach does not signify, however, that each statement is the retraction of the last, but that truth inherently has two sides, that reality is Janus-faced, and that adherence to truth and reality involves the avoidance of all over-simplification and com-prehending things in their complexity.

Thus Marvell, in 1650, could write that great "Horatian Ode" in which he carefully weighs the virtues of the King and of Cromwell, seeing the poi-gnancy of one and the power of the other, including both within an intellec-tual vision that is able to choose, at the end, the side of destiny, without ceas-ing to regret the necessity of the destruction of ancient institutions. And alongside the paradoxical vision of that Ode, Marvell could then place, perhaps only a few years later, his great poem "The Garden," in which the joys of intel-lectual peace are praised as the center of existence. Thus, in the famous cen-tral stanzas of "The Garden," the speaker finds his harmony, both physical and mental, in an easy relationship with the created universe:

> What wond'rous Life in this I lead!
> Ripe Apples drop about my head;
> The Luscious Clusters of the Vine
> Upon my Mouth do crush their Wine;
> The Nectaren, and curious Peach,
> Into my hands themselves do reach;

> Stumbling on Melons, as I pass,
> Insnar'd with Flow'rs, I fall on Grass.

And while the body enjoys that fortunate fall, the mind, withdrawing from these lesser (physical) pleasures, discovers and creates its own happiness:

> Mean while the Mind, from pleasure less,
> Withdraws into its happiness:
> The Mind, that Ocean where each kind
> Does streight its own resemblance find;
> Yet it creates, transcending these,
> Far other Worlds, and other Seas;
> Annihilating all that's made
> To a green Thought in a green Shade.

The mind, that is to say, contains within itself the images drawn from the outer world; yet it creates, transcending these, worlds of the human imagination, which arise from the creative and unifying power that Marvell suggests in the word *annihilating*. There is an allusion here to the mystical usage of the word, as Crashaw has used it when he speaks of "soft *exhalations* / Of *Soule; deare and Divine *annihilations.*" But of course the word is used by Marvell in a characteristically playful sense, for in mystical annihilation all sensory images are destroyed and the soul ascends into the realm of pure spirit. In "The Garden" the process of annihilation blends the greenness of nature with the abstract purity of thought. And even as the soul ascends upward in Marvell's poem, thought remains still allied with sensory things, as we may see from the next stanza, where the soul does not leave the physical, but remains connected with the body through the tree:

> Here at the Fountains sliding foot,
> Or at some Fruit-trees mossy root,
> Casting the Bodies Vest aside,
> My Soul into the boughs does glide:
> There like a Bird it sits, and sings,
> Then whets, and combs its silver Wings;
> And, till prepar'd for longer flight,
> Waves in its Plumes the various Light.

Then in the next stanza Marvell's quiet humor reminds us that the mind is still within the world of man, as he humorously recalls Adam's happy state, before Eve, the cause of all his woes, was created as an help meet for him:

> Such was that happy Garden-state,
> While Man there walk'd without a Mate:
> After a Place so pure, and sweet,
> What other Help could yet be meet!
> But 'twas beyond a Mortal's share
> To wander solitary there:
> Two Paradises 'twere in one
> To live in Paradise alone.

And finally, in stanza 9, perhaps a symbol of numerical perfection, Marvell returns gently and easily into the world of time as he presents his image of the floral sun-dial, and concludes:

> How could such sweet and wholsome Hours
> Be reckon'd but with herbs and flow'rs!

Less wholesome hours, no doubt, await the speaker in the outer world, but the mind's happiness remains within, a sure retreat that underlies the varied explorations conveyed in all his other poems.

As at the end of a long avenue, one catches a distant glimpse of this ideal in the poem that might be regarded as the most obviously Mannerist of all Marvell's works, the one entitled "The Gallery," which Jean Hagstrum has suggested must be influenced by the famous volume of Marino's poetry entitled *La Galeria,* where Marino bases his poetry upon various paintings and sculptures, or gives in similar terms imaginary portraits of his own. Following this mode of action Marvell here presents to us the art gallery of his soul, hung, he says, with various portraits of his Lady:

> *Clora* come view my Soul, and tell
> Whether I have contriv'd it well.

It opens with the characteristic gesture of all Mannerist art: he urges the viewer to watch closely and to judge whether the work is well "contrived." Here in his Soul, he says, she is first painted in the dress "Of an Inhumane Murtheress," tormenting her lover with "Black Eyes, red Lips, and curled Hair." Then on the other side he says she is drawn as a great Renaissance nude:

> Like to *Aurora* in the Dawn;
> When in the East she slumb'ring lyes,
> And stretches out her milky Thighs;

In the next painting she is shown as an "Enchantress," and in the next she sits afloat "Like *Venus* in her pearly Boat," as in some painting by a Botticelli. "These

Pictures and a thousand more," he says, form in his Soul "a Collection choicer far / Then or *White-hall's,* or *Mantua's* were." That is to say, choicer than King Charles's collection in his palace at Whitehall, or the collection of the Duke of Mantua which Charles had purchased. Then he concludes with a significant movement of the mind toward a scene that forms the deep and inner center of all Marvell's poetry, in the close revealing the ideal that underlies his art:

> But, of these Pictures and the rest,
> That at the Entrance likes me best:
> Where the same Posture, and the Look
> Remains, with which I first was took.
> A tender Shepherdess, whose Hair
> Hangs loosely playing in the Air,
> Transplanting Flow'rs from the green Hill,
> To crown her Head, and Bosome fill.

The memory of the green hill, the pastoral landscape, the effort to regain the vision of a lost garden—this is the deep theme of Marvell's poetry, the center of security which lies within his mannered, stylish surface, which is in fact guarded and treasured within that surface. Here Marvell joins the central quest of many of the most significant writers of this mid-century era of turmoil. On the one side he joins the pagan Paradise of Robert Herrick, with the many "fresh and fragrant" girls that live like flowers and live with flowers throughout the *Hesperides.* And on the other side he joins Henry Vaughan, Thomas Traherne, and John Milton in *Paradise Lost*—all in their own ways keeping a kindred image of a pastoral Paradise before their inner eyes. And other writers too, notably Izaak Walton, in his *Compleat Angler,* where he gives us a georgic pastoral, in which the art of fishing provides the setting for a truly religious retreat into an inner Paradise, where man is at one with Nature and with God.

The meaning of this central quest of the mid-century may be suggested in Marvell's small poem "Bermudas," where the longing for the earthly Paradise represents a search for peace amidst the cruel controversies of the age, the ravaging of England by the Civil Wars, the efforts at repressive persecution by whichever side was temporarily dominant in the religious conflicts of the day. Here we have the imagined song of the Puritan refugees from King Charles's High Church policy, refugees who found peace in the remote Bermudas, as others did in Massachusetts:

> What should we do but sing his Praise
> That led us through the watry Maze,
> Unto an Isle so long unknown,

> And yet far kinder than our own?
> Where he the huge Sea-Monsters wracks,
> That lift the Deep upon their Backs.
> He lands us on a grassy Stage;
> Safe from the Storms, and Prelat's rage.
> He gave us this eternal Spring,
> Which here enamells every thing;
> And sends the Fowl's to us in care,
> On daily Visits through the Air.
> He hangs in shades the Orange bright,
> Like golden Lamps in a green Night.
>
> .   .   .   .
>
> And in these Rocks for us did frame
> A Temple, where to sound his Name.
> Oh let our Voice his Praise exalt,
> Till it arrive at Heavens Vault:

It is a Puritan Psalm of Thanksgiving in praise of the Creator's bounty and goodness, by which they have been enabled to reach a place amid these remote rocks to praise their Lord. One should note that, as in *Paradise Lost,* the meaning of Paradise lies in the human response to nature and not in the beauties of nature itself. The physical imagery of nature's beauty is meaningless unless man lives in a state of joyful harmony, with gratitude toward the Creator. Or rather one might say that outer nature has no beauty except as man receives it gratefully within the mind.

Such an attitude toward the meaning of Eden we may see developed in Marvell's symbol of the Mower, whose pastoral existence has been destroyed by love of his particular Eve, named Juliana. In "The Mower to the Glo-Worms" we see that these beneficent works of nature now shine in vain,

> Since *Juliana* here is come,
> For She my Mind hath so displac'd
> That I shall never find my home.

And he continues in "The Mower's Song":

> My Mind was once the true survey
> Of all these Medows fresh and gay:
> And in the greenness of the Grass
> Did see its Hopes as in a Glass;
> When *Juliana* came, and She
> What I do to the Grass, does to my Thoughts and Me.

But now he reproaches the meadows for growing in luxuriance when he is pining away with frustrated love. They ought, he feels, to be fading away like him, but they have instead disloyally forsaken him and have gone their own way. The pastoral condition, we see, depends upon man's state of mind: it is by this that nature becomes either a Paradise or a ruin. Externally, the Mower as he mows is simply doing his usual job: to reap crops, to clear the land for further crops. This is his natural function. But now his function is perverted by sorrow and pain: and so in "Damon the Mower" he sees nature falsely and recklessly seeks revenge upon it for a state of mind which creates his own fall and ruin:

> While thus he threw his Elbow round,
> Depopulating all the Ground,
> And, with his whistling Sythe, does cut
> Each stroke between the Earth and Root,
> The edged Stele by careless chance
> Did into his own Ankle glance;
> And there among the Grass fell down,
> By his own Sythe, the Mower mown.

But his own self-destruction is only a symbol of man's general corruption of these natural harmonies, as the Mower declares in his tirade against artificial gardens:

> Luxurious Man, to bring his Vice in use,
>> Did after him the World seduce:
> And from the fields the Flow'rs and Plants allure,
>> Where Nature was most plain and pure.
> He first enclos'd within the Gardens square
>> A dead and standing pool of Air:
> And a more luscious Earth for them did knead,
>> Which stupifi'd them while it fed.
>
> . . . .
>
> 'Tis all enforc'd; the Fountain and the Grot;
>> While the sweet Fields do lye forgot:
> Where willing Nature does to all dispence
>> A wild and fragrant Innocence:
> And *Fauns* and *Faryes* do the Meadows till,
>> More by their presence then their skill.
> Their Statues polish'd by some ancient hand,
>> May to adorn the Gardens stand:

> But howso'ere the Figures do excel,
>   The *Gods* themselves with us do dwell.

Marvell has in his poetry many other symbols of this kind of "fragrant Innocence," always threatened or overcome by some corruption. Thus even the small girl whom he celebrates in "The Picture of Little T. C. in a Prospect of Flowers" must grow up, damage mankind by her beauty, and then die, despite her Eden-like beginning:

> See with what simplicity
> This Nimph begins her golden daies!
> In the green Grass she loves to lie,
> And there with her fair Aspect tames
> The Wilder flow'rs, and gives them names:
> But only with the Roses playes;
>   And them does tell
> What Colour best becomes them, and what Smell.

Like Adam she names the other creatures, and as with Adam the world of mortality awaits her, as Marvell makes plain in the last stanza:

> But O young beauty of the Woods,
> Whom Nature courts with fruits and flow'rs,
> Gather the Flow'rs, but spare the Buds;
> Lest *Flora* angry at thy crime,
> To kill her Infants in their prime,
> Do quickly make th'Example Yours;
>   And, ere we see,
> Nip in the blossome all our hopes and Thee.

Thus in one way or another she is threatened with the fate that has overtaken the innocent Nymph who complains for the death of her fawn in the enigmatic, fascinating poem that has attracted so much attention by critics and scholars of this century, beginning with Eliot's remark in his fine essay on Marvell:

> Marvell takes a slight affair, the feeling of a girl for her pet, and gives
> it a connexion with that inexhaustible and terrible nebula of emo-
> tion which surrounds all our exact and practical passions and
> mingles with them.

Everyone agrees that the poem must have some symbolic significance—but hardly anyone agrees on what this is. It seems to have some local significance for the English Civil Wars in its opening lines:

> The wanton Troopers riding by
> Have shot my Faun and it will dye.

The Troopers are the marauding cavalrymen of the Civil Wars, on both sides, for the word "Troopers" was a general term: one could speak of Cromwell's Troopers or of Prince Rupert's Troopers. In either case they are wanton in their unruly lack of discipline, in their carelessness of others' rights. But what does the fawn represent? Some have found in him the symbolism of Christ, since the Nymph says

> There is not such another in
> The World, to offer for their Sin.

And a little later she echoes the phrase of Jeremiah (2:2) when she says that the fawn "seem'd to bless / Its self in me." These religious implications are enforced by the garden imagery that follows a little later, imagery that clearly echoes the Song of Solomon, particulary the verses:

> My beloved is gone down into his garden, to the beds of spices,
> to feed in the gardens, and to gather lilies.

> I am my beloved's, and my beloved is mine: he feedeth among
> the lilies.

> (6:2–3)

So we find the fawn in a garden of roses and lilies, and the Nymph says:

> Among the beds of Lillyes, I
> Have sought it oft, where it should lye;

and she finds the fawn feeding upon the roses. The purity of the fawn, and the fact that it dies "as calmely as a Saint," have led some to see in the poem profound Christian implications. But on the other hand the pagan and classical implications are equally strong: similar stories about the deaths of pet deer occur in Virgil and Ovid; the Nymph's tears will be placed "in *Diana's* Shrine," and the fawn will go to a pagan Elizium. The Nymph imagines herself turned into a statue like that of Niobe, forever weeping. Furthermore, she is not weeping just for her pet deer, but also for the faithless man who gave him to her: "unconstant *Sylvio,*" a seducer who talks the old Petrarchan sweet talk:

> Said He, look how your Huntsman here
> Hath taught a Faun to hunt his *Dear.*

The point is that the fawn and the Nymph are both destroyed by "false and cruel men," and the whole poem thus becomes a lament for lost innocence, whether destroyed by war or by human infidelity, whether it exists in pagan or in Christian story. Wanton men kill the very innocence that prays for their salvation.

The end of innocence, the destruction of the pastoral garden, and the search for their recovery in the mind—these are Marvell's deepest themes. His abrasive political satires and his great political poems on Cromwell have all been made possible by the existence of the interior retreat which he describes in the latter half of his long pastoral poem, "Upon Appleton House." Here in the fourth section of that poem (which is clearly divisible into six main parts: the House, the History, the Garden, the Meadow, the Wood, and the Vision of Maria) the speaker's mind plays over the meadow, inventing from its images a fanciful entertainment, a theatrical presentation of worldly scenes, a playful nightmare, where at first man seems to drown in the abyss of greenness:

> To see Men through this Meadow Dive,
> We wonder how they rise alive.

It is a world of flux and change, mingling images of the ideal and the actual, creating a "scene" that seems to change by some mechanical devices such as were used by Inigo Jones in the Court entertainments that we have discussed [elsewhere]:

> No Scene that turns with Engines strange
> Does oftner then these Meadows change.
> For when the Sun the Grass hath vext,
> The tawny Mowers enter next;

Enter, that is, like theatrical performers. And as they mow the meadows we have suggestions of blood and death as the edge of the scythe cuts into the peaceful birds nesting on the ground. Then another change brings in a battle scene, intricately "wrought":

> The Mower now commands the Field;
> In whose new Traverse seemeth wrought
> A Camp of Battail newly fought:
> Where, as the Meads with Hay, the Plain
> Lyes quilted ore with Bodies slain:
> The Women that with forks it fling,
> Do represent the Pillaging.

The word "traverse" means literally the action of the mowers as they make their ways back and forth across the field; but "traverse" in the language of Marvell's time could also mean a curtain. It is upon this curtain, as though it were a tapestry, that the "Camp of Battail" is "wrought," "Camp" being used here in the old sense of *champ,* that is, a field of battle, as the word "Plain" in the next line makes clear. In this curiously inverted analogy, Marvell is saying that as on some great curtain, the Meads are quilted over with fallen hay just as on a battlefield the plain "Lyes quilted ore with Bodies slain"—the word "quilted," of course, carrying on the imagery of handicraft and artifact. At the same time it is relevant to feel something of the military sense of the word "traverse," which means, of course, a barrier in a fortification. Finally, the word "represent" in the last line carries on the imagery of theater or tapestry.

In spite of these threats, however, it is all only a harmless pastoral scene, as the next stanza tells us:

> And now the careless Victors play,
> Dancing the Triumphs of the Hay;

(with a pun on the word *hay,* meaning also a rustic dance)

> Where every Mowers wholesome Heat
> Smells like an *Alexanders sweat.*
> Their Females fragrant as the Mead
> Which they in *Fairy Circles* tread:
> When at their Dances End they kiss,
> Their new-made Hay not sweeter is.

Pastoral, yes, but as we continue reading we find that further hints of the world of time and death are brought in, as the hay suggests to the poet a resemblance to Pyramids on the *"Desert Memphis Sand,"* and also to the Roman camps which rise "In Hills for Soldiers Obsequies." But again the scene changes as the next stanza shows:

> This *Scene* again withdrawing brings
> A new and empty Face of things;
> A levell'd space, as smooth and plain,
> As Clothes for *Lilly* strecht to stain.

The reference to the paintings of Sir Peter Lely maintains the vision seen through the world of art forms, but soon the actual world comes in upon this levelled space as the poet mentions the bull-ring at Madrid, or sees in the field a pattern for "the *Levellers,*" that radical left-wing sect which threatened the hierarchies of society in Marvell's day.

Thus throughout the contemplation of the meadow a conflict is set up between the imagery of art forms and the actuality of war and death, as though the pastoral scene were living on the verge of destruction—and then suddenly it is destroyed, as a flood overtakes this "painted World":

> Then, to conclude these pleasant Acts,
> *Denton* sets ope its *Cataracts;*
> And makes the Meadow truly be
> (What it but seem'd before) a Sea.

In the midst of this comical catastrophe, while the whole world turns topsy-turvy, we discover that behind the Mannerist facade of art lies something deeper:

> But I, retiring from the Flood,
> Take Sanctuary in the Wood;
> And, while it lasts, my self imbark
> In this yet green, yet growing Ark;

It is the ark of the contemplative mind, where the poet (wittily, with a play on the word "imbark") finds his refuge; although even here nature is fallen, as the woodpecker knows, acting as moral judge of the world within the wood:

> He walks still upright from the Root,
> Meas'ring the Timber with his Foot;
> And all the way, to keep it clean,
> Doth from the Bark the Wood-moths glean.
> He, with his Beak, examines well
> Which fit to stand and which to fell.
>
> The good he numbers up, and hacks;
> As if he mark'd them with the Ax.
> But where he, tinkling with his Beak,
> Does find the hollow Oak to speak,
> That for his building he designs,
> And through the tainted Side he mines.
> Who could have thought the *tallest Oak*
> Should fall by such a *feeble Strok'!*
>
> Nor would it, had the Tree not fed
> A *Traitor-worm,* within it bred.
> (As first our *Flesh* corrupt within
> Tempts impotent and bashful *Sin.*)

The whole passage, particularly the witty inversion of the relationship between flesh and sin in the last two lines, gives a clear instance of Marvell's unique tone of serious wit, of playful morality, the tone that Eliot long ago gave its classic description, when he spoke of Marvell's wit as maintaining "this alliance of levity and seriousness (by which the seriousness is intensified)." Then Marvell sums up this attitude in two lines:

> Thus I, *easie Philosopher,*
> Among the *Birds* and *Trees* confer:

Easie is the right word, meaning, at ease, detached from care, free from pain, annoyance, or burden, free from pressure or hurry. The poet's mind is wholly in harmony with nature, and as he reads thus "in *Natures mystick Book*" the artifice of the theater is turned into the robes of nature herself as the speaker is garbed with a costume that reminds one of some Court Masquer:

> And see how Chance's better Wit
> Could with a Mask my studies hit!
> The Oak-Leaves me embroyder all,
> Between which Caterpillars crawl:
> And Ivy, with familiar trails,
> Me licks, and clasps, and curles, and hales.
> Under this *antick Cope* I move
> Like some great *Prelate of the Grove,*

(*antick* meaning both "fantastic," as in a masque, and "antique.")

This then is the center of the mind's security, as the poet lives in physical and mental harmony:

> How safe, methinks, and strong, behind
> These Trees have I incamp'd my Mind;
> Where Beauty, aiming at the Heart,
> Bends in some Tree its useless Dart;
> And where the World no certain Shot
> Can make, or me it toucheth not.
> But I on it securely play,
> And gaul its Horsemen all the Day.

(A foreshadowing of the time when Marvell's satires will play their bitter wit against the leaders of Charles II's regime.) And finally, this natural harmony reaches its climax in a pastoral ecstasy, as the speaker implies his realization that he cannot stay forever in this sanctuary, through his hyperbolic imagery of joyous bondage and happy crucifixion:

> Bind me ye *Woodbines* in your 'twines,
> Curle me about ye gadding *Vines,*

> And Oh so close your Circles lace,
> That I may never leave this Place:
> But, lest your Fetters prove too weak,
> Ere I your Silken Bondage break,
> Do you, *O Brambles,* chain me too,
> And courteous *Briars* nail me through.

Now, gradually, we become aware that in the poet's vision the outer world itself has undergone a magical transformation:

> For now the Waves are fal'n and dry'd,
> And now the Meadows fresher dy'd;
> Whose Grass, with moister colour dasht,
> Seems as green Silks but newly washt.

In this renewed world there comes to complete the scene the perfection of human beauty and virtue in the figure of the young Fairfax daughter, Marvell's student, who by a fortunate coincidence is named Mary. Calling her by the name Maria, Marvell universalizes the young girl into a figure of the highest humanity, and declares, through hyperbolic rhetoric, that this virtuous human beauty is necessary to unify and perfect the created world:

> 'Tis *She* that to these Gardens gave
> That wondrous Beauty which they have;
> *She* streightness on the Woods bestows;
> To *Her* the Meadow sweetness owes;
> Nothing could make the River be
> So Chrystal-pure but only *She;*
> *She* yet more Pure, Sweet, Streight, and Fair,
> Then Gardens, Woods, Meads, Rivers are.

But as he recapitulates the scenes of his poem he insists that human nature must rise above even these superb physical beauties, for the perfection of human nature lies in heavenly wisdom:

> For *She,* to higher Beauties rais'd,
> Disdains to be for lesser prais'd.
> *She* counts her Beauty to converse
> In all the Languages as *hers;*
> Nor yet in those *her self* imployes
> But for the *Wisdome,* not the *Noyse;*
> Nor yet that *Wisdome* would affect,
> But as 'tis *Heavens Dialect.*

Grasping thus in imagination the vision of an ideal harmony of the natural and the human, Marvell is able to see the whole estate as an image of interior restoration:

> 'Tis not, what once it was, the *World;*
> But a rude heap together hurl'd;
> All negligently overthrown,
> Gulfes, Deserts, Precipices, Stone.
> Your lesser *World* contains the same.
> But in more decent Order tame;
> *You Heaven's Center, Nature's Lap.*
> *And Paradice's only Map.*

The words apply to the estate, to Mary, and to the inner condition of the speaker himself. At the close of this long, pastoral-meditative work, Marvell has attained an ideal vision by creating, for a time, a vision of nature seen through the lens of art, with an effect of "dream-like sublimation or high-spirited play," in the words of Arnold Hauser. Thus Marvell's "Upon Appleton House" may be said to represent, better than any other English poem, the "revolution in sensibility" which Hauser has found in Mannerism:

> The essential to be borne in mind is the heterogeneous and con-
> tradictory nature of reality as seen by mannerism in general. In man-
> nerist art things are seen alternately in concrete and abstract form,
> now as substantial, now as insubstantial, and now one and now
> the other aspect is uppermost. Appearance and reality, truth and
> illusion are inextricably interwoven, and we live in a borderland of
> wakefulness and dream, knowledge and intuition, sensuous and
> ideal awareness; it is this that matters, not precise determination
> of the boundaries between the various provinces of being. The point
> is the difference between the two worlds we belong to, between
> which there is no making any final and exclusive choice.

DONALD M. FRIEDMAN

Knowledge and the World of Change: Marvell's "The Garden"

In an essay intended to correct the tendency to read "The Garden" as if it were a collection of Neoplatonic commonplaces, Professor Frank Kermode has argued that it is in fact an "anti-genre" poem, written in reply to and in criticism of the *libertin* garden poems of sensual indulgence associated with Saint-Amant, Thomas Randolph, Thomas Stanley, and other contemporaries. We have seen [elsewhere] that Marvell is given to evaluating a literary form by writing his own version of it, thereby exploiting it and criticizing it at the same time. But Kermode's idea is slightly more radical than that; although he acknowledges the existence of a genre of seventeenth-century garden poetry whose distinctive feature was the exaltation of the contemplative life over the life of action, he feels that Marvell aimed "The Garden" specifically at the poets of the *jouissance*, and that matters of diction, metre, symbol, and convention can and should be referred to the dominating idea of criticizing the assumptions of the *libertin* genre. Kermode has received support from an unexpected quarter; in conscientious pursuit of a major theme of Horatian poetry through the seventeenth, eighteenth, and nineteenth centuries in English poetry, Miss Maren-Sofie Røstvig has written two lengthy and well-documented volumes on what she calls the *"beatus-ille* theme." She demonstrates that during the seventeenth century, poems about the pleasures of retirement and the excellences of the contemplative life are so numerous that they appear to be a genre in themselves. Miss Røstvig makes clear the relationships of this genre not only to Horace's *Odes* but also to Stoic philosophy in general; she recognizes the sources of the

From *Marvell's Pastoral Art.* © 1970 by Donald M. Friedman. Routledge & Kegan Paul, 1970.

genre in Christian literature and the importance for its symbolism of Neoplatonic philosophy. And she does not ignore the political and social significances
of the poetry she is writing about; she considers "the poem of the happy country
life the most typical expression of the Royalist and Anglican spirit of the seventeenth century." As this quotation makes clear, her work is devoted particularly
to the poetry of rural retirement, a theme which appears to have grown tremendously in importance during the mid-seventeenth century, perhaps in response
to the galling pressure of public events, but which we may certainly see as a
limb sprung from the pastoral tree. The rejection of the life of affairs had always
been an implicit tenet of pastoral poetry; in Horace the preference for simplicity
and ease in country life is raised to the level where it becomes a commanding
ethical viewpoint. Naturally enough such a view is easily connected with Stoic
ethics; for English poetry it was fortunate that some of the forms of Stoicism
were absorbed as fully and congenially into Christian ideas of morality as were
more rarefied Platonic metaphysical doctrines.

However valuable the work of Kermode and Røstvig may be in keeping
us from reading Marvell's octosyllabic couplets as if they were versified *Enneads,*
it would be unwise to allow their emphasis on genre to obscure the importance
of Marvell's originality of treatment. Rather than devote his energies to discovering novel and witty ways to express familiar pastoral themes, Marvell chose
to invent the figure of the Mower, and to use him to probe the meaning of man's
relation to nature. In the earlier poems, such as "Young Love" and "The Gallery,"
Marvell used a common form in order to subject it to uncommon scrutiny—
and to suggest the complicated questions the forms created but did not attempt
to answer. I think it likely, therefore, that "The Garden" represents an enterprise similar to these others. Marvell is quite obviously writing a poem whose
type would seem thoroughly familiar to his audience (especially if this audience
were made up of Lord Fairfax, Lord Westmorland, and their friends—that is,
if "The Garden" was written and circulated during Marvell's stay at Nunappleton, which seems very probable). But further, with typical ingenuity and
the integrity of a mind that cannot relax before it has seen the farthest possible reach of a problem, he is forcing the garden poem to absorb and contain
all the meanings that he saw the genre to possess potentially.

A year before the publication of their *Andrew Marvell,* Miss Bradbrook
and Miss Lloyd Thomas collaborated on an article entitled "Marvell and the
Concept of Metamorphosis." They suggested there that "the concept of
Metamorphosis, the basis of the poem, fuses the modern psychological idea
of sublimation and the modern theological idea of transcendence into
something more delicate." I am not sure that this fusion really occurs in "The
Garden" or that the idea of metamorphosis in the poem is "the poetical answer

to the problem of Time and the decay of beauty." But it can be shown very con-
vincingly that not only the separate events of the poem but also many individual
images, puns, exempla, and analogies are related and held in their respective
places by the omnipresent poetical mode of transmutation. "The Garden" is
full of plants, gods, men, and words that change from one thing into another
and are seen at times as one thing, at times as another, and sometimes as both.
The effect is to insist on the reality of both states of a metamorphosed entity,
but more clearly to delineate the reality of the process itself of change. "The
Garden" is "about" mutability only in so far as it uses the phenomenon of change
as its universal metaphor—as a key signature, as it were.

The first two lines of "The Garden" exhibit the characteristics of symbolic
reference, pure punning, and ironic statement that will pervade the entire poem:
"How vainly men themselves amaze / To win the Palm, the Oke, or Bayes" (ll.
1–2). To notice that "vainly" means "in vain" and "from vanity" at once and
with equal force is to enter into the fictive viewpoint of the speaker of the poem.
The two meanings constitute something more than a pun, for they represent
two kinds of judgment. The second (from vanity) is that of a man assessing
the behaviour of other men according to standards he has learned in the world
he has quitted for the Garden. The first (in vain) implies a knowledge superior
to that world, a knowledge that creates a vantage-point from which all human
activities can be viewed in comparison with all *possible* forms of action, not
just those that experience provides. Both judgments are important, but it is the
latter that is to set the tone for the poem, for it justifies the transition from a
mocking portrait of men's actual pursuits to the praise of the way men *should*
choose, in the light of the Garden's lesson.

The pun on "amaze" is of a different quality but it, too, is related to both
of the viewpoints we have just described. Its first set of meanings refers to the
effects ambition and purposeful activity have on the men who suffer from
them—"to amaze" meant "to bewilder," "to infatuate," "to drive oneself stupid."
When all these senses are understood in apposition to the meanings we have
just observed for "vainly" the impression of hectic futility is deepened and begins
to appear pathetic. And that sense is reinforced by the other meaning of "amaze,"
which is "to trap oneself in a maze." This is the life of action seen from the
Garden; and there is a sort of grace note in our realization that a maze would
normally have been a proud part of any formal garden. How much less harmful, we are made to feel, is the maze of box-hedges than the endless and
meandering prisons of greed and striving.

The first mention of the objects of all this futile strife raises the criticism
from the level of contemporary society to a consideration of the life of action
as a constant type in human history. "The Palm, the Oke, or Bayes" are,

respectively, the classical (and therefore classic) reward for military victory, the civic crown for valour, and the traditional prize of the poet. It becomes clear immediately that Marvell is not criticizing courage or poetry but the ways in which men seek to outdo each other to win an honour that is symbolized by the leaves or fronds of a tree. The witty stance of the poem will be to pretend that the honour is truly *in* the leaves, that they are not so much the symbol as the reality; the joke is, of course, that men could much more easily and more satisfactorily "win" what they compete for by retiring to the Garden and consorting with the trees themselves. The brief catalogue of trees not only establishes a background of classical reference for the poem but presents its claim to be able to judge men not only as they follow the ignoble pursuits of business and litigation but the admired callings of warfare and the arts. In either case, it is the desire to excel that is shown to be vain, or perhaps just the intensity of any desire. For it will be demonstrated that the plants offer rewards when no effort has been made to win them; and often they reward effort with a prize it has not sought (as in Marvell's revision of the myths of Apollo and Pan). The task of the first stanza is to make it apparent that the usual criteria of human achievement are irrelevant in the Garden, and indeed that achievement must be redefined in the terms insisted on by the contemplative paradise. The futility of human endeavour is underlined in the second couplet: "And their uncessant Labours see / Crown'd from some single Herb or Tree" (ll. 3–4). To sacrifice all other human and supernatural values for a symbol that is more beautiful, intrinsically, than the thing it symbolizes is the best measure of man's inspired stupidity. Not only is the crown of leaves either inadequate or far too rich for the dreams of ambitious mankind, but it is made from a tree "Whose short and narrow verged Shade / Does prudently their Toyles upbraid" (ll. 5–6). The point is that the economy and simplicity of the trees (as evinced in the small circle of their shade) is an implicit criticism of the excesses and hectic activities of the men of "uncessant Labours." Marvell follows this with an image of the activity that the trees oppose to the weaving of crowns and chaplets for the heroes of the world: "While all Flow'rs and all Trees do close / To weave the Garlands of repose" (ll. 7–8). The amazing thing about these lines is that they set up with magnificent economy and with absolute nonchalance the contrasted values that will be forced into conflict in the first three stanzas of the poem, only to be transcended by the mythological allusions in stanza 4. Moreover, they show a tactful awareness of Kermode's "anti-genre," since the central image is one that can be duplicated in several *libertin* poems.

It is obvious that "repose" is introduced as the state preferred by trees and preferred by the mind of contemplative man to the active life of field and city. As Justus Lipsius declared in a book of widespread popularity in the seventeenth century, gardens "be ordained, not for the body, but for the mind: and to recreate it, not to besot it with idlenesse: only as a wholsome withdrawing place from the cares and troubles of this world." One could multiply instances of this thought, from Sir William Temple's *Upon the Gardens of Epicurus,* Sir Thomas Browne's *Garden of Cyrus,* and from uncounted poets and essayists of the century who looked to the green and ordered garden for a symbol of the natural, contemplative life. Here Marvell is proposing that the life of rational retirement seeks and finds its own "crowns" in the "inter-wreathed bay" formed by the instinctive motions of the trees, the "closing" of their vegetable loves [to use Eldred Revett's phrases from *Poems,* 1657]. The important thing to note is that these are not rewards for effort, but gratuitous gifts given because of the very nature of trees, which is to grow into garlands for the contemplative life—or so at least the poem pretends.

But we must also notice that in weaving "the Garlands of repose" the trees behave as they do in, for example, Thomas Randolph's "A Pastorall Courtship," in which

> The lofty *Pine* deignes to descend,
> And sturdy *Oaks* doe gently bend.
> One with another subt'ly weaves
> Into one loom their various leaves;
> As all ambitious were to be
> Mine and my *Phyllis* canopie!

The difference is sufficiently marked in the last couplet; but perhaps a more representative example of the vigorously amorous landscapes drawn by the naturalist poets is this, from Thomas Stanley's "Loves Innocence":

> See how this Ivy strives to twine
> Her wanton arms about the Vine,
> And her coy lover thus restrains,
> Entangled in her amorous chains,
> See how these neighb'ring Palms do bend
> Their heads, and mutual murmurs send.

In Randolph and Stanley, and in Saint-Amant from whom Stanley took so much, the need was often to create a landscape that in its natural ardour would match and incite the passions of the lovers who inhabited it. The pretence was that all was natural, therefore all was permitted; trees and flowers can hardly be accused of sin, and if man in the Golden Age was as innocent as the trees the analogy must hold for human sexuality. Such, at least, was the half-joking, half-serious, philosophy that lay behind lines such as these from Saint-Amant's "La Jouyssance":

> Sous un climat où la nature
> Monter à nud toutes ses beautez
> Et nourrit les yeux enchantez
> Des plus doux traits de la peinture,
> Nous voyons briller sur les fleurs
> Plustost des perles.

Again, in "La Metamorphose de Lyrian et de Sylvie," Saint-Amant's Ovidian tale of the elm and the ivy, we find:

> Et son corps s'attachant à l'arbre qu'il contemple
> Se change en mille bras tournoyans a l'entour,
> Dont il acquit le nom de symbole d'amour;
> Bref, ce fidelle amant n'est plus qu'un beau lierre,
> Qui, sur la tige aimée, en s'elevant de terre,
> Cherche en sa passion, qu'il tasche d'appaiser,
> La place où fut la bouche, afin de la baiser.

A recent French critic of the *libertin* and *précieux* poets defines, as a distinctive trait of Saint-Amant, Théophile de Viau, and others, "the interplay of amorous and sensuous delights in woman's beauty with those in nature, so that the naiad's serenade in her crystal dwelling, the caressing waters, the fluid hair of a woman, the whiteness of hands . . . the games of love and those of fancy are all made of the same delicate and transparent substance" (Odette de Mourgues, *Metaphysical Baroque and Précieux Poetry*). Randolph and Stanley may have learned a great deal from this technique; and it is clear that Marvell knew it well and, in "The Garden," was exploiting it only to turn the tables on the entire convention in order to celebrate the delights of natural beauty at the expense of female beauty.

Because this is not the exclusive aim of the poem the second stanza relinquishes the subject (to take it up again in stanza 3) in favour of the exploration of the mythology of the Garden itself.

> Fair quiet, have I found thee here,
> And Innocence thy Sister dear!
> Mistaken long, I sought you then
> In busie Companies of Men.
> Your sacred Plants, if here below,
> Only among the Plants will grow.

> Society is all but rude,
> To this delicious Solitude.
> (ll. 9–16)

The joint goddesses of pastoral contemplation are discovered in the Garden,
"Ther wher noe thronging multituds / Disturbe with noyse" [to quote Lord
Fairfax's poem "The Recreations of My Solitude"] and where innocence is defined by the lack of worldly ambition. The active and acquisitive life is
remembered and judged in the word "then"; and the "busie Companies of Men"
refers both to tumultuous crowds and perhaps to the business "companies" that
were an important economic phenomenon before and during the Civil War
period. In the first stanza Marvell made fun of human passion in so far as it
was misdirected; in the third stanza he will consider both the physical realities
of lust and its highly artificial manners. In stanza 2, then, he creates a kind of
parodic version of his own love-affair with the trees, which partakes of many
of the characteristic traits of human lovers, but which the poem must pretend
is saner and more exalted. "Delicious" casts an ironic light back upon the earlier
part of the stanza, since the speaker relishes the supposedly pure delights of
quiet and innocence with quite as much sensuous fervour as the "Fond Lovers"
of stanza 3. In "The Garden," I think, this is meant to be understood as a piece
of self-conscious humour, but the personification of virtues as beloved creatures
was taken seriously by other poets, as in Drummond's

> Deare Wood, and you sweet solitarie Place,
> Where from the vulgare I estranged liue,
> Contented more with what your Shades mee giue,
> Than if I had what *Thetis* doth embrace;

or, even more passionately,

> I hugg my Quiet and alone
> Take thee for my Companion,
> And deem in doing so, I've all
> I can true Conversation call,

from Fane's "To Retiredness," where "Conversation" carries quite definite sexual overtones. This is not to say that Fane and Drummond were not aware of
the joke implicit in the hyperbole; but Marvell is alone in turning the joke
against the point of view his poem is trying to establish, and making the pursuit of innocence as passionate as any of the more earthy quests he is criticizing.

The notion of plants that grow on earth as living emblems of gods who
have left it because it has grown corrupt is venerably founded in classical

tradition. But Marvell converts the idea to his own uses by deliberately confounding the abstract values of Quiet and Innocence with their vegetable insignia; in the Garden, he implies, trees and what they represent are once again united harmoniously. Lord Fairfax had a different explanation for the peculiar affinity of the pastoral gods for gardens:

> Times past Fawnes Satyrs Demy-Gods
> Hither retird to seeke for Aide
> When Heaven with Earth was soe att odds
> As Jupiter in rage had laide
> O're all a Deluge these high woods
> Preseru'd them from the sweling floods.

In both poets the mythology serves the idea that informs the closing lines of "The Mower against Gardens"; the gods of peace and fertility have abandoned the "busie Companies of Men" and lend their influence only to the calm and ordered pastoral of the country garden.

The same point is made once more in the last couplet of the stanza, but in a way that permits Marvell to comment wittily on the pretensions of "civilization." As we have seen, it was at least a continuing debate in the seventeenth century whether primitive societies were indeed replicas of the Golden Age or mere rough conglomerations of ignorant and vicious savages. The heroic visions of the sixteenth century were gradually giving way before the accumulation of factual evidence brought back by wide-ranging exploration; and the view that society was the means to progressive civilizing of human instincts was gaining ground. But Marvell, by taking solitariness as the standard of individual and moral value, can turn and call society "rude" with infinite aplomb and with a full awareness of the point of his paradox. It is the final blow to the "Companies of Men," and he can now attend to the phantoms of courtly lovers that still haunt the paradisiacal Garden.

> No white nor red was ever seen
> So am'rous as this lovely green.
> Fond Lovers, cruel as their Flame,
> Cut in these Trees their Mistress name.
> Little, Alas, they know, or heed,
> How far these Beauties Hers exceed!
>
> (ll. 17–22)

We do not have to know much Petrarch, or Donne, or Carew, to realize that "white nor red" stands for all the worlds, both real and conventionally literary, of passionate lovers. And the synecdoche itself implies a judgment on these worlds in so far as they can be reduced so easily to their trivial components of white and red. In contrast, the "am'rous . . . green" is extended and made to seem meaningful by the addition of its adjective; the phrase also functions as a corrective to the view that fails to see true passion and fruitful love in the plants of the Garden rather than in the painted mistresses of the world outside. The corrective is applied in terms that blend mockery with stern disapproval; we know that "Fond" can mean both "loving" and "foolish," but this kind of foolishness is drawn for us as callous brutality to the sensitive and animate trees. The pun on "Flame" helps to describe the lovers and their inane situation since it refers both to the passion of love that "burns" those in love, and the mistress herself (as in our rather dated use of "flame") who is traditionally cruel in her denial and disdain of the posturing suitor. The word-play, then, characterizes the lovers as dupes caught in the hopeless toils of an elaborate and pointless game, but dupes who compound their guilt by revenging their pains upon innocent nature, and by the same tortures they have undergone. The custom of cutting names, initials, and entwined hearts into trees has not yet disappeared, but the basis of Marvell's objection to the practice is not simply that of the conservationist. He is also pointing to the greater stupidity that thinks to preserve and celebrate a name in this fashion when it is only performing an act of desecration against a tree whose "name" is infinitely more significant than any human name can be. The lovers' mistake is announced quite bluntly in lines 21–22; but the justification for the superior beauty of the trees must be found in the preceding and the following stanzas. In stanza 3 Marvell is content to display his speaker's feelings as he promises, "Fair Trees! where s'eer your barkes I wound, / No Name shall but your own be found" (ll. 23–24). Of course this is meant to be a joke, but, as we have just seen, the concept that lies behind the joke is a serious one. Marvell is conscious of the fact that wounding the "barkes" is in some ways akin to dealing "between the Bark and Tree"; no matter how pure the passion that inspires it, it is still an interference with nature. He tries to redeem the act by swearing that *this* lover will carve only the trees' own name. The idea must be seen as part of the parody, since nothing could be more irrelevant to the pure love of nature than behaviour modelled on the deeds of fleshly lovers. Even so, the only name that may properly be graven into bark is the name of the thing itself, a recognition that the tree transcends the categories applied to it by the mind distracted by passion of any sort.

Marvell will not have done with these trees, and in stanza 4 goes on to the most important instances in history and mythology that reveal the true nature of the relation between passion and trees. Here the pun is raised to a level well above simple word-play; it begins to assume the proportions of a symbolic analogy, and the various puns in the stanza are the primary means whereby

Marvell converts the traditional myths into evidence for his metaphor of metamorphosis: "When we have run our Passions heat, / Love hither makes his best retreat" (ll. 25–26). In "The Garden" the puns are marshalled to give the sense of physical passion driving the lover through the exhausting flames of desire, while at the same time the lover drives himself through the predestined course of lust and frustration. The result is the "retreat" of "Love" to the Garden; and it is intended that "Love" be understood both as a generic word and as the personification. The mention of the God of Love will provide the transition to the following lines and their mythological innovations. Miss Bradbrook and A. H. King have commented on the meanings of "retreat" and have shown that the predominant sense is that of retiring gratefully from the field of amatory combat. Marvell follows the image with a catalogue of the gods who thus abandoned an initial desire for the higher satisfactions of the Garden: "The *Gods, that mortal Beauty chase, / Still in a Tree did end their race*" (ll. 27–28). As Miss Bradbrook points out, "*Race* is a pun on *contest,* and *family, seed.*" The pun refers to the myths of Apollo and Pan retold in lines 29–32 and the "*Gods*" are the Olympians who were notoriously fond of earthly maidens.

Marvell's argument is taken from Ovid; and rarely has the phenomenon of change been interpreted with more purposeful wit.

> *Apollo* hunted *Daphne* so,
> Only that She might Laurel grow.
> And *Pan* did after *Syrinx* speed,
> Not as a Nymph, but for a Reed.
> (ll. 29–32)

To begin with, King makes it perfectly clear that "Only" and "for" have the force of "for no other end or purpose than," as is shown in *Hortus*. Marvell takes up the Ovidian paradox in the form that Randolph gives it in: "Love Laurell gives; *Phoebus* as much can say, / Had not he lov'd, there had not been the Bay," and changes it into another and different paradox by asserting that Apollo pursued Daphne just so that she might become the laurel tree. Miss Bradbrook interprets this to mean that Marvell "finds, as the gods find, that the only lasting satisfaction for the instincts is an activity which does not employ them for their original purpose. Apollo hunted Daphne for the laurel crown of Poetry and Pan sped after Syrinx to capture Music. Desire is only to be quieted in the permanence of Art." King offers a slight objection when he says, "Apollo and Pan do not see in the laurel and reed objects of natural contemplation. Apollo, god of poets, is interested in laurel wreaths, the reward of poets; an interest condemned in the first stanza of the poem. And Pan wants the reed as a musical instrument." I think Miss Bradbrook is closer to the truth, and primarily because the rest of "The Garden" will make it clear that the mind and the soul (which are meant to take precedence over the passions according to the pagan and Christian traditions, and according to the ethic of Marvell's pastoral as well) attain their highest and happiest states when contemplating the creations of their own faculties. In this sense the most perfect meaning of "Apollo" is the abstract idea of "poetry," and of "Pan," "music." It is difficult to avoid the conclusion that, among many other concerns, Marvell is thinking of the nature of his own art in "The Garden," and the gods of poetry and music might be expected to have a prominent part in its symbolism.

Moreover, I think King is mistaken in taking his readings of "Only" and "for" too literally; that is, he assumes that the ambiguous words refer to the intentions, felt as such, of Apollo and Pan. Yet surely the prevailingly ironic mode of the poem makes it easier to believe that the passions of the gods have been frustrated and then redirected by the intelligible order of the universe, or whatever power governs the Garden and makes trees more beautiful and more valuable than human beauties. The main point of the stanza is that the gods "that mortal Beauty chase" are destined to·have their folly reproved by the truths embodied in nature. The order that enforces this ironic teaching is the same one, presumably, that decides, in Miss Bradbrook's words, "that the only lasting satisfaction for the instincts is an activity which does not employ them for their original purpose." Hers is the more cautious statement, but I cannot help feeling that the meaningful metamorphoses described in this stanza are meant to reveal a governing concept in the worlds of the gods and of men. The lusts of Apollo and Pan are rewarded with the emblems of art, and the implication is that every kind of passion directed toward objects lower in the scale of values than the perfectly abstract forms of contemplation will be purified in the Garden. For, besides the underlying allusions to the Garden of Eden and to all the gardens that appear in Western literature as the types of pristine innocence and perfection, there is in "The Garden" a continuing reference, I believe, to the garden as a symbol of *sapientia,* or wisdom, as opposed to *scientia,* which is merely worldly wisdom or knowledge. It is important to notice now that the linking of contemplation and gardens is not gratuitous; the fact that the mind is so often said to achieve pure perception in the natural setting of the garden is simply the other side of the truth that the garden itself is not only conducive to contemplation, but is the very *place* where contemplation can attain wisdom.

The first four stanzas have brought us through the snares of the active life and the more deceptive lures of passionate love. Marvell's *persona* has shown us the nature of his conversion to the worship of the quiet and innocence of the Garden, and what remains is to trace the stages of his refinement from knowledge of the senses to the pure apprehensions of the intellect. With due regard for the decorum of this Platonic ascent, stanza 5 is devoted to portraying the life of the senses in the setting of the Garden, where carnality does not obtain.

> What wond'rous Life in this I lead!
> Ripe Apples drop about my head;
> The Luscious Clusters of the Vine
> Upon my Mouth do crush their Wine;
> The Nectaren, and curious Peach,
> Into my hands themselves do reach;
> Stumbling on Melons, as I pass,
> Insnar'd with Flow'rs, I fall on Grass.
>
> (ll. 33–40)

Before attending to details, we must notice that the basic metaphor for Nature in this passage is the one that distinguished the pastoral settings of the Golden Age; it is a Nature that gives of herself freely and bounteously, in recognition of her sympathetic ties with the human creatures who live by her bounty. In "Bermudas" island fruits behave with the same passionate benevolence, but there is a distinction: "He makes the Figs our mouths to meet; / And throws the Melons at our feet" (ll. 21–22). "Bermudas" differs from "The Garden" in that sustaining nature in that poem is directed and inspired by the will of God. In "The Garden" the various fruits are rendered animate so that they can express the projected attitudes of natural things toward the innocent contemplative, one who has shown his faith and renounced the world of carnal desire and material greed. His reward is to be nourished lavishly while he remains utterly passive, the grapes crushing their wine against his mouth and the peaches putting themselves into his hands. It is made to appear that nature is as possessive of her true lovers as human mistresses can be. And this, of course, is part of the point of the stanza; for the poem will grow more complicated and more profound as we move away from this idyllic, but mindless and unproductive, scene.

[Pierre] Legouis is the only critic to notice that almost all the fruits mentioned in stanza 5 were grown in England only through careful cultivation; Damon the Mower would have called them the products of vicious artifice rather than of "willing Nature" (a phrase that, nevertheless, describes this stanza impeccably). The point is that the Garden is not the epitome of simple, pastoral nature; it is the achievement of nature working with all her skills as creator, and is designed according to the principles of order that man tries only to imitate. It is as superior to the ornate garden of "The Mower against Gardens" as it is to the chaotic society of the "busie Companies of Men." But the fruits of this Garden are as sophisticated as they are animate, and we may assume that Marvell meant to convey certain meanings by his choice of particular plants. The apples in stanza 5 are, of course, impressive in that they do not wait to be plucked by disobedient man or woman; they fall of their own will, and therefore they precipitate no "fall" in the theological sense. The grapes do not entice man to drunkenness, nor are they related to Dionysiac worship. Their wine is given as the free gift of a joyous and vivid nature, delighting in its ability to enamour its human suitor. The nectarine and the peach as well convey themselves into his eager hands, as if to feed a hunger of which he has not yet grown aware.

The only difficulty in the stanza arises in the last couplet, where [William] Empson's remark that "Melon, again, is the Greek for apple," is misleading in that it suggests that the apple here is the cause of another, if less guilty, fall: "Stumbling on Melons, as I pass, / Insnar'd with Flow'rs, I fall on Grass" (ll. 39–40). Marvell may indeed be playing on the Greek etymology, but the Christian idea is badly suited to the meaning of the couplet as I interpret it. He might rather have in mind the legend of Atalanta and Hippomenes, for Marvell has the habit of remembering all the examples of the symbolic event he is describing. But when L. W. Hyman follows Empson's interpretation, even to the point of repeating the derivation of "Melon," and says "when he stumbles on melons . . . he is falling into carnal sin," some disagreement is called for. Hyman later modifies this statement, but nowhere does he say, as I think one must say, that this fall on grass is entirely without sin, as that word is understood in any of the ethical or theological systems Marvell would have known.

The "Grass," we know, is flesh, and as such it again signals the inherent identification between created nature and the man, at least, who is still part of nature by choice and by instinctive sympathy. The speaker in "The Garden" falls on grass—that is, relapses into a passive, vegetative dependence upon the loving nurture of earth. Neither disobedience to God's commandment nor a fall into lustful sexuality is involved here; indeed, heterosexual passion has been banished from the Garden from the moment the lover offered up his devotion to the trees. They return his love, and so the imagery of stanza 5 is redolent of sensual indulgence. The point is that it is a conscious parody of the love-relationship between man and woman; and the humorous innocence of the last line can be understood only if the element of parody is appreciated. This fall is an innocent piece of mimicry; just as the grass cushions the fall and keeps both man and the world from shock, so the human figure falls not from immortality to mortality, as Adam did, but from ordinary mortality into a form of mortal life raised to the heights of passive sensitivity and supine enjoyment.

It is the apotheosis of life in the flesh, but there is nothing sinful about it. The only problem is the flowers that entangle the passing feet of the poem's "I." Empson says that the flowers are "the snakes in it [the grass] that stopped Eurydice," but I think we need not more but fewer mythological allusions if we want to clarify the poem. If the grass is the fundamental element in man and in nature, and the fruits are the active, animate nutrients that sustain the human-natural relationship, then the flowers are the signs of the outward beauties of the natural world, the lures that attract only the purified senses. In a passage in "The Mower's Song" the flowers appear as the heraldic emblems of the meadows themselves: "That not one Blade of Grass you spy'd, / But had a Flower on either side" (ll. 9–10); and we have seen [elsewhere] how in "The Coronet" Marvell made a clear and careful distinction between fruit and flowers (l. 6), with the implication that fruits are the substantial products of creative genius, and flowers merely the decorative and substanceless shadows of these fruits. If this is indeed a consistent concept in Marvell, then to call them the "snares" in this earthly paradise is thoroughly justified. The speaker has been overcome by the passionate courtship of the Garden, and he has succumbed most easily to the temptations of the eye; his susceptibility has its antecedents in the Spenserian pastoral and in Christian doctrine as well. Though Marvell seems to be describing a snare that catches at the feet of the speaker and brings him to the ground, it would be well within the limits of intelligibility and decorum for a metaphysical poet to speak of eyes entrapped in flowery snares. Thus the stanza concludes with a vision of man as a sensuous creature abandoning his will, his freedom, and even his consciousness to the blandishments of a supremely beautiful nature. It is the high point of earthly perception; but the next step on the ladder leads up to the level of the rational intellect, and that is indeed where stanza 6 begins.

The diction of these eight lines proceeds with a degree of ambiguity unusual in Marvell, while the concepts the stanza deals in both explicitly and implicitly are delicate and elusive in their own right. The trouble starts with the very first line: "Mean while the Mind, from pleasure less, / Withdraws into its happiness" (ll. 41–42). Following as it does the lush and riotous terms of concrete description in stanza 5, the phrase "pleasure less" carries an air of cool, unquestioning dismissal that minimizes the impression made upon us by that paean to the senses. If it is only "pleasure less," we feel, then the mind must indeed have resources immense beyond imagining. We note, too, that pleasure is tacitly contrasted with happiness, as if the latter state were somehow more exalted and more real than pleasure, which begins to appear as simple indulgence. A similar idea of the mind's happiness is expressed by Henry More:

> But senses objects soon do glut the soul,
> Or rather weary with their emptinesse;
> So I, all heedlesse how the waters roll
> And mindlesse of the mirth the birds expresse,
> Into myself, 'gin softly to retire
> After hid heavenly pleasures to enquire.

And in Cudworth we can find yet another definition of happiness that also sheds light on the development of the ideas of "The Garden" through this and the following stanza:

> Now our onely way to recover God & happines again, is not to soar up with our Understandings, but to destroy this *Self-will* of ours: and then we shall find our wings to grow again, our plumes fairly spread, & our selves raised aloft into the free Aire of perfect Liberty, which is perfect Happinesse.

But Marvell is not so strictly doctrinal as this; nor does he leave us long in doubt about the nature of the happiness the mind seeks. To understand its "withdrawal" we must know something of the character of the mind itself, and Marvell gives us this information in the parenthetical—"The Mind, that Ocean where each kind / Does streight its own resemblance find" (ll. 43–44). The idea that the seas contained exact replicas of all the animals to be found on land was, as many editors have remarked, a commonplace of medieval and Renaissance natural philosophy. But Marvell is using the comparison to reveal the mind's power to create a mental reality as complete and consistent as the reality of the physical world. It is important that we be made to feel that the world of the mind's images (if that is what it is stocked with) is as complex and alive as the world of real creatures. Of course "kind" meant, primarily, a genus; but the word was used commonly to refer to the different genres of poetry and drama; and since, presumably, the abstract kinds of poetry would be as real in the mind as the more concrete kinds of animals, it is possible that Marvell intends a general statement about the correspondence between the structure of the mind and the nature of all universal concepts. For we must be careful to remember that the metaphor of the mind as an ocean simply names an analogy; it does not insist that we think of the mind as an enormous underwater menagerie. The mind contains the kinds in *its* way as the ocean allegedly contains the kinds in *its*. It is equally important to notice that the emphasis is put on "kinds" rather than creatures; the ocean shelters *typical examples* and the mind too deals in ideas rather than specific parts of experience. But the implications of the couplet carry further; the "kinds" of earth, after all, are material in so far as they are embodied in individual creatures. For the mind's abstract mental forms to have a "resemblance" to individuals requires another act of metamorphosis. The mind must transmute the essence of the earthly kind into an idea that retains that essence yet strips it of its material qualities.

> Yet it creates, transcending these,
> Far other Worlds, and other Seas;
> Annihilating all that's made
> To a green Thought in a green Shade.
>
> (ll. 45–48)

The mind is pictured here as a creator, and the analogy to Divine creation is unavoidable. But the mind is also, it seems, uncircumscribed by the actual creation of God as we have seen it on land and in the seas in lines 43–44. It creates its own "garden of the kinds," a new earth and a new ocean to contain the creatures of its mental generation. "Transcending" can mean both "to overpass" and "to exceed," as Miss Bradbrook points out, but I am not sure that she is right in saying that it does not also carry the theological sense of going beyond normal human experience. It is true that the events of "The Garden" are intelligible entirely within the terms of the Christian universe; even the symbolism of stanza 7 is not truly mystical in character. Nevertheless, the mind as it is described in stanza 6 appears to be capable of unlimited creation. The only admissible qualification is that it does, in fact, create "other Worlds, and other Seas," as if its imaginings are, or must be, modelled on the created universe whose shape and essence have been impressed upon the mind by the senses. In other poets the imprisonment within the senses was indeed the key to the mind's freedom of imagining. Benlowes, for example, says:

> Man may confine the body, but the mind
> (Like Nature's miracles, the wind
> And dreams) does, though secur'd,
>   a free enjoyment find.
>
> Rays drawn in to a point more vig'rous beam;
> Joys more to saints, engoal'd, did stream;
> Linnets their cage to be a grove, bars
>   boughs esteem.

In any case, the poets and philosophers who accepted the assumptions of Christian Platonism were at one in believing that the mind (or the soul) could achieve its proper end and function only by turning from the distractions of sense. They were aware, nevertheless, that the mind's powers of imagination can operate only upon the qualities and meanings of "events" they have met in real experience. There is some uncertainty about whether the mind is meant to contemplate only the ideal truths communicated to it through its resemblance to the Divine Mind, or whether it imitates the Divine by contemplating its own creations. The problem of knowledge, as it affected the relations between knowing intellect and known object, absorbed the best thinkers of the seventeenth century; the habit of analogical thinking was strong enough even in the late Renaissance for Platonic philosophers to find a solution to the problem in the literal identification of knower and known. Others thought the mind affected its objects in such a way that it might almost be said to create the things it contemplated. For example, in J. Hall's elegy for Lord Hastings, which appeared with Marvell's in 1649, Hall speaks of the quality of Hastings's intellect:

> as if that every Thing,
> Stript of its outward dross, and all refin'd
> Into a Form, lay open to his Minde:
> Or if his pure Minde could suddenly disperse
> It self all ways, and th'row all Objects pierce.

To be sure, this is hyperbole dictated by the occasion and the need for high-flown terms of praise; but in a sober and encyclopedic treatise, *The True Intellectual System of the Universe,* we find Cudworth discussing the apprehension of "secondary attributes" in very similar terms:

> But sensible things themselves (as for example light and colours) are not known or understood either by the passion or the fancy of sense, nor by anything merely foreign and adventitious, but by intelligible ideas exerted from the mind itself, that is, by something native and domestic to it.

Marvell would have heard many similar opinions at Cambridge during his stay there, for although the Cambridge Platonists did not form so cohesive a school as many histories of philosophy pretend, they held a good many epistemological and ethical ideas in commmon. And Cudworth's concept of the powers of the mind to affect objects outside it would lend itself to the interpretation of the "annihilation" of created things of which Marvell speaks in line 47.

It should be remembered that none of this contradicts the picture of the mind as "withdrawing" from the world of sense. The latter was a necessary act, as we can learn from Henry More:

> For they will be in the flaring light or life of the body as the starres
> in the beams of the Sunne scarce to be seen, unlesse we withdraw
> our selves out of the flush vigour of that light, into the profundity
> of our own souls, as into some deep pit. . . . Thus being quit of pas-
> sion, they have upon any occasion a clear though still and quiet
> representation of every thing in their minds, upon which pure
> bright sydereall phantasms unprejudiced reason may safely
> work, and clearly discern what is true or probable.

But this withdrawal did not hamper the mind's abilities to judge and create; on the contrary, it provided precisely the same atmosphere of retirement and freedom from temptation that the Garden provides for man seen as a complete entity. In this state of freedom, the mind can perform its dual function of "creating" forms for the world of sense, and understanding the forms of the ideal universe. But at this point in "The Garden" Marvell is not yet concerned with the mind as the intermediary between ideal perfection and the less perfect world of creatures. Stanza 6 concentrates on the mind's "Annihilating all that's made / To a green Thought in a green Shade" (ll. 47–48). There are both am- biguities and contradictions within this couplet; the contradiction is in the use of "annihilate" to describe what is essentially another act of metamorphosis. "All that's made" is reduced (or simply changed) to a green thought; it is not destroyed and turned into nothingness. I think it is unlikely that Marvell meant "Annihilating" to carry the impression of "obliterating." For one thing, the idea of not-being was noxious to the Platonic philosophy that dominates the poem; and it was equally untenable within a Christian context. And, finally, "a green Thought" is very far from nothingness to the mind in the Garden. Rather, Marvell seems to have used the term to parallel in force and audacity the previous word, "transcending." Extraordinary powers are thus predicated of the mind, powers that appear to equate it with the faculties of the Divine Mind. And it is possible that the lines constitute a deliberate use of hyperbole, whose irony will be revealed in the next stanza when the soul attains a higher state of apprehension than the mind does in stanza 6. The point is that even when "all that's made" has been transformed into the peculiar idiom of the mind's ideas, there is yet another way of perception and understanding, yet another avenue open to the solitary contemplator.

The ambiguity is in the phrase "all that's made," since we do not know whether this refers to the Creation itself or to the "other Worlds, and other Seas" whose progenitor is the mind. As we have noted, the ambiguity is clearly intended; it is an instance of Marvell's typical desire to express a complicated concept by rendering it in all its complexity and refusing to resolve it for the sake of a clarity that would be untrue to the lines of the question itself. The mind has already transcended the "kinds" of earth and sea; it would not be difficult to accept the assertion that it has changed the material creation into purely mental phenomena. But the syntax will allow us also to believe that lines 47–48 mark a second step in a process only begun in lines 45–46, and that the mind is now performing its function of transmutation on the very worlds and seas with which it originally passed beyond the limits of actual experience. This time it abandons altogether the categories of "Worlds," "Seas," and even "kinds"; in contemplating its own creations it has reached the point where it must impose its own categories of apprehension upon them. Thus all that the *mind* has made becomes "a green Thought in a green Shade."

I doubt that it would be profitable to speculate too freely on the meanings that attach to "green" in this line. The "green Shade" obviously looks back to the reproving shade cast by the evergreen trees of the Garden down on the inanities of the "busie Companies of Men"; but this time it is neither "short" nor "narrow verged." It has so widened its scope under the pressure of the mind's creative impulse that it now overshadows all that is and all that the imagination can call into being. The symbolism of the colour in this line is clearly delimited; this green shade does not shelter ideas of fickleness, or even of hope, and it seems to have little to do with love of any kind, even the pure and unassertive love of the trees that cast the shade (in the mind's eye). By the same token, "a green Thought" can have little to do with any of these significations; it must have some reference to the symbolic value of green as the sign of growth and the essence of naturalness. Thus the correspondence between the mind and the principles of order represented by the trees is driven home by a metaphor of metamorphosis that makes its point by using unexpected epithets. The mind, in transforming nature into intellectual phenomena, has paralleled the trees' transformation of human passions into fruitful attitudes toward nature. It is thus like the trees in several important ways, and can therefore be said to put its "green Thought" in the "green Shade" that inspired it at first. But the following stanza makes it clear that the "green Shade" is still but the furthest reach of the powers of the natural reason; its enclosing coloured shadow is unilluminated by the intelligible truths through whose reflected light the soul shines. [In his article "The Doctrine of Charity in Mediaeval Literary Gardens"], D. W. Robertson Jr. mentions that both the trees in the Garden of Eden and their shadows had perfectly recognizable connotations, and that the Tree of the Knowledge of Good and Evil (which by definition is the symbol of mortal, or human, knowledge) "is frequently associated with *scientia* (as opposed to *sapientia*) for worldly wisdom is conducive to a false sense of security." It is my contention that the tree that shelters the winged soul in stanza 7 is the tree of *sapientia* (the Tree of Life). It is to this higher, this ultimate, form of wisdom that Marvell turns in the climactic passage of "The Garden."

The sensuous life of stanza 5 was depicted with intense particularity of place and object, but the intellectual metamorphosis of stanza 6 took place only within the mind, while we lost contact with the realities of the Garden itself. The very first word of stanza 7 redirects our attention forcefully to the *place* in which this experience occurs, as if to remind us that the symbols and metaphors are all along rooted in the basic figure of an actual garden, and also as if to enforce the paradoxical connections between physical acts and their philosophical significances: "Here at the Fountains sliding foot, / Or at some Fruit-trees mossy root" (ll. 49–50).

The exact spot Marvell specifies for the transformation of the soul that is about to take place is a fine example of his talent for choosing particulars that will also be expressive of a wide range of meanings. The fountain and the fruit tree are familiar landmarks of the pastoral landscape; but they are, as well, Christian symbols of spiritual regeneration and the site of man's lapse from grace. The soul is obviously on the point of entering into divine wisdom, as contrasted to the purely intellectual apprehension of stanza 6. Furthermore, as Robertson remarks, "a well or fountain appears often beneath the Tree of Life"; and, finally, the association of sin with the Tree of Knowledge is clearly absent from this scene—the soul is purified both of the clay of the flesh and of the lesser understanding of the unaided intellect, and has passed beyond knowledge to the edge of wisdom. As evidence that the presence of the Tree of Life in a garden signified the ultimate separation of the soul from worldly bonds we may adduce the following, from Walter Mountague's *Miscellanea Spiritualia* (1648):

> They then who live in this holy Garden of Speculation, may be said to be already under the shady leaves of the Tree of Life; this state of separation from the world, seeming to be in such an order and relation to the supreme beautitude, as *Adams Paradice* was to Heaven, as it is in a maner of integrity of ease, and passeth away out of this life by a kinde of translation to glory.

In contrast, Cowley gives the attributes of the Tree of Knowledge thus:

> The sacred *Tree* midst the fair *Orchard* grew;
> The *Phoenix Truth* did on it rest,
> And built his perfum'd Nest.
> That right *Porphyrian Tree* which did true *Logick* shew,
> Each *Leaf* did learned *Notions* give,
> And th'*Apples* were *Demonstrative*

So clear their *Colour* and divine,
The very *shade* they cast did other *Lights* out-shine.
                    ("The Tree of Knowledge," ll. 1–8)

But Marvell's allusions to the biblical tree are part of an attempt to increase the drama of the final metamorphosis of the speaker.

Casting the Bodies Vest aside,
My Soul into the boughs does glide:
There like a Bird it sits, and sings,
Then whets, and combs its silver Wings.
                    (ll. 51–54)

We need not comment again on the image of the soul as having wings or even as being a bird; nor, perhaps, does the concept of shedding the body's restrictive covering need further elucidation. But it is suggestive that the bird of the soul sings; for it is fair to say that this is a reference, once more, to the art of poetry. To a Renaissance poet "song" always meant "poem." Furthermore, one suggestion inherent in the "longer flight" of line 55 is that this refers as much to this different kind of poetry (the kind that Marvell implies he has not written in "The Coronet") as it does to the final flight of the soul to its reunion with God.

The final couplet, "And, till prepar'd for longer flight, / Waves in its Plumes the various Light" (ll. 55–56), leaves no doubt that the naturalistic description of the bird has been subsumed in the Christian (and, in this case, Platonic and Plotinian) image of the soul shining with the reflected light of God. In this convention, as we have seen in "On a Drop of Dew," Divine Light is always single, pure, white; while its reflections in the phenomena of the world are many-coloured, as they are less perfect than their source. Thus the religious tone of the stanza is maintained and brought to its complete expression; it is no less important to recognize that the soul is left in the world of phenomena. The "various light" signifies the earth; and its illumination of the soul's "Plumes" indicates that the soul still contemplates the creation that surrounds it. Perhaps the waving of the plumes is a very refined symbol of the act of writing poetry; but at the very least it suggests that the preparation required for "longer flight" will be both long and demanding. For Marvell this would be true of both the apprenticeship to poetry and the life of spiritual education that leads to salvation.

The transition in the final stanza of "The Garden" from the world of speculation we entered in stanza 4 back to the imagined garden of the opening is not so abrupt as the exclamation that begins the penultimate eight lines.

> Such was that happy Garden-state,
> While Man there walk'd without a Mate:
> After a Place so pure, and sweet,
> What other Help could yet be meet!
>
> (ll. 57–60)

We have returned, with a jolt, to the speaker's voice and to the detached, ironic viewpoint of the first three stanzas of the poem. The view is over the entire experience we have passed through in the Garden, from sense to intellect to the soul's perception; and as yet we are not sure to what condition of knowledge we are meant to have attained. We find that it is a sort of worldly wisdom, but wisdom informed with the sense of what is possible to human faculties. Nevertheless, the tone is nostalgic, for we have emerged from the vision of pure apprehension into the world of natural beauty. And to reinforce the nostalgia Marvell picks up again the rather subdued allusions to Eden in stanza 5 and recalls the myth of Adam in almost literalist fashion. The contemplative Garden we have just left is characterized as Eden before the creation of Eve, apparently to allow the poem's wit to modulate back again into the mode of the rejection of erotic love. But it is interesting that the absence of a "Mate" is rejoiced in; there is no mention of a "Mistress," something we might expect if Marvell is merely making fun again of the "Fond Lovers" of stanza 3. The implication is, rather, that the introduction of Eve into the Garden disturbed the delicate balance and sympathy that existed between man and the living nature of the Garden in the central part of the poem. But the implied statement is not followed by a lament for lost innocence and quiet; rather, it provides an excuse for the most forthright bit of word-play in the entire poem—"What other Help could yet be meet!"

> But 'twas beyond a Mortal's share
> To wander solitary there:
> Two Paradises 'twere in one
> To live in Paradise alone.
>
> (ll. 61–64)

This can be called an elegant form of misogyny—or even misanthropy—but it is not so intent on deprecating Woman that it ignores the opportunity to probe the idea a bit with more puns. It was indeed "beyond a Mortal's share" to wander in Paradise; or at least it proved to be once Eve's sin had made Adam mortal. And "one" in line 63 may be taken to mean Adam as well as the Garden of Eden; the joy of possession of the Garden might well have been doubled if it had not been shared—the mathematics is fairly simple.

Nevertheless, there is undoubtedly a sense of sorrowing yearning after the eternally lost world of innocence and natural sympathy that pervades this stanza. It is almost desperate, as we realize when it attempts to revise one of the Christian world's basic myths; the wit is in the expression of the attempt, not in the wish itself. "To live in Paradise alone," aside from being the direct antithesis of the world's usual vision of eternal bliss, is a state that can be achieved only in the imagination; neither the mythical nor the real world will accommodate this kind of solitude.

It is this recognition that governs the strangely complicated conceits of the ninth, and final, stanza. The floral sundial has bewildered many readers, not only because of the puns and ambiguities that go to make up its description, but because of its ostensibly emblematic position in "The Garden." It certainly represents a return to the actual garden created by human skill, and we shall see that the structure and meaning of the dial are both indicative of a newly-discovered relationship between art and nature. This "Gardner" has nothing in common with the "Luxurious Man" who distorted nature to abet his illicit desires. The sundial is a work of the imaginative intellect in that it imposes an order on nature that becomes symbolic of the meanings that creatures alone cannot express. Not only the flowers but the bee as well contribute to the emblematic function of the sundial, and together they assume a degree of control over time itself: "How well the skilful Gardner drew / Of flow'rs and herbes his Dial new" (ll. 65–66). As Miss Bradbrook mentions, "well" implies both that the work was done skilfully and that the gardener was right to undertake it. In both senses there is no irony in the praise for the gardener and for the dial. It is made of decorative emblems ("flow'rs") and useful, even medicinal, herbs—so that it combines beauty and utility, the twin shibboleths of Renaissance poetic. Both the point of a sundial is that it measures the passing of time, even if such measurement is taken by living creatures who are the mortal subjects of time: "Where from above the milder Sun / Does through a fragrant Zodiack run" (ll. 67–68). King's article is indispensable to an understanding of the puns in this couplet, in that they are based quite clearly on the parallel passage in *Hortus,* as most of "The Garden" is not. He explains that *Sol ibi candidior fragrantia Signa pererrat* "shows that *milder* means less dazzling than up in the sky . . . and that *fragrant* must be stressed, meaning that the zodiac up there is not fragrant." And since the sundial measures hours, the comparison to the zodiac is one between the lesser and the greater, where both are scales to judge the passing of time. For the flowers to pretend to measure the passage of the months is daring enough, but Marvell then turns to "th' industrious Bee" who, "as it works . . . / Computes its time as well as we." King points out the pun on "time" and "thyme," but the important thing to note is that the bee is as busy here as were the "busie . . . Men" who were repudiated early in the poem; yet nothing in the bee's industry is found false to nature or to the values of the Garden. The conclusion must be that this is the proper and natural use of time, and that the living creatures can subject time to their measurement. In the comparative "Computes its time as well as we" the pun is vital, since the two terms of the comparison are the bee's collecting nectar from the thyme blossoms and man's measuring out his time under the influence of nature. Both are natural creatures and both have learned how to deal most profitably with the forces that rule them: "How could such sweet and wholsome Hours / Be reckon'd but with herbs and flow'rs!" (ll. 71–72). Time is no longer a threat, but a reality that is always, in the Garden, qualified by the epithets "sweet and wholsome." And the herbs and flowers have proved themselves to be not only the proper setting for contemplation and the approach to wisdom, but a real means of conquering time through natural beauty. The final couplet suggests that the floral sundial is the only *possible* means to measure time, as if the phenomena of aging and decay could not be understood—perhaps would not exist—without the intermediary influence of nature and its creations.

From stanza to stanza the poem proceeds by a series of free variations on the theme of change and transmutation; and many of the individual metaphors and puns are based on the trope of calling something by another name, or on viewing a common tradition from an uncommon viewpoint. The most important example, of course, is the series of transmutations the speaker goes through during the poem. He rehearses the life of man as it would have been understood by Plato, and he ends his saga with strong intimations of Christian salvation. The poem leaves him, and us, with a corrected view of the meanings implicit in nature; for we have come far from the conventional treatment of the garden as the setting for contemplative and rural retirement. Rather, that is only Marvell's starting point; as we saw in the "Mower" poems, he is more concerned to understand the relationship between the inevitably abstract mind and the recalcitrant materialism of the world of the senses. The analogies he finds and the sympathetic correspondences on which he bases his metaphoric diction are both supported by his perception of the underlying "naturalness" of man. But that perception is only the beginning of the problems that are raised and dealt with in the "The Garden." The paradoxical outcome is that man must transcend his natural faculties if he is ever to understand nature correctly and live harmoniously with her.

ROSALIE COLIE

Visual Traditions behind "Upon Appleton House"

I. LANDSCAPE

"Upon Appleton House" is a poem about a house and the estate crowned
by the house, mutually supporting and honoring each other. From very different perspectives, the poet provides us with different views of the topography:
we see the house itself, as a study in architecture; the ruins of an earlier "house,"
still visible as a pile of masonry on the estate, seen in the poem as a "quarry"
and even a "chaos"; the formal gardens next the house; the water-meadows by
the river, with the rural activities appropriate to such a scene; the wood, cut
by a straight alley; the river in its bed and out of it. Nunappleton offers just
such a landscape as Pliny laid out as the proper sort for a painting, with considerable differentiation and variety in both view and function. The estate
satisfies its master and its master's poet with *"Lordship . . . of the Eye,"* its landscapes seen in accord with mood and moral.

As one runs through the standard topics of seventeenth-century landscape
painting, both fantastic and actual, topothesical and topographical, one
discovers that the locales of this poem can be classified according to recognizable
and accepted visual genres of landscape depiction. In the repertory, there are
many pieces showing individual buildings, painted both as a record for their
owners and as a form of praise to his greatness. Some were large enough to show
the estate's principal activities taking place around an architectural center.
Ruins-pieces form a genre, often designed to induce melancholy or nostalgia;

From *"My Ecchoing Song": Andrew Marvell's Poetry of Criticism.* © 1970 by
Princeton University Press.

there are many examples of bucolic scenes of sheep, cattle, and mowing; and
georgic scenes of sowing, reaping, harvesting, and gleaning. There are forest-
pieces with many variations, some not unlike Marvell's different views of his
variegated enchanted wood; there are river-landscapes, often with angler or
anglers; there are panoramas or prospect-pieces which present many of these
elements in one picture.

According to visual tradition, pastoral and georgic scenes, with human
figures going about their natural activites, were regarded as stressing the pros-
perous nature of a given countryside, as the browsing cattle, the mowers, or
the fishermen in this poem demonstrate the balanced economy of Fairfax's estate
and the benevolence of local Nature. Figures were, we discover, generally
deliberately included in a landscape to increase its mood of well-being; well-
being did not always extend to ecstasy, as in this poem it happens to, but neither
was it uncommon for a figure in a woody landscape to be beside himself with
one rapture or another. Different activities suit different sorts of well-being,
as in Ruisdael's magnificent *Grainfields,* or his pictures of linen bleaching
across wide fields. In Adriaen van de Velde's *Farm by a Stream,* the house,
the cows, the sheep, and the horses all make up a small but sufficient unit, the
prosperity of which is evident; in the same painter's *Summer,* many elements
gather to show the varied richness of that season (the season of "Upon Appleton
House")—mowers, haycocks, sheep, and shepherds, horsemen and footmen
are all present, as well as a ruin and a town in the background. As for the wood-
scenes, there are many lovely ones in the repertory of Dutch seventeenth-century
landscape—entrances to forests, some showing a dark and mysterious wood,
some a light glade within the gloom, the sun brightening a particular spot or
dappling the floor of the forest. Most forest-landscapists are inclined, like the
poet in this poem, to note some specifics of their wood—as Wolfgang Stechow
pointed out [in *Dutch Landscape Painting in the Seventeenth Century*], on the
whole they painted woods, not trees, and some, like Gerard David and
Altdorfer, painters in an earlier tradition closer to miniature, went so far as to
paint leaves, not trees. Had he been a painter, Marvell's foliage-style would
doubtless have taken after theirs, since he was careful, he tells us, to note each
leaf in his environment. It is not wholly a surprise, then, to discover that he
had access to an important book on miniature-painting: Ralph Thoresby the
antiquarian, who acquired many of Fairfax's books and manuscripts, had a
manuscript copy of a major book in the miniature-tradition, Edward Norgate's
Miniatura, "dedicated to the Lord's Daughter Mary," which Marvell may well
have known. This book is a professional study of "the art of limning" small:
Norgate's subject ranges over pictures "by the Life, Landskip, and History," with
directions for perspective drawing and for mixing colors. In view of Marvell's

famous tendency to miniaturize, this book may have some importance in his education as well as that of his little pupil; it may even have something to do with this poem.

Forests were variously depicted: some painters favored very dense forests, as Vroom did; others favored open paths through a wood, even lanes and alleys of the formal sort which, as Marvell tells us, divided Fairfax's wood as the Red Sea was divided. Hackaert's picture in the Rijksmuseum (*The Alley*) shows a road passing a pond, with woods on the far side; there is a similar picture in the Wallace Collection. Hobbema's *Road into a Forest* might be an analogue to Marvell's wood at Appleton, the wood, edged with arable, dark from without but light within. There are, also, dawn-pieces in the repertory of landscape-painters, to which the poem's garden-scene offers an analogue; and evening-pieces, the last, like Marvell's river landscape, often with a still sheet of water to show the day's final piece. In Aert van der Neer's evening pictures in the Mauritshuis and in the Boymans Museum, just as in Marvell's poem, the water's stillness helps give the evening its mysteriousness and fulness.

Such topical scenes are often related—in Marvell's poems are overtly connected—to specific historical or mythological events. Landscapes as settings for biblical scenes and Ovidian metamorphoses are common enough: Marvell's poem offers analogues to both subjects. By means of imagery, the mowers metamorphose into Israelites crossing the Red Sea, later miraculously gathering food in the desert. The poet turns into a Noah, then a Solomon, in the retreat of his wooded ark. In late sixteenth-century paintings, a small biblical scene was often "planted" in a landscape, so subdued and understated as to be hardly noticeable at first glance. In Alexander Keirincx's painting, what seems a wooded landscape with river and roads, turns out to be a Temptation of Christ. The wilderness and woods seemed to be the appropriate setting for saints and hermits: like such a holy figure, the poet becomes in his wood "some great Prelate of the Grove," in Marvell's magnificent conflation of Christian with pagan imagery. Though the "prelacy" is consistent with one iconographic tradition, the poet blends it with others; he takes advantage of the wood as the proper habitat for ecstasy, and assumes many other roles in that passage, finally allowing himself to metamorphose into the very landscape. As such a Proteus, he descends from an Ovidian rather than a meditative source.

Though the traditions of generic landscape-painting lie in the middle-ground of Marvell's poem, the poet draws on many other visual conventions as well. Indeed, it would be difficult not to: the more one knows of poetic description, the more frankly ecphrastic it turns out to be, closely related to visual renderings schematized by tradition. It was as difficult for poets to write a pastoral wholly independent of visual traditions, for instance, as for painters

to show a pastoral scene without recourse to verbal sources. Pliny's descriptions of ancient pictures set models for later imitations in both painting and
poetry, for which Horace's tag could always be cited in justification. Homer's
description of Achilles' shield gave ecphrastic exercises their respectability, and
parallels in minor genres, for instance from the Anthology, were common also.

One can, then, see "Upon Appleton House" as no less a gallery-poem than
Marvell's lyric "The Gallery"; the house-poem is a coherent series of pictorial
descriptions, this time not of a lady in different symbolic poses, but of a landscape seen from different perspectives. The Appleton gallery contains many
variations upon the theme of topography, as biblical scenes (Exodus, the Flood,
Solomon, a *pentimento*-Crucifixion) and classical scenes (the pyramids, a
Roman camp, Roman tumuli, the Nile) are interspersed among more conventionally representational views. In one image, Sir Peter Lely is introduced (stanza
56); shortly after that, an ecphrastic passage from *Gondibert* is recalled. But
not only are large-scale views introduced with their suggestions of epic painting; the poet also provides lovely miniatures: the nuns embroider pictures,
taking Isabella as their model for the Virgin; Mexican feather-pictures are referred to; and emblems occur as well. In these ways, the exotic is set in contrast
to the standard, the sacred or near-sacred to profane and profaning notions.

II. MINIATURES AND EMBLEMS

Critics noting Marvell's "miniaturism" have found examples in "Upon
Appleton House." Kitty Scoular's finds have been most valuable in this respect.
As her work suggests, Marvell's visual imagery drew from the rich resources
of moralized picture, and as we examine these in this poem, we recognize not
only his remarkable skill in diminishing, but also his ability to underscore the
themes of his poem by the intellectual meaning of the traditional images he
used. The texture of his poem turns out to be very closely woven, as his
emblematic images demonstrate. The tortoise, for instance, appears in the
emblem literature in various ways relevant to Marvell's themes. Miss Scoular
gives us Wither's tortoise, whose modest and suficient house is his shell; one
could add Henry Peacham's sensitive creature, or Rollenhagen's, Typotius',
or Camerarius' to the list, all of them used to symbolize qualities for which
Marvell honored his patron. In the wonderful illustration to Zacharias Heyns's
"Vivitur parvo bene," though, is the very finest analogue to Marvell's tortoise-
imagery, as well as to his theme of containment and proper occupation; there,
on the authority of Pliny, a picture is presented of the tortoise-shell put to various
uses: "There be found Tortoises in the Indian Sea so great, that one shell of
them is sufficient for the roufe of a dwelling house. And among the Islands

principally in the red sea, they use Tortoise shells ordinarily for boats and wherries upon the water."

Heyns's emblem shows a man in a boat on the sea, evidently made of a tortoise-shell, and another emerging from his tortoise-shell "house," propped up so that it seems to be the shell of the man himself, borne on his back as the fishermen carry their coracles in Marvell's poem.

Other images have their emblematic analogues: Miss Scoular prints Beza's neat geometrical emblem of the cube within the circle: the stability of the cube, as well as the perfection of circle and sphere, are endlessly attested in other sources. In Freitag's emblem book, the stork sacrificing its nestling obviously relates to Marvell's heron who sacrifices its first-born to the Lord, so curiously letting it drop from the high nest in Appleton wood. Emblematic storks, cranes, and herons turn out to represent a cluster of qualities relevant in the thematic structure of this poem: the stork is a conspicuously good provider, the parent-birds of their young and the young in turn of their parents. The married storks are, also, images of fidelity. Storks, herons, and cranes are all provident; Camerarius shows us the heron, like Lord Fairfax, flying above the storm. The stork's and heron's sacrifice may be a way of referring to the Fairfax's earlier loss of a child, since Thoresby records the burial of another daughter, Elizabeth, "ob. inf." beside the heiress Mary.

In the case of the stork, Marvell has provided the nearest equivalent in native British birds to the classical emblem: his stock-doves too are local, though their qualities are assimilated to those of the emblematic dove. Doves are religious, faithful in marriage, chaste in widowhood, and good providers. They are, also, sensible retirers (like the tortoise); according to Camerarius, when threatened, doves take refuge in woods. His picture shows a pair flying thither, as one asumes Lord and Lady Fairfax, honored in the poem's stock-dove reference, made their retreat to the country. The halcyon, used in the poem to praise Mary Fairfax, shares some qualities with the dove: she nests on the sea, of course, but also finds her needed solitude there, as the dove finds hers in the wood; the halcyon is also a faithful mate and a provident parent. Its floating nest was, in an earlier seventeenth-century poem, likened to the island England. Miss Scoular reproduces Camerarius's lovely nesting halcyon, but the bird is in most emblem books, and descends from Pliny and Ovid. Another provident parent is the woodpecker; according to Pliny, the "spight," or woodpecker, goes catlike up a tree, carefully placing its stroke, as Marvell's bird does; in Jacob Cats's woodpecker emblem, the woodpecker, like a lover aiming for the be-loved's heart, pecks firmly through the hard tree. Like the heron's, the hewel's sacrifice in the poem is reverential; the tinted oak falls without hatred or bitterness, to keep the forest clean. The bird is, in an archaic technical term, a "holt-felster," in charge of the health of the health-giving wood.

The nightingale too is prominent in the emblem repertory, chiefly as an educator of its young, training them in their remarkable birthright. Pliny's description of the nightingale's traditional tuition is often illustrated in emblem, most sweetly in Camerarius' version.

I can find no rail in the pictured emblems, although the characteristics of other low-nesting birds seem to have been assimilated to Marvell's local bird. The usual emblem-equivalents are the lark and the quail, with the last of which Marvell specifically associates his little bird. Peacham shows the careful partridge-mother teaching her birds to fly the nest as the mowers approach, and Camerarius' lark does the same thing. Valeriano notes that the rail is precocious and provident, two qualities notably absent in this poem's rails; and Pliny calls the little bird "amphibious," which ties in to another major theme of the poem. In "Upon Appleton House," the humility and innocence of the bird are stressed, as are its failures to adapt rather than its powers of accommodation. The rail is not here used to demonstrate moral adaptability, although the theme is otherwise stressed in the poem before its clear enunciation in the last stanza. The tortoise and the crocodile offer hints that the poet to some degree approves of moral amphibiousness, a necessary quality for life in the human world. The emblem books offer many models for amphibiousness; frogs, tortoises, and especially crocodiles, are all approved, not reproved, for their adaptability.

Birds and animals do not provide the only emblematic parallels to the imagery of this poem: Camerarius' systematic emblem book stresses the meaning of grass and mowing, to reinforce the biblical and classical implications clearly legible in the poem. When grass is cut, it waxes richer—"Surget uberior"; haycocks reward labor ("Non metentis sed serentis"). Following Paul's great image, grain is the emblem of the Resurrection: "spes alterae vitae." The emblem from De Jode's *Microkosmos,* showing a hamadryad in a hollow tree, illustrates the notion that man is an inverted tree; Cats's river-god, with sedge on his head and his body fusing with bank and river, has his analogues in classical and neo-classical art as well as in Ovid (*Metamorphoses* 9.3) and Virgil (*Aeneid* 8.31–35).

In general, the emblem books provide interesting corroboration for the themes of the poem as well as analogues to Marvell's graphic vignettes; but in this range of reference, as in so many others, Marvell alters his traditional sources in favor of problematics. The birds in this poem do very odd things, after all: why should the stock-dove, so clearly associated with his lady patron, weep *before* experiencing widowhood? What is the heron's attitude to its sacrifice, or the woodpecker's? There is an unexplained element to many of

these scenes, whose emblematic language of reference was perhaps more intelligible to the circle in which the poem was written than to more general readers.
When one consults the emblem books, particular obscurities about these birds
seem somewhat to be cleared up, but not altogether. Though the cryptic emblem
literature offers some straightforward help in filling in the hints made in the
poem's imagery, no "source" seems to provide an exhaustive gloss to Marvell's
intentions. His meaning is elusive, even with these useful aids.

Marvell's miniature scenes offer a scalar contrast to the set of large landscape pictures of which the poem is chiefly built. His gallery holds great and
small, each kind of picture observing the conventions of its genre, and com-
plementing other kinds. For all their obscurities, the emblems are noticeably
exact, as the tradition demanded. Marvell's mysteriousness is well within the
emblem tradition, though, which notoriously combined an exact observation
with an esoteric thought or generalization: part of the test, in emblem-writing,
was to puzzle or trick the reader as well as to enlighten him. Emblem pictures,
of course, shared some content with the ordinary, undidactic landscape: Lebei's
emblem, "Eunt anni more fluentis aquae," for instance, with its two fishermen,
river-god with sedge and urn, might as well point to well-being as to transience;
one needs the motto to read the lesson as the writer intended.

Comparing Marvell's imagery to its emblematic analogues shows that he
made use of two opposed tendencies in emblem-technique, utilizing both the
precision and the fixedness on one hand, and the ambiguousness and
mysteriousness of the tradition on the other. Nor was his manipulation of landscape conventions merely standard or routine, even though his descriptions do
fulfil the criteria for such genre-scenes. Indeed, the standard element of
Marvell's scenes is the least remarkable thing about them: it is their deviations
which command our chief attention.

III. DEVIATIONS IN PERSPECTIVE, METAMORPHOSES, AND ANAMORPHOSES

In visual and intellectual ambiguity, the poet could and did find particular
resources for his own presentation of the fluidity of both material and intellectual worlds. In *adunaton,* rhetoric offers a standard mode of inversion, on which
the poet certainly relied, as in his stanza 60, about the Nunappleton flood:

> Let others tell the *Paradox,*
> How Eels now bellow in the Ox;
> How Horses at their Tails do kick,
> Turn'd as they hang to Leeches quick;

> How Boats can over Bridges sail;
> And Fishes do the Stables scale.
> How *Salmons* trespassing are found;
> And Pikes are taken in the Pound.

This is the familiar commonplace of the world-upside-down, a classic literary signal of topsy-turvydom, of handy-dandy, of a morally upset universe in which things do not keep their accustomed or assigned places, but waywardly rearrange themselves in ways disruptive to conventional thought. The tradition has its long history, this particular image occurring (also with stress on its literal truth) in Ovid's *Metamorphoses;* (with stress on the overwhelming nature of love) in Virgil's eighth *Eclogue*; (with stress on its figurative element) in Horace's *Odes*, II, ii and IV, vii, there to suggest the disaster attendant upon civil war. As Mr. Allen has pointed out, this kind of imagery was regularly associated in Latin poetry with the chaos produced by civil war in a country, especially the countryside. An even more relevant storm, also metaphorically connected to the disastrous effects of war upon the agrarian economy, is that of *Georgics* 1, when the reapers face the rain-flood sweeping away their harvest. From this storm, the heron escapes by flying above the clouds and the cranes by flying into the valleys.

In Marvell's poem, the facts in the end reverse the function of this upside-downing, modify the frightening references to civil war. If this world-upside-down, this world in flood, is designed to invoke the civil war raging outside the boundaries of the estate, it retracts its utterance too: the disasters suggested by the imagery turn out not to be disasters at all, but simply the seasonal observance of georgic providential behavior—commended by, among others, Pliny. This flood-after-reaping restores the proper relation between harvest and replenishing, prevented in the *Georgics* by the disastrous natural flood. At the same time, though, the image is not simple: the landscape is made into a double scene, the high seriousness of its biblical and classical references dissolving into the happier context of the real episode, merely seeming catastrophic but in fact beneficial. The original disproportion of the scene sinks back into normality, as we learn that what would be a world-upside-down, in another and more ordinary context, is here simply regular and beautiful. The poet plays with his and our own literary expectations, ultimately to empty the great *adunata* of their paradoxical meanings.

Marvell's way with this standard *topos* for inversion should give us pause, since his manner in this stanza is a model for much else that he does in the poem. The more one studies it, the more the poem's use and abuse of order demands attention, most obviously in the many images of inversion. For in this poem, there are many worlds-upside-down, many men-upside-down: in the wood, whither the poet retires to escape the flood, he experiences an extraordinary identification with the birds and plants of that thick landscape, an identification which involves his own metamorphosis. To himself, and to us forced to observe with his eyes, the poet's form and nature, his real "being," seem fully to merge with the elements of his environment. Had he wings, he would fly, he says; inverted, he would be a tree.

Yet, although the imagery inverts so much, and so strikingly conveys the poet's sense of freedom from the gravity even of himself, and all the cares the self must bear in the ordinary world, we discover that the man in the poem is in fact never turned upside down: he stays upright through everything. However high his raptures, he walks upon the ground, moves from here to there; even when he seems prone in ecstasy he is mysteriously on his way to somewhere else. It is true that in one sense nature's order is inverted in the wood-ecstasy, but that inversion is intellectual, not actual. Attributing high powers to nature, this man wishes to be turned into bird or tree, elements on the scale normally regarded as lower than a man. But even in the poem's fiction, we learn that the scale of creatures can be altered only in imagination: the poet throughout remains a man, simple and complex. He does not fly; he is not a tree. Only in his imagination can the rules of nature be altered to suit a passing psychological need.

In the meadow scene, the poet sees the mowers as inverted men: they "dive" through space, through the meadow as if through a sea, losing their sense of spatial relation, losing their sense of themselves. In the final stanza of the poem, the fishermen are inverted, "rational *Amphibii*" appearing on the scene like Antipodeans, in a multiple image of inversion. On Cleveland's authority at least, men on the other side of the world were deemed to wear their shoes on their heads; the Yorkshire fishermen habitually carry their coracles on their heads, or backs. Both behave peculiarly, wearing on their heads what they ought to have beneath them, shoes or boats; but, in the normal way, Antipodeans are antipodal to Yorkshiremen walking right side up. One pair of feet is, from the other's perspective, always upside down. This pairing is not a mirror-reflection, though: Antipodeans, even with shoes on their feet, are not mirror-images of Yorkshiremen with boats on their heads. Only when men upside down oblige by wearing shoes on their heads can the images mirror one another. Then, if they do, the men are twice antipodal, doubly upside down: their feet against one another are antipodal, and their pseudopoda in the air make them seem antipodal to themselves. They are doubly topsy-turvy, and since this is so, they are not topsy-turvy. They mirror each other, but only by verbal sleight-of-hand. There are too many possibilities in this image for readers to keep straight, or

to interpret as they read—the salmon-fishermen and the Antipodeans are grotesque, decorative figures thrust into the poem to remind us, at its peaceful end,
that things are simple nowhere in the world, that all men are sometimes, in some
perspectives, upside down. In contrast to the diving mowers who emerge from
the meadow to stand up straight in the poem, the figures in the final stanza
retain some degree of mystery, of oddity, as they move offstage and out of view,
trailing their ambiguity behind them, leaving readers at the poem's end aware
of the mystery even in daily occupations.

For somehow, it is not as comforting as it ought to be that most of the
things inverted in this poem are not in fact inverted; readers' stability is not
increased by the righting of the men and worlds upside down. Even when right
side up, these figures do not behave conventionally: in the abracadabra of their
positioning lies their peculiar meaning, pointing to the world's instability, the
illusion in all perspectives, even those taken from Appleton, upon the multiple
lives of men. Gradually, though, the conventions of upside down and right side
up cease to matter as much as they normally do in the world. These topsy-
turvydoms come to seem artifices and constructs like anything else: the river
floods the land, the fish swim through buildings—but the flood is an artful
one produced to georgic prescription. The mowers are not divers, even if the
meadow is later flooded; but in the mowers' lives some uncertainty comes, as
they must question their occupation after the death of the baby rail. The poet
is not a tree, but he understands the book of nature written on the leaves around
him, and is the better for it.

To say all this, though, is to speak after the riddle has been set and studied,
after the effect of the bizarre images has come to seem normal, and the grotesque naturalized. In the developing poem, readers certainly think and feel
catastrophe as the flood comes up over the land and the fish swim in the stables.
It is somehow disturbing to realize that all this is *not* crucial, or that our emotional reactions to the evident meaning of the words used are continually under-
cut and undermined by what the poet does next, by the shifts of context and
tone from one passage to its successor. By such stratagems the poet works to
involve his dutiful readers in the very unbalancing of which the poem speaks.

IV. SCALAR SHIFTS AND OPTICAL ILLUSIONS

Shifts provide one kind of puzzle for the reader expecting, from his ac-
quaintance with other house-poems, an orderly cosmos displayed for his admiration and edification. Scalar disruption contributes to the muddle, as when,
for instance, grasshoppers are seen to contemn the men "beneath" them. This
seems an inverted world, in which grasshoppers are larger than men; but it turns

out, only, that the grasshoppers are sitting, in their usual small shapes, on top of the grass grown taller than men. Inverted, but not inverted; and the poet involves himself in this scene as a figure wandering in this world. As he enters the meadow scene—in the first person, now: "to the *Abbyss* I pass"—he seems to see the haymakers from a great distance, themselves mere grasshoppers in the tall grass. At that point, the grasshoppers are introduced as "Gyants there": to a cinematic generation, such a shift from distant prospect to close-up is familiar enough, but such switches were rarer in Marvell's time, though some analogues can be profitably cited.

Among the visual analogues is the curious painting in Hartford, attributed to Ruisdael, an extraordinary view of thistles and other weeds, seen from such a perspective as to dwarf the postulated beholder with respect to the towering plants. In the poem, the grasshopper shift turns out to be deceptive itself: the creatures are not giants at all, and as we realize that, an element of sanity returns to the meadows that they had seemed conspicuously to lack.

There are other shifts of focus in the poem. We are shown the mowers at a considerable distance, but the rail killed by the scythe moves instantly to the foreground as "bloody *Thestylis*" seizes it to convert it into lunch. Rubens's great landscape in London, where the partridge hide in the clearing, and are enormous compared with the actually more imposing landscape elements depicted in the distance, may be compared to this. One thinks too of emblem conventions, where illusionistic perception is so often abandoned in the interests of thematic emphasis, and small things bearing heavy symbolic weight are seen as monumental.

In the famous image of the grazing cattle sent to crop the stubble-fields, the same movement occurs from small to great. At first we see the cows from afar; they are like fleas, or like stars in the night sky. The flea image is turned inside out: the fleas emerge from a subsidiary position in the original metaphor to be transformed into something huge, as if seen through a microscope. And what huge things are they seen to resemble? Cows, of course, so that the total circularity of the image is established. "Multiplying Glasses" are the means used to telescope tenor and vehicle of this image: we are made to consider the fleas through a microscope, where they appear disproportionately large—like that classic page tipped into Hooke's *Micrographia*, where the flea is depicted as enormous. We then turn to look up, not down, at the stars; through a telescope, not a microscope: the image itself works in reverse, too. Unlike fleas, constellations are made up of huge bodies which look small to us who are so distanced from them. By the many kinds of opposition exploited here, all scale is somehow obliterated. We are made to lose our measuring-rod, so that the cows lose their reality between the very small and the unbelievably huge.

Marvell's incisiveness in describing small objects calls up another kind of art, the minute precision of the still-life painter. That artist consistently used magnifying glasses and microscopes to observe and render his subjects; for his art, fleas could be on the bovine scale of Hooke's engraving. Normally, the still-life painter does not falsify the scale of his picture, but maintaining the illusion of a fixed perspective, strives for a highly developed representational illusionism. Marvell's details are the result of exact vision: in the "Hazles thick," for instance, the poet sees not the whole thrush upon her nest, but its "shining Eye," distinct from the surrounding leaves, a sharp eye which in its own right catches and holds the sharp eye of the poet. Montaigne and his cat; Marvell and the thrush—who plays with whom, who observes whom?

In his communion with the wood, the poet knows all nature, even down to the individual leaf:

> No Leaf does tremble in the Wind
> Which I returning cannot find.
>
> (stanza 72)

Like the still-life painter, the poet seems to accord each thing the attention due it as itself, to honor the individuality and individuation of each bird, each leaf— and of each element, whatever it may be, of his scene. This attention, however, is in the poem quite inconsistent, notably selective. Only now and again can the poet demonstrate his sense of the autonomy of each individual thing in the environment: in the wood episode, as in the sixth stanza of "The Garden," the poet's revelation of nature's unity does not prevent him from recognizing nature's separate elements. The greater his absorption into nature, the more precise, apparently, his appreciation of its particulars. From intense awareness of individuals the poet's cosmic identification emerges; in turn, the cosmic identification brings understanding of the value of individuals.

Later in the poem, in the evening, a panoramic still life is rendered as a miracle wrought by Maria. Again specific elements are honored; each fish in the river is, somehow, separately delineated:

> The stupid Fishes hang, as plain
> As *Flies* in *Chrystal* overt'ane;
>
> (stanza 85)

What had fluctuated is brought to stasis, as the halcyon-girl stills the fluid scene; the rapidly changing elements of earlier passages, the lapping, relaxed particulars of the river scene just before Maria's entrance, are at this point all arrested, frozen into a moment of still life, caught at an instant of immobility as a painting catches its shifting actuality.

Though optical instruments were at first considered to be clarifiers of sense-experience, isolating and distinguishing new facts about the natural world and, by extending the sense of sight, making possible great advances in the taxonomic effort of the Renaissance, in Marvell's hands optical techniques are used to very wayward ends. Seeming to sharpen a reader's perceptions, so that with the poet he sees for a moment the thrush's black eye, in fact these devices are confusing and puzzling. After all, the grazing cattle are neither constellations nor fleas, but by these similes, the poet expressly prevents us from more than a fleeting glance at the cattle plain. In the wood and stream, the opposite is the case: the details are plain enough, but their aggregate is confusing: "the hatching *Thrastle's* eye," the separate leaves, "the stupid Fishes" are all so separated from their environment that we have difficulty in piecing their world together. Here, pieces are missing from the picture-puzzle. An analogue to this technique is, for instance, a plate by Hoefnagel, to which E. H. Gombrich has drawn attention [in *Art and Illusion*]. Each element in the picture is shown for itself, detached from the others, some flying, some sitting on a flat ground, some casting shadows in one direction, some in another, some casting no shadows at all. In the wood passage, some of the poetic elements are so distinct and detached from environment that they seem entirely without context. Though the thrush sits on her nest—and nests are clearly important in this poem—the poet leaves us to work out where the specific nest may be, and indeed what the connections are from nest to nest. Disjunction is of course typical of many ranges of this poem's operation: the cattle are detached from scale, the bird's eye is detached from the bird, the hewel's curiously hierophantic, unexplained activity quite detached from the usual forest-behavior of that bird.

There are other devices borrowed from optical techniques in this poem beside the microscopic separation of an element from its accommodating background. Of the cattle, the poet says they

> seem within the polisht Grass
> A Landskip drawn in Looking-Glass

that is, the cattle seem to be elements of a picture drawn on backed glass, so that when someone uses it as a looking-glass, he sees the cattle on his own reflection, "As Spots, so shap'd, on Faces." By this means, the poor cattle are again transported from context, this time into a double picture of a sort not yet met in the poem, in which a rural landscape is transposed into a face. To read the landscape-face picture as one, the beholder must see the cattle as disfiguring facial spots. In this passage, the poet refers deliberately to anamorphosis: somewhat earlier, in stanza 56, he had achieved an anamorphic effect simply by verbal means, without invoking the visual arts at all, when he gave us at once "A new and empty Face of things" and a full depiction of an active rural scene.

Mirrors characteristically repeat pictures, repeat what is before them: the "mirror" at the poem's end, the still river reflecting the scene outside it, has its double function too, something like the looking-glass of the cattle image. This time, though, instead of two pictures interpenetrating one another, the river presents a picture of the world to the world, a picture so perfect that the things reflected in the river seem to lose their identity in their reflections, or in the reflection of themselves. Therefore, all things "doubt / If they be in it or without." And if they *are* in it, of course they are antipodean. Even in his image of perfect stillness, serenity, and rest, the poet cannot resist raising questions of ontology and epistemology, so that things themselves are for a moment animated to question and to doubt, along with the readers working their way through the poem.

Visual imagery—and mirrors, of course—provide the vocabulary in classical as in modern languages for understanding and perception. With the systematization of linear perspective, the problem of point of view, both as an organizing device and as a limiting one, became paramount in the visual arts and lent its language to that of epistemology, too. To see things "in perspective" requires that things be organized and rendered in specific relation to each other; the perceiver must have a fixed viewpoint, a rooted stance, must have taken a decision about his place in relation to the world. It may, though, be something else, the indication of a decision not taken, for any given perspective implies only a limited view of things; and a picture or drawing may suggest that there is much more than can be shown, just out of the viewer's range.

Perspective itself is an honest illusion—a deceit, as some Renaissance critics wrote—by which things are made to look true, even though their actual relation may be something quite other than what the eye from a given point can perceive. In a picture, perspective implies a conventional, expected falsification, even as it observes the illusionistic "truth" of phenomenal vision. Perspective is, then, a severely limiting device; the beholder of a perspective view must reorganize his "picture" whenever he shifts his position, since with each shift on his part, perspective relations also shift. As Jurgis Baltrušaitis pointed out in his fascinating book (*Anamorphoses*), once one has learned to present visually "true" perspectives, it is but a short step to producing deforming perspectives, manipulating the science of optics to heighten the illusion not of proportion only, but also of disproportion, deformation, and irregularity. "Anamorphic" pictures, which broke up conventional forms and relations by geometrical means, insisted upon the relativity implied in the rules of perspective, but by using at least two points of view to organize a picture, brought to the beholder's attention questions of irregularity normally unasked, at least in pictorial form. In order to compose a picture of this sort, its beholder had to discover the exact position from which the various pictorial elements would fall into place in a "normal" perspective. In some pictures, of which Holbein's *Ambassadors* is the most famous example, no single position can bring the different elements into one focus. Still other pictures manipulated pictorial scale so as to preclude the possibility of a fixed point of view.

Such pictures are rarely important as works of art, though Holbein's picture is an exception. Normally, they are intellectual exercises rather than pleasing pictures, which have involved a great deal of careful planning on the part of their designers. They force questions upon beholders willy-nilly. There are other kinds of double or multiple pictures, of which the human landscape is one of the most common sort. Other kinds of displays were possible in the seventeenth century, such as the catoptrical instruments which showed, in rapid succession, several different tableaux. After these had been shown serially, all could be composed into one grand final synthetic picture of an officially important subject. In metamorphic and anamorphic pictures, several perspectives are offered; some mental energy is required of the beholder in putting the disparate elements into a consistent context. In catoptric displays, the beholder stays in one place, as it were, watching the set scenes metamorphose without having to solve them himself. "Upon Appleton House" offers analogues to both kinds of display. Sometimes perspectives must be forcibly arranged by the viewer; sometimes he can stand passive before shifts of scene which do not demand his attempts to control them, as in magic lantern performances.

V. MAGIC LANTERN AND MASQUE DEVICES

The meadow scenes seem much like a catoptric or magic lantern performance; Marvell may have known the magic lantern device, for as early as 1618 such a performance had been put on at the English court by Cornelis Drebbel, and others had tried the trick subsequently. Drebbel had projected pictures of himself in different costumes from beggar to king, one figure metamorphosing into the next through the social scale. As the poet enters the meadows, he pauses as if to focus on his view, trying out several perspectives, in the first of which men seem like grasshoppers, and then grasshoppers are seen as giants. After a time he achieves a "normal" focus, in which the haymakers' progress is seen, presented in diminutive form (i.e., like a magic lantern performance) and as a highly stylized, choreographed formalization of reality (i.e., as a masque):

> No Scene that turns with Engines strange
> Does oftner then these Meadows change.
>
> (stanza 49)

After many "turns" of mowing, rail-killing, and triumphal dance, the players withdraw to leave the stage empty for another series of changes, in a different mode altogether:

> This *Scene* again withdrawing brings
> A new and empty Face of things;
>
> (stanza 56)

By moving ungraded from one operation to the next, all the bustle of horses, haycarts, pitching and tossing has been avoided, so that the accomplished mowing brings us naturally to a "Table rase and pure," a blank canvas ready for the painter. This blank canvas is also the world empty on the First Day of Creation: for a moment, the painter is like the deity, with all creation in prospect. Onto this set, the "Villagers in common chase / Their cattle": the animals enter as if from nowhere, on Creation's Fifth Day, or into the bullring at Madrid. The one is nature plain and pure, the other manifest artification, the subtle arts of a highly developed civilization, in which the primitive behavior of bulls has been subjected to rigorous and ritualized control. In this stanza there are other switches: the tempo, at first nervous and quick, slows down utterly as the cattle's movement becomes imperceptible:

> They feed so wide, so slowly move,
> As *Constellations* do above.
>
> (stanza 58)

The cattle vanish from the poem as the stars vanish in the morning, again without fuss or explanation; and the last meadow scene begins:

> Then, to conclude these pleasant Acts,
> *Denton* sets ope its *Cataracts;*
>
> (stanza 59)

This language of staging and scenery recurs in the poem, as for instance the poet dresses for his priestly part in the wood, and in the final scene at the riverside, where

> Men the silent *Scene* assist,
> Charm'd with the *Saphir-winged Mist*
>
> (stanza 85)

until, at the very end, the professional fishermen lead in the night and lead the principals off the stage.

Magic lantern performances exploit scalar shifts, projecting a tiny original as unbelievably huge; masques, too, are lifesize presentations of a series of emblematic scenes. In magic lantern presentations, one scene can be made to melt into another, as the anamorphic body-landscape melts from scene to human shape. In such pictures, a natural scene is characteristically converted into a reclining man or a huge human head: conversely, a human figure can be seen to be made up of animal or vegetable elements, as in the many arcimboldesque paintings of the sixteenth century. In various ways, the poet makes use of the body-landscape trick, as when he makes himself metamorphose into wood-elements and into the stream: he uses even himself, in this poem, to call into question the principles of definition, limitation, and boundary. The superposition of forms points to forms' ambiguities: nothing seems to be itself, or itself alone.

Devices like those used in masque and magic lantern performances permit the poet to shift from one scene to another without gradation or transition, to alter sharply differentiated episodes into one another. Focus once achieved, the poet could maintain a single perspective for a time; he could shift perspective radically too, by shifting his own apparent focus. Drebbel made himself his own subject in his magic lantern entertainments; Marvell presents himself as a character in his invention, too.

In the meadow scene, the poet begins as an observer, well outside the action he observes. As critic and commentator, he is clearly separate from the mower-masquers, whom he seems to manipulate acccording to his fancy, as the inductor does. His little world is very much his theater: by his highly stylized framing of the scenes, the simple behavior of simple men, even down to their sweating, is raised to the level of courtly entertainment. What could be more detached from the actual activity of mowing than this graceful pastoral? Lest we take it as only that, though, a radical disjunction jars us into realizing the artificiality of the artifice: one of the actors refuses to be manipulated by the poet, and turns on him, to expose him to our view. The poet's previous metaphors, addressed to the readers who overhear his inventions, ought to have been inaudible to the *farouche* Thestylis, who has nonetheless caught his drift and herself imaginatively extends the poet's metaphor by her reading—counter to the nostalgic tone he then affects—of the events taking place. By this trick, scale and perspective both shift, and with them the psychological or tonal angle. Though the poet has indeed called the mowers "Israelites," by the time Thestylis burst into the poem, he had abandoned that image and become absorbed in the small tragedy of the rail's death. Thestylis irrupts upon the language of pastoral sentimental identification, the lament for a creature dead ere its prime. Her speech calls attention to the very *writing* of the poem: she carries the poet's biblical metaphor to an area into which he had not planned to take it, and we realize, suddenly, that another imagination might have gone another way, that the poem might, in another poet's hands, have been quite different. Her untimely comment also has the effect of calling into question not just the limits of the poet's aesthetic attention and thus the limitations in this kind of poetry, but also the whole process of figural reading, mocked in her speech. More important, she effects a major reversal of role, the poet becoming for a moment an actor in *her* drama. Hitherto effaced and neutral, although in fact manipulating the whole scene, the poet finds himself rudely recast, forced into evidence in the poem he writes, his scale suddenly dwarfing the mowers', even as Thestylis' seizing the little rail dwarfs that tiny bird, till then so much in the foreground.

The poet's apparently involuntary intrusion into the scene has affinities with the painted self-portraits in which the artist seems almost accidentally to be a part of his picture. More important, though, is the poetical self-criticism involved in the behavior permitted Thestylis: the poet, intent on "creating," on finding his many various figures for the scene he presents, has forgotten, as it were, the "Israelites" of a few lines before, gone on in his prodigal versatility to quite another range of reference, when he is sharply recalled to his tonic, the metaphor, which of all those given, finally dominates the mowing scene. His sympathy for the rail is cut off, as Thestylis forces back on him the providential implications of his metaphor from Exodus. Pastoral sympathies must be abandoned before the providence of the Lord; one language must give way to another, one theme to another. Extended to refer to the state of England at large, the metaphor forces both poet and readers to count the cost of passing from bondage to the rule of saints.

In the wood, the poet-director frankly takes on the role of actor in his "mask" there, but he is at the same time an audience for scenes displayed for him, in magic lantern sequence, by the wood environment. Nightingale, doves, thrush, heron, and woodpecker go through their gestures for him. According to his imagery, he becomes first a Solomon who knows every leaf and feather of his world, and who understands the language of its creatures. At this point, the poet assumes the costume appropriate to his part:

> And see how Chance's better Wit
> Could with a Mask my studies hit!

that is, he wears a mask for his part, takes his place in a masque of nature. The poet becomes the landscape, ceasing simply to be a figure enhancing the landscape to turn into the elements themselves of that landscape:

> The Oak-Leaves me embroyder all,
> Between which Caterpillars crawl:
> And Ivy, with familiar trails,
> Me licks, and clasps, and curles, and hales.

The still-life elements, even to the caterpillar, absorb him into their decorum. Although he does not stay "still," as he ought if he were pictured, he moves in a garb appropriate to a picture of a wood:

> Under this *antick Cope* I move
> Like some great *Prelate of the Grove.*
>   (stanza 74)

The word "antick" manages semantic references both to miming and to antiquity; the player plays at a natural priesthood, in the shape of a druid, identified as the *numen nemoris.*

In yet another way, the imagery tends to gather the poet cryptically into the several habitats of the wood. He himself asks to be covered with woodbine and vines, "chained" and "nailed" in a natural crucifixion, gentle if prickly, by "Brambles" and "courteous Briars." By these small chains, he requires nature to gather him into its artifice, that he may maintain his rapture as long as possible—longer than he can expect it naturally to last. In his piscatory experience, the poet once more fuses with nature, this time with another landscape, as he becomes one with the riverbank, crowned with ("vocall") reeds:

> Oh what a Pleasure 'tis to hedge
> My Temples here with heavy sedge;
> Abandoning my lazy Side,
> Stretcht as a Bank unto the Tide;
>   (stanza 81)

These alterations of scene are very different from the abrupt, dramatic changes of the meadows. There, the scenes changed so rapidly as to affect balance as well as sense of dimension and proportion, whereas in the wood and stream scenes, the poet melts in and out of the landscape, loses and finds "himself" in the nature he contemplates. Once again, as in "The Garden," the poet has managed to bring literary figures to life in his poem; before our eyes, he shows himself becoming one with nature. This absorption of the poet into his scene is in radical contrast to his jutting-out when Thestylis interjects him into the meadow scene. In the wood, the poet is enchanted and shares his enchantment with us, while Thestylis had made the audience turn to laugh at the poet, so brutally exposed to ridicule just as he was most absorbed in his poetizing, most secure in safe stage management.

What has happened is that by these devices, especially because he was willing to use them against "himself," the poet raises questions of place and of volition fundamental to the theme of the poem. On the one hand, the magic lantern devices and the masque episodes involve activity on the poet's part, who manages them for us, and activity on the reader's part as well, who must make sense of context and reference; on the other, poet and reader seem both to lose their volition as they watch the effortless metamorphoses taking place. In the wood and stream episodes, we are invited to share the poet's delicious languor, to abandon mental activity, to "let be" with nature herself.

Visual devices are used to many ends in this poem, not the least of them their stress on the world's instability, on the fluidity of material things, and the relativity of human perception. In the contrast between activity and passivity, even between styles of activity and passivity, we can perceive the differences between voluntary and involuntary commitments to one's situation as given; we can perceive, further, the difficulties involved in what is "voluntary" and what is not. Choice and destiny are recognized as the problems they are for any responsible man, although in these scenes neither choice nor destiny is more than the fleeting subject of the poem.

In the wood episode, for instance, the poet subdues his claims upon human rights to aspire (if one can say that for a "downward" wish) to wood and stream ecologies. Or, he subdues his own personality to the demands of the landscape—reversing thereby our normal expectations of literary *pathétique*—and thereby relinquishes some of the privileges of his humanity. By becoming "one" with these scenes, the poet illustrates in himself the amphibiousness with which the poem is concerned; he demonstrates man's need to be part of more than one environment, more than one ecology, more than one world. Though the nature into which the poet is absorbed, or permits himself to be absorbed, is traditionally lower than his own, he is by no means diminished by that absorption. Rather the opposite: as in "The Garden," the poet is recreated by his days' recreation, having given himself wholly to nature divinized at Nunappleton. Interestingly enough, as we examine this absorption of the poet into landscape, we find it working both ways. The poet, like the pastoralist, makes nature reflect his wishes and objectify his fantasy, but he bends to its powers as well. The wildwood will not submit to pastoral, then, but works its own poetic enchantment on the poet, earlier an enchanter himself. In yet another way, not wholly unlike his treatment by Thestylis, the poet allows himself to seem manipulated by the elements of his own poem.

There are many other kinds of connection one might make with this episode: in his passive descent into nature, the poet does not recapitulate, though he does recall, Isabella's passive descent into the cloister. She was absorbed for a time in the life "within," and thus forced her manly lover to strenuous activities of reclamation. Isabella was victimized by art; Marvell asks to be drawn into eternal nature itself, both of them "suckt in" by very different means, to very different moral contexts. The poet must be reclaimed too, we find: another Fairfax is required to free him from his delicious relaxation by the streamside to a more strenuous posture, to a less passive life. At the end of the stream episode, another metamorphosis takes place, as the kingfisher flies across the scene to transfix the Wharfe landscape as the halcyon stills the sea. Isabella's will had been sucked out of her by the art and will of someone more sophisticated than herself; this bird permits its hallowing color to be drawn out of it, to infuse and transfix the landscape. Like the poet, the bird "becomes" its scene:

> The viscous Air, wheres'ere She fly,
> Follows and sucks her Azure dy;
> The gellying Stream compacts below,
> If it might fix her shadow so;
> The stupid Fishes hang, as plain
> As *Flies* in Chrystal overt'ane.
>
> (stanza 85)

The halcyon fuses with Mary Fairfax, as the two enter the scene together and jointly arrest the landscape in a convention familiar in masque-production, where, for better or for worse, players and dancers were often immobilized, as in *The Tempest,* or *Comus.* This enchantment, to stillness and perfection, is just the opposite of the enchantment with which the nunnery episode had ended, with the nunnery vanishing like a false castle (stanza 42). Again, the proper masque-ending serves to put to rights an unpleasant episode and to crown a lovely one.

At the stream, natural things achieve stasis in an educative moment in which things are transformed from what they are to what they ought to be. With this stilling, we return to human scale: the poet and his pupil walk lifesize through their landscape, to meet the recessional fishermen bringing the day's labor to a close. Now, the figures are not diminished, as the mowers and cattle had been, nor grotesquely enlarged, as the grasshoppers and the rail had been. This evening light does not deform, as for instance, Charles Cotton's evening had done:

> The Shadows now so long do grow,
> That Brambles like tall Cedars shew,
> Mole-hills seem Mountains, and the Ant
> Appears a monstrous Elephant.

As night comes down on Marvell's scene, things are in their proper proportion; the poet and his charge can go "in" quite naturally although, as we watch them go, their "in" is "out" to us, as their figures follow the choral procession offstage.

DAVID KALSTONE

Marvell and the Fictions of Pastoral

I might have called this essay "Polyphemus Restored." The one-eyed knave of epic poetry barged into pastoral at its very beginnings. A refugee from the Homeric world, he appears twice in Theocritus. He is not a natural herdsman, and yet the grotesque Cyclops is as native to the eclogue as true pastoral singers are. His poetry is among the most frequently imitated in Renaissance pastoral. And, as we shall see later on, he has a special importance for Marvell, one which helps us understand a great deal about the place of pastoral in the Renaissance and even in modern verse. For the moment we need only keep him in mind as an intruder who, in another sense, belongs, even though the pastoral spirit totally eludes him.

The French critic Roland Barthes, in general remarks about earlier literature, speaks of writing which "assumes that nature can be possessed, that it does not shy away or cover itself in shadows, but is, in its entirety, subjected to the toils of language" (*Writing Degree Zero*). This kind of writing he opposes to modern poetry which gives its readers a "closed nature," one of "fragmented space, made up of objects solitary and terrible." Or as a contemporary poet [A. R. Ammons] puts it: "I look and reflect, but the air's glass / jail seals each thing in its entity." These are extreme statements—of "the surrendered self among unwelcoming forms"—which we tend to think of as particularly modern. Yet the contrast Barthes describes is one to which the best writers of pastoral poetry were always alive: a contrast between the comforts which the very existence of pastoral assured to them (nature *is* comprehensible) and the lively doubts great writers have about patterns and fictions.

From *English Literary Renaissance* 4, no. 1 (Winter 1974). © 1974 by *English Literary Renaissance*.

Probably one reason for the remarkably intense interest in Marvell these days is *his* awareness of such problems. If we are alive to the pleasures and perils of pastoral, it is in large part because he and Milton have helped us to understand them. Writing at the moment when pastoral was in danger of becoming mere pedantry or mere aristocratic masquerade, these two poets were at once great practitioners of the form and its formidable critics. Extremely self-conscious about the history of the genre, they used that self-consciousness to revive and—for their moment—recreate it. Even in the frailest province of the genre, the erotic pastoral, Marvell is able to transform what others trivialize; to recall chords of natural harmony and strain which belong to our deepest experience, in poems of such surface ease that they appear to be about flirtation rather than love, self-pity rather than suffering.

Renato Poggioli is right to see Marvell's short poems as a last chapter in the history of the love complaint, just as *Comus* and "Lycidas" are climactic examples of the pastoral masque and pastoral elegy. And Poggioli's term for what lies beneath Marvell's pastoral, "the pastoral of the self," though it is somewhat misleading (is the "self" ever absent from such poems?), still suggests the expressive force which lies in wait for us in even some of the simplest lyrics.

I begin with "Damon the Mower," a kind of outcropping of erotic pastoral. This is where Polyphemus comes in. With Marvell, as with Milton, memories of classical pastoral may be so vividly present as to have almost the force of metaphor. If "Damon the Mower" seems mysterious, it is because there are a number of presences behind the poem, contradictory spirits which account for its cosmic surface and serious undercurrents: the Cyclops of Theocritus, a pastoral intruder; Daphnis, the pastoral god of Virgil and Theocritus; and, from Virgil's second *Eclogue*, the complaining shepherd Corydon. There is also the mower himself, drawn from another world to replace the traditional herdsmen. To feel these disparate presences is to sense how much Marvell is trying to include and how much freedom he exercises over material he thoroughly understands.

"Damon the Mower" belongs to a family of poems consisting of pastoral invitations, given and, most often, refused. In its simplest form we know the convention from Marlowe's "The Passionate Shepherd" whose invitation, "Come live with me and be my love," offers in a very guarded way a fantasy of leisure and fulfillment. Offers—gifts, an attractive life—are at the center of such poems. Marlowe's shepherd aims them at a refined taste, one which would value madrigals, coral clasps, and amber studs.

> And I will make thee beds of roses
> And a thousand fragrant posies,

A cap of flowers and a kirtle,
Embroidered all with leaves of myrtle.

A gown made of the finest wool,
Which from our pretty lambs we pull,
Fair linèd slippers for the cold:
With buckles of the purest gold.

He includes gestures which would be, in the perfumed chambers of London, either trite—everyone there has shoes with golden buckles—or decadent, "beds of roses." He freshens these gestures by placing them side by side with reminders of the first innocence of love and the freedom and playfulness which should accompany it. In his country setting, a pun, "And I will make thee beds of roses," purges away jaded associations. The passionate shepherd guarantees a delicate conspiracy with nature, one in which wishes are fulfilled, but also one in which he and his love remain at a proper distance from nature—spectators, innocent libertines, pageant-masters.

The pastoral invitation is at least as old as Theocritus. But the catalogue of gifts in his hands was not so entirely seductive, not so entirely a sign of the controlled interplay of civilized and simplified desires. In his eleventh *Idyll*, Theocritus sets one of the earliest versions of "Come live with me" as part of the wooing of Galatea by the grotesque, one-eyed Polyphemus, who wants her to feed her sheep with his. He offers his thousand sheep, milk, cheeses, cool water distilled of the whitest snow. His boastful persistence, his monstrous bristly eye, and his blindness to his grotesque position subvert the delicacy of his offers and betray whatever frail connections to nature his language claims. The catalogue of gifts becomes an ironic clue to the wooer's self-inflation. From the examples of Theocritus and of Marlowe, it should be clear that even the simplest of pastoral formulae can serve extremes of dramatic purpose—giving an elegant example of fantasy, as Marlowe does, or a comic deflation of it, as does the earliest Greek example.

But I am interested in some poems which go a step further, poems where the invitation is part of a larger drama examining such offers of gratified desire. In such pastorals, fantasy is mulled over, the temptation to fulfilled wishes all but refused. The poem acts out a clarification of feeling. This kind of plot lies behind Marvell's rich and amusing "Damon the Mower" and proves a vehicle for his critical treatment of pastoral love. Its prototype—one which Marvell explicitly recalls—is Virgil's second *Eclogue*; and Virgil, as in those infinitely receding perspectives of Chinese boxes, remembers, as if to comment upon, the lamenting Cyclops of Theocritus. Polyphemus becomes the Latin poet's suffering Corydon, and with that stroke the comic side of the pastoral courtship is toned down, converted to serious uses in love poetry. But Virgil's great innovation—as Brooks Otis [in *Virgil: A Study in Civilized Poetry*] teaches us to see it—is to put the courtship song, the "Come live with me," almost into brackets or quotation marks. Corydon *reports* his proposal as part of a series of reflections. He is talking to himself as much as offering country pleasures to Alexis, and repeating his pastoral invitation helps clarify his understanding of love. With this brilliant retrospection Virgil frames Corydon's pastoral promises, and the poem itself becomes a lens for the examination of feeling.

Virgil's second *Eclogue* belongs to Corydon, who "burned for the handsome Alexis." His invitation to rural pleasures is less courtly than Marlowe's later version was to be, and less a spectator sport as well:

> How pleasant then
> to live with me in some mean country dwelling,
> chase deer, and drive the kids with green hibiscus,
> and like Pan, fill the forest with our music.
> > (trans. Stephen Orgel)

The poem includes both complaint and invitation. Corydon promises gifts—lilies, poppies, narcissus, fragrant dill, cassia, sweet herbs, soft hyacinth and yellow marigold—and presents himself in a way that has some mythological or heroic resonance:

> My songs are such as, summoning his herds,
> Amphion sang in Attic Aracynthus.
>
> . . . .
>
> The flute I have of seven hemlock stalks
> the famous Damoetas gave me as he died,
> saying, "You shall now be its second master,"
> Damoetas said, and dull Amyntas envied me.
> > (trans. Stephen Orgel)

In his complaint he plays through a range of possibilities: warnings ("learn to mistrust complexion; white privets fade, the blackberries are garnered"); enticements ("my thousand sheep graze the Sicilian mountains; summer and winter alike bring ample milk. . . . I too shall gather downy quinces, chestnuts my Amaryllis used to love, and add the waxy plums"), and threats ("Is it not better to suffer Amaryllis' unhappy rage and arrogant disdain, endure Menalcas, black for all your whiteness"). In other words he tries a number of voices and attitudes, reproaches and doubts as well as promises. In some ways he makes himself ridiculous.

Throughout, the poem is full of loving detail from country life, the specific things precious to Corydon and, so, worthy of being offered: the pipe with its seven hemlock stalks, downy quinces, waxy plums, sweet odors of laurel and myrtle. But this precise and particular gathering has a strange effect upon him; the details accumulate behind a flash of insight in a Latin adjective very hard to translate. Suddenly Corydon turns upon himself: *"rusticus* es, Corydon; nec munera curat Alexis,"* which one translator renders as "Ah, peasant Corydon! Things will never move him." That version comes close but doesn't quite give us the double point of Corydon's adjective. He is *rusticus*—in one sense, clownish, making a fool of himself; Alexis will never care for his gifts or his kind of life. But he is *rusticus* in another sense, a countryman whose resources are not to be undervalued. This single word crystallizes, more than at any other point so far in the poem, Corydon's sense of love as a madness, something he must escape as dangerous to the balance of his life. He is now able to see Alexis as being as insane as he himself is; the same word, *demens,* can describe the condition of the frustrated pursuer and the pursued so foolish as to flee Corydon and Corydon's countryside ("Even gods have loved the forests; Dardanian Paris too: then let Minerva live in the castles she herself created, but let me keep the woods"). At the close of the poem a series of calls to order alternate with feelings of desire ("One certain lust drives every creature"). More and more the pressures are reduced as he assesses what he has done to a life he values: "The south wind, desperate, upon my flowers, the wild boar set loose in my clear springs." Corydon is drawn again to the rich repose and engaging activity of the country: "Look, the bullocks draw the plows home, the late sun lengthens the growing shadows. . . . Corydon! Corydon! what madness overcomes you? You have left the vine unpruned upon the leafy elm . . . why not prepare instead to plait with twigs and reeds some useful everyday device? If this Alexis scorns you, seek another." The poem itself—the act of singing—becomes a restorative, a return to the familiar Virgilian richness, a world in which Thestylis prepares garlic and thyme and fragrant herbs for reapers weary in the heat. If Corydon has not reached a state of repose by the end of his monologue, still it is by envisioning the familiar rhythm of tasks and pleasures that the poem holds out hope of performing its exorcism.

Virgil's eclogue grows in wonderful ways, the gathering of details drawing Corydon away from his driven state. What it promises is not simply a return to nature, but also a clarity of vision which Corydon's sense of nature allows him. The poem can end satisfactorily at this point, the singer's performance itself a potent healer. It is exactly here, at the close of the poem, that Marvell, who has Virgil's eclogue in mind, makes his most significant departure:

> Only for him no Cure is found,
> Whom *Julianas* Eyes do wound.
> 'Tis death alone that this must do:
> For Death thou art a Mower too.

When Damon the Mower makes this half-jesting, half-grim discovery, in a sense his occupation's gone; that is, he cannot be so simply restored to natural tasks as Virgil's speaker can. Whatever clarity of vision those last lines offer, they also suggest a separation from nature which, at the outset of the poem, Damon never suspected. This is only the most striking example of something the poem as a whole prepares us for—a version of pastoral surprising in its implications.

For one thing, Damon's song is controlled, even corrected by the presence of a detached narrator. Virgil's eclogue opened with a similar master of ceremonies, one who characterized Corydon's verses as "rough," but then vanished from the poem, allowing the complaint recuperative powers which counter that opening description. But Marvell's narrator intervenes in the penultimate stanza, and his introduction, too, peculiarly adjusts our feelings:

> Heark how the Mower *Damon* Sung,
> With love of *Juliana* stung!
> While ev'ry thing did seem to paint
> The Scene more fit for his complaint.
> Like her fair Eyes the day was fair;
> But scorching like his am'rous Care.
> Sharp like his Sythe his Sorrow was,
> And wither'd like his Hopes the Grass.

We may hear in these lines a confident and sympathetic call to order. But we also cannot miss the elaborate arrangement of nature's backdrop which *seems* to "paint the Scene." The narrator takes a dry view of love's little theater, its neat arrangements serving to make nature fit for Damon's complaint. The song which follows has many of the elements of Corydon's in Virgil's eclogue: the heat; the lizards; the pastoral gifts; a heroic boast; and an admiring glimpse of the speaker's own reflection—Damon's in his scythe, Corydon's in the water at the shore. (In this last example even the phrasing is the same: "nec sum adeo informis"; "Nor am I so deform'd to sight, / If in my Sithe I lookèd right.") Yet if some of the scenery and gestures are familiar, we listen to Damon differently. Marvell exaggerates the figure and his connection to nature, so that we are always aware of Damon's complaint as a performance in the pastoral theater; his very extravagance must give us a way of interpreting and judging his song. Even before he has said a word, the narrator's introduction, with its elaborately parallel similes, has tuned us to Damon's high frequencies: "Like her fair Eyes the day was fair; / But scorching like his am'rous Care." Damon's ingenuity will find emblems all around him: the only moist and cold are his tears and Juliana's icy breast. His speech sets up parallels of rhythm and sound which elaborately and humorously reflect the disproportion of his desire: "Not *July* causeth these Extremes, / But *Juliana's* scorching beams"; "Tell me where I may pass the Fires / Of the hot day, or hot desires."

There is an intensity and pleading wonder about the poem which promises something more than the weak appeals of Renaissance shepherds invoking the pathetic fallacy. But it is only toward the end that we understand the root of Damon's extravagant sense of displacement. The extreme way in which he puts his complaint is the reverse side of his sense of being a controlling and worshiped deity in nature. Virgil's Corydon was tied to the countryside by the loving details of his tasks and his music. But when Damon thinks of the past, it is with a fine heroic swing, releasing energies which lie behind his sense of dazed and injured merit: "I am the Mower *Damon,* known / Through all the Meadows I have mown." With that decisive enjambement (and the emphatic *known*), he entirely alters the movement of the poem and displays his true sense of swagger in nature. Earlier details fall into place: the grasshoppers which stop piping; frogs that won't dance; the gifts of chameleon and harmless snake. All these testify to Damon's comic awkwardness, to the naive braggadocio with which he takes nature to be his deliberate and delicate servant: "On me the Morn her dew distills / Before her darling Daffadils."

The force of the poem, then, lies not only in the entrance of Juliana, but in the illusory confidence which her appearance dispels. Damon is more than a shepherd. In fact he dismisses shepherds as merely industrious capitalists. His scythe—at least this is *his* way of thinking about his activity as mower—"discovers wide / More ground then all his Sheep do hide." *Discovers* turns him into a fine explorer and for the moment conceals any destructive motion in cutting down the hay; the prize itself becomes a golden fleece, the mower a Jason. ("With this the golden fleece I shear / Of all these Closes ev'ry Year.") Damon's confident position in nature allows him his mock heroic boasts and his dazzling transformations. He turns himself and his scythe into planets of their own world:

> Nor am I so deform'd to sight,
> If in my Sithe I lookèd right;
> In which I see my Picture done,
> As in a crescent Moon the Sun.

We have come a long way from Virgil's Corydon, who with a similar phrase glimpses his own image in the sea, and in one sense we seem closer to the dangerous side of the myth of Narcissus. But more likely, and more important, what Marvell seems to have in mind is a bow to the originator of the boast, the Cyclops of Theocritus' sixth *Idyll*: "For truly I am not even ill-favoured, as they say; for of late I looked into the sea, and there was a calm, and fair, as my judgement goes, showed my beard and my one eye, and it reflected the gleam of my teeth whiter than Parian marble" (trans. A. S. F. Gow). In Damon, Marvell restores the Polypheme's comic boastfulness, though with larger claims to being an imaginative center, a mythmaker in his world ("as in a crescent Moon the Sun"). Polyphemus sputters an end to his speech: "But to ward off the evil eye I spat three times into my bosom as the hag Kotyttaris taught me." Damon, on the other hand, asserts himself as a natural god. He is poised between grotesque and heroic expectations—perhaps an inevitable pairing for anyone who intrudes in the world of nature. In Damon, Marvell appears to be deliberately including all the variants and possibilities his predecessors saw in the figure of lamenting lover: the suffering and self-restoring song of Corydon, the god-like claims of Daphnis, and the comic short-sightedness of Polyphemus. These very human contradictions—all present in one singer—are insisted upon.

What I would like to suggest is the essential, the inevitable flaw of the mower's position in nature—a delicate disproportion apparent to the reader though it does not become so to the mower himself until the end of the poem. In all the comic delicacy and attractiveness of Damon's boasts, we sense the strain, the reliance on bravado to skate over the tension in words like *discover*. Damon claims his scythe *discovers* the ground. But when the narrator enters again—Damon no longer speaking but described within his frame—the outside speaker finds another word for mowing: "While thus he threw his Elbow round, / Depopulating all the Ground."

Unlike Virgil's Corydon, Damon, once enlightenment comes, makes no restorative return to pastoral tasks. He is "the mower mown." Virgil's Corydon has a past and future in Arcady: other lovers, Menalcas, Amaryllis, perhaps another Alexis. But the history of Marvell's mower jolts him out of the reach of pastoral comforts; his suddenly seems a decisive and timeless enterprise. The mower's final words—delicately cavalier in tone—pay a self-pitying tribute to Juliana. But beneath it all is a note of discovery of what it means to be a mower. "Death thou art a Mower too," besides being an unhappy sigh, is also a different sense of occupation from "I am the Mower *Damon*, known / Through all the Meadows I have mown." In the last stanza we are allowed to glimpse for a moment the serious flaw revealed by Damon's love complaint. It is the appearance of love which exposes his precarious mastery. It is perfectly appropriate that the breaking of illusion should be expressed in terms of the gap between self-pity and healthy performance of pastoral tasks, between sighing and scything. For a mind which clownishly, delicately, sees itself as a master in nature, Juliana's aloofness is indeed a drought or death.

In a poem of light surface—and this is his way—Marvell asks us to think about the source of the elaborate metaphors pastoral love poets invent in love complaints. Why do we talk this way about love? Marvell links these extravagant meditations in a landscape with the essential flaw in human nature—a pristine, even attractive egotism which allows us to feel the identity of nature and our own thoughts. Polyphemus is recalled precisely to raise such beguiling questions. The poet may share in Damon's song, identify it with Virgil's vision of expressive and restorative powers in nature. But he also steps back and in his narrative frame does more critical maneuvering than is usual in such complaints. By calling back one of the oldest intruders in pastoral, the Cyclops, he suggests many of the difficulties and perils of adopting the pastoral mask. But then, all along, we know he has only half assumed it. In the brilliant substitution of mower for shepherd he embodies most clearly the creative and self-deceptive powers of mythmaking about one's place in nature. His doubts are those that pre-Christian pastoralists did not care to raise. Damon's song—so amusing and attractive an example of pastoral complaint—also allows the understanding that in our own delectable, even innocent egotism we prepare the grounds for the most stylized and extravagant expressions of desire.

Marvell's wariness about the symbols of pastoral lyric pervades his poetry. We seldom hear him assume a pastoral role directly—that is, without the ironic framework provided by a third-person narrator or the dialogue form. In "The Coronet" he turns explicitly to an alternative. To "weave a chaplet" for the Savior's head, he dismantles

> all the fragrant Towers
> That once adorn'd my Shepherdesses head.
> And now when I have summ'd up all my store,
>   Thinking (so I my self deceive)
>   So rich a Chaplet thence to weave
> As never yet the king of Glory wore:
> Alas I find the Serpent old
> That, twining in his speckled breast,
> About the flow'rs disguis'd does fold,
> With wreaths of Fame and Interest.

In "Damon the Mower" too, a snake which "kept within, / Now glitters in its second skin." A deliberately ambiguous *within* allows the reader to imagine not only a snake stretching itself happily out from shade into scorching sun, but also to glance at Damon's own fall from nature, human nature becoming the serpent's "second skin." When, in another familiar poem, the soul locks the body in eternal debate, the body's closing metaphor stresses the ambiguous place of a civilized or creative mind in nature:

> What but a Soul could have the wit
> To build me up for Sin so fit?
> So Architects do square and hew,
> Green Trees that in the Forest grew.

The very refinement of seventeenth-century awareness—everything which may be conveyed by *wit*—becomes potentially destructive. Marvell, when writing a pastoral, using its now very civilized and highly developed vocabulary, also calls us back to the source of pastoral metaphors, to Damon's exaggerations. We are always alive to the pleasures and perils of pastoral.

There are, of course, exceptions, and these have their beauty and critical value. "The Garden" comes immediately to mind as a poem where, for once, the restorative powers of pastoral song are at work, one of those rare moments when the mind is in accord with the passionless green of nature. If in "The Coronet" wreaths are serpentine and dangerous, in "The Garden" trees and flowers weave the garlands of repose. But what is most important here is again Marvell's detachment, his only halfway donning the pastoral mask, while winning his meaning from traditional pastoral material. "Society is all but rude, / To this delicious Solitude." The speaker may have withdrawn from competitive sophistication, but *delicious* shows him relishing some of its vocabulary. It would be equally wrong to think of the poem, as Poggioli does, as an abandonment of erotic pastoral for a new "pastoral of the self." "Two Paradises 'twere in one / To live in Paradise alone": those lines from the penultimate stanza come almost as a jingling summary of a view earned in a most entertaining and sophisticated manner. The *'twere* of love's exclusion is merely a subjunctive. Far from excluding love, the poem achieves its brief ecstasy—or rather is launched into it—by reinterpreting and including some important myths of erotic pastoral.

Every reader of "The Garden" must sense a special wit and rise in poetic temperature with the Ovidian conceits of stanza 4:

> When we have run our Passions heat,
> Love hither makes his best retreat.
> The *Gods,* that mortal Beauty chase,
> Still in a Tree did end their race.
> *Apollo* hunted *Daphne* so,

Only that She might Laurel grow.
And *Pan* did after *Syrinx* speed,
Not as a Nymph, but for a Reed.

What wond'rous Life in this I lead!
Ripe Apples drop about my head.
                                    (ll. 25–34)

The preceding stanzas have been primarily satirical—cool glances at the world's ambitions and the feverish pursuit of love. Stanza 3 wittily proposes that "No white nor red was ever seen / So am'rous as this lovely green." But the following stanza takes up that promised *am'rous* in a surprising way. It is Ovid and tales of lovers' metamorphoses which, ironically, launch us into the ecstasies of the garden. The speaker uses the tales of nymphs transformed—for one thing— to satirical purpose, continuing the jests about driving passions. Part of the fun lies in the spectacle of powerful gods plunging against trees or falling among reeds, thwarted in their erotic pursuits.

But Marvell recalls these figures of erotic pastoral for other reasons. The tone of the stanza is philosophical and retrospective: "When we have run our Passions heat." Besides referring to passion's warm weather, *heat* is also a racing term. The speaker is saying from his perspective inside the garden that love has a fixed or predestined course which we all have to run. Then, gratefully, "Love hither makes his best retreat." *Retreat,* too, has its double sense: a driven, strategic withdrawal, on one hand, and, on the other, the dedicated considered withdrawal of religious retreat. Passions give way to the more permanent beauties of the garden, its trees, laurels, and reeds. They are the end of the *race* of the gods: another pun allowing us to see both pursuit and offspring. Each of these three puns *(heat, retreat, race)* refers us both to transitory driven states and to transformed, permanent conditions. So too Apollo and Pan, inflamed gods, have turned their frustrations into the poet's laurel and the musician's reed. Here is wit with a serious point, one aided by Marvell's syntax: "*Apollo* hunted *Daphne* so, / Only that She might Laurel grow." *Only* taken one way stresses Apollo's comeuppance and frustration; but seen another way it suggests the necessary connection, the fruitful plan, behind the transformations of Daphne and Syrinx.

What the speaker suggests is that the strong desires we suffer in the world outside the garden have their most permanent value when they are transformed by the poetry of Apollo and the music of Pan. This suggestion marks a rapid change in the poem and catches us perhaps unawares. The poem began with examples of the futility of erotic love, and it ends by showing us that erotic love is purified and transformed in the garden, thus contributing to the garden's delights. The witty handling of myth and, above all, the brilliant set of puns add a startling dimension to the speaker's pleasure. As the poem moves on, the garden is revealed as a retreat from which he gains perspective on the passions of the world. Its repose allows him to see things clearly and in their complications; hence the double meanings which make words themselves into complex lenses. Words denoting passionate states yield another, cooler meaning. In that state of excitement, not subject to the single-mindedness of the lovers and adventurers outside, the speaker is launched—by the only rhyme link between stanzas ("Not as a Nymph, but for a Reed. / / What wond'rous Life is this I lead")— into the wonderful state in which the entire garden begins to move and presses itself upon him in an innocent pleasure, a liberation of the mind perfectly embodied in the two halves of the line "To a green Thought in a green Shade." What the speaker is describing is exactly what has happened in this poem. Retreating, he has not only recognized objects in the garden, but allowed them to suggest complicated observations about the world and about the garden itself. His wit and his puns have allowed him to view civilized experience from multiplying perspectives, to leap in a single word or phrase or through reference to pastoral myth, from the achieving to the achieved experience. This is his own creation of "other Worlds, and other Seas," an experience he is then able to describe metaphorically and with some exhilaration in the second half of the poem.

I began this essay by pointing to Marvell's critical view of pastoral myth-making. "Damon the Mower" is not the only example, but it is certainly a striking one, of Marvell's difficulty in finding a satisfying pastoral mask, a satisfying stance or role which does not destroy as it creates in nature. "The Garden" becomes for him a model of the proper, the *inclusive* use of pastoral detail, the speaker in this rare moment not cast as the self-enclosing, single-eyed Polypheme. But it is equally important to stress the fact that it is a witty grasp of the implications of pastoral tales and vocabulary which allows him that freedom. He refers us, this seventeenth-century gentleman, to the image-making power of the first man who was able to see in the laurel the form of a desired and imprisoned maiden; he refers us as well to the sublimated wishes and passions which lie behind a richly gathered tradition. In his hands, as in the hands of most of the great practitioners of the genre, pastoral is not merely a bundle of attitudes such as country is better than city, gardens are better than streets. It provides a language and vocabulary for the activity of the spirit and a touchstone for everything which might distort it.

Marvell, not always but very often, sees the pastoral speaker as by nature an intruder. For him, as for Milton, pastoral is part of a fallen world whose richness nourishes an essential fiction-making activity. He is rarely—except in

"The Garden"—fully at rest with pastoral's recuperative powers. He tests one stance after another: the nymph's lament over her dead faun, which makes of pastoral materials a self-cherishing monument; Damon's complaint; or the poet's explorations of "Upon Appleton House," with his complicated attempts at satisfaction in different pastoral theaters. He relishes pastoral song, the expressive power of pastoral landscape, and yet remains wary of "the surrendered self among unwelcoming forms." Conscious of our intrusions—what we try to *make* of nature—he can go on to invent, like the fictional Polyphemus, lyrics in which true pastoral recreation so often eludes him.

It is an odd literary achievement. Odd, because the restlessness or wariness I have described does not seem to destroy the pleasure Marvell takes in reviving or giving life to certain conventions like the one behind Damon the Mower's lament. This quality—which may be pejoratively described as a kind of juggling—is one which angers many of my students these days; it is also one which has enticed critics to produce in the past two years a greater concentration of books on Marvell than we have ever had. Marvell is on the threshold of modern poetic problems, and yet because of his extraordinary wit and poise the reader never needs to feel them as such. If Damon the Mower is deprived of his pastoral recreation, if the nymph is imprisoned by her pastoral complaint, the reader in each of these cases is not. Precisely by showing up the limits of their points of view, by giving them up as literary hostages, Marvell is able to restore what engaged him in Virgil and Theocritus: the power of pastoral fictions both to express and temper our cravings, our fantasies, our desires. He anticipates the condition which came to govern modern pastoral, the human figure as an intruder, a kind of Polyphemus at large in the natural world. But he does not share the related notion that by virtue of our intrusions we are almost excluded from the pleasures of pastoral fiction. In the poetry of Robert Frost and Wallace Stevens we become the intensest spectators in order to claim even a momentary sense of nature's relation to mind; we must become convinced that the hostility, the changeability of nature is also within the grasp of the imaginer. It is a long way from the momentary assurance of Marvell's green thought in a green shade to Stevens's momentary exultation in a scene which excludes us almost entirely:

> Today the air is clear of everything.
> It has no knowledge except of nothingness
> And it flows over us without meanings,
> As if none of us had ever been here before
> And are not now: in this shallow spectacle,
> This invisible activity, this sense.
> ("A Clear Day and No Memories")

ISABEL G. MacCAFFREY

The Scope of Imagination
in "Upon Appleton House"

In the ninth stanza of "Upon Appleton House," Marvell locates the subject
of his poem in language of grave import:

> The House was built upon the Place
> Only as for *a Mark of Grace;*
> And for an *Inn* to entertain
> Its *Lord* a while, but not remain.
>
> (ll. 69–72)

Fairfax's attitude toward his house (confirmed by lines of his own composing
which Marvell's echo or anticipate) indicates an awareness of his own mortality.
"Inns are not residences," as Marianne Moore observed; Fairfax's true home
is elsewhere. Line 72 balances upon *a while,* precariously signaling the temporal limits of a human life. In the poem's opening stanzas, Marvell develops
the idea of spatial limitation through a sequence of geometrical conceits that
allude to the economy of Nature as a model. These first ten stanzas, therefore,
establish the terms to be explored in the perambulation of the estate; the tenth
names nature and art as rivals in landscape architecture.

> But Nature here hath been so free
> As if she said leave this to me.
> Art would more neatly have defac'd
> What she hath laid so sweetly wast;

From *Tercentenary Essays in Honor of Andrew Marvell,* edited by Kenneth Friedenreich.
© 1977 by Kenneth Friedenreich. Archon Books, 1977.

> In fragrant Gardens, shaddy Woods,
> Deep Meadows, and transparent Floods.
>   (ll. 75–80)

Gardens, woods, meadows, floods: on these stages, where art and nature mingle, the speaking pictures of Marvell's philosophical poem will unfold. It opens and closes with emblems of humility: and spherical or hemispherical enclosures that define the limits accepted as legitimate and inevitable by the poet and the master of the house he celebrates.

Marvell's imagination is characterized by its resistance to external limits, and its submissiveness to the symbolic limits that express the soul's sense of its own disabilities. Much of his poetry is devoted to the exploration of limit; and the dominance of the theme suggests why so many of the poems fall under the rubric of pastoral. The dream of a perfect congruence between man and nature is one of the great myths of mankind, and it offers contexts for considering the urgent epistemological questions that obsess so many postmedieval imaginations.

> From this the poem springs: that we live in a world
> That is not our own, and much more, not ourselves.

The pastoral paradigm provides an *as if* that negates this chilly aphorism: let us imagine a world that belongs to us, that mirrors ourselves. The belatedness of Marvell in the tradition meant that he came to pastoral with a deep sense of both its virtues and its dangers, and his pastoral lyrics reflect this ambivalence. His paradises seldom remain intact. The Mower Damon, boasting of his privileged position as nature's favorite son, is already the victim of an alienating love. The Mower in "To the Glo-Worms," his mind "displac'd" by love of Juliana, regards with the melancholy of an outsider the "courteous Lights" of a creaturely world from which he is now exiled. Inveighing against gardens, he attacks the propensity of fallen man, "that sov'raign thing and proud," to reverse the beneficent relationship, established in Eden, between himself and nature. Instead of gazing into the mirror of natural innocence, he narcissistically forces Nature to give him back his own image. This is a version of idolatry: "The Pink grew then as double as his Mind; . . . The Tulip, white, did for complexion seek."

Yet Fairfax makes a garden at Nunappleton, and is not rebuked. It is the vocation of Adam. The dilemmas confronting the makers of gardens in a fallen world are also the dilemmas of poetry-makers. In both cases, there is a problematic relationship between imagination and its materials; and that relation is a specialized version of a larger problem—the disjunction between the human mind and the world in which it finds itself. The issues raised by Sidney in the *Apology* two generations earlier are firmly joined in Marvell's poetry. Does the imagination outsoar nature, as Sidney claimed, voyaging through the zodiac of wit and concocting its golden worlds beyond the range of the too-much-loved, imperfect earth? Or does the infected will that we inherit from Adam force us to accept a humble role, curbing the erected wit and, as Bacon recommended, bowing and buckling the mind to the nature of things? These are crudely formulated versions of questions considered with great subtlety within the limited but intense range of Marvell's lyrics. And "Upon Appleton House" is a "sober frame" for a meditation upon the claims of imagination, that presumptuous defier of limits.

All truly sober frames exist in the symbolic dimension that acknowledges the transience and "lowness" of their makers. Hence the careful geometries, spatial and temporal, of the opening stanzas. Marvell's architectural conceits are complemented by allusions to emptiness and fullness that comment on the contrast between a self-regarding art detached from its true sources, and the art which respects purposes which lie beyond it. Nature's artfulness exhibits a perfect decorum of form and content.

> The low roof'd Tortoises do dwell
> In cases fit of Tortoise-shell:
> No Creature loves an empty space;
> Their Bodies measure out their Place.
>
> (ll. 13–16)

The only truly "empty space" is inside the skull of a presumptuous human being, represented by the comic hubris of the "Forrain *Architect.*" Launched upon strange voyages in the spaces of his own brain, he illustrates the extravagance of an "unrul'd" imagination:

> That unto Caves the Quarries drew,
> And Forrests did to Pastures hew;
> Who of his great Design in pain
> Did for a Model vault his Brain.
>
> (ll. 3–6)

The violence perpetrated upon the landscape manifests the architect's conceit, in two senses of the word. It is an extreme instance of imagination's metamorphosing power: caves become quarries, forests pastures, in the interests of a "great Design" which has forgotten its origin in the patterns of created nature, the divinely designed universe. The architect's swelled head, "vaulted" by the pressure of his own conceit, is a model for a "hollow Palace" (l. 19), the epithet looking back to the hollowing out of artificial caves in stanza 1, and the condemnation of "empty space" in 2.

In contrast, the sober frame of Nunappleton, and the poem that celebrates it, are modeled upon the true "great Design."

> all things are composed here
> Like Nature, orderly and near.
> (ll. 25–26)

"Upon Appleton House" is an example of what it explores; the poet's design and God's are concentric structures. Images of enclosure and fullness express this "orderly and near" composition, imitating "the Beasts [that] are by their Denns exprest" (l. 11): *"Romulus* his Bee-like Cell" (l. 40), and Nunappleton itself, based upon a *"holy Mathematicks"* (l. 47) whereby "Things greater are in less contain'd" (l. 44). The immortal soul lives within its temporary house; the inn entertains its lord but a while. Many stanzas later, the poem closes with a series of concentric spheres: tortoise shells, men beneath their boat-roofs, the globe of earth suggested by the reference to the Antipodes, and the "dark *Hemisphere"* (l. 775) of the vaulted heavens. Thus in the course of his argument Marvell moves from the admonitory image of the tortoises in their "cases fit" to the extravagantly reconfirmed vision of men accepting the injunction to imitate nature's humility; having "shod their *Heads* in their *Canoos"* (l. 772), they have truly become *"Tortoise* like" (l. 773). The second image mocks the first, and at the same time affirms it; the progress of Marvell's imagination as it moves from the simple relationships of the opening stanzas to the metamorphosed and reimagined conceits of the close provides the poem's plot.

It is not, of course, a narrative plot, but a circular, meditative expatiation upon a perambulation—a walk through the estate of Nunappleton, and through the human imagination, the state of man. In the process, Marvell is able to consider the history of human arts, which can be seen as efforts, most of them unsuccessful, to reconstruct or regain paradise. History is supplemented by geography and topography, and the experiences of the contemplative observer offer examples of the dangers and pleasures of imagination in the foreground of the poem's action.

Appleton House itself is the second edifice to have been built on its site, and Marvell's contrast between it and its "Quarries," the former nunnery buildings, gives him his first opportunity to consider man's efforts to make his own world. His purpose here, as throughout the poem, is to define the paradoxical human condition. The definition must ultimately refer to God, and man's creaturely dependence upon his maker is everywhere reiterated, most crucially and perilously in Marvell's exploration of the human urge to imitate God's making, to evade limits and draw a map of salvation. The nuns who enclose themselves from the world, like the gardeners in "The Mower against Gardens," attempt to remake Nature in a human image. "Like themselves they alter all" (l. 215). They also practice corrupting "arts" that pervert natural order in the interest of "curious tasts" (l. 182)—*curious* bearing, in this context, its full weight of theological portent. Marvell's language has a deliberate, suggestive duplicity; the nuns, "handling Natures finest Parts" (l. 178), prepare a banquet of sense that compares unfavorably with the subtler delights offered by Created Pleasure to the Resolved Soul. The lines in stanza 22 on the preserving of fruit work metaphorically in two directions: the nuns intend the preservation of "mortal fruit" as a parable for the salvation of souls, but to the narrator's severer contemplation it offers an instance of presumption and the perversion of art.

The nunnery is one of Marvell's false paradises: "Within this holy leisure we / Live innocently as you see" (ll. 97–98). That it should be also false art is predictable. The reference to virginity as an analogue of the retired life, unexamined and artfully composed, is familiar to us from "The Picture of Little T.C." and "The Nymph Complaining" and, in a different form, "To His Coy Mistress." It is inverted at the end of "Appleton House" in the prophecy of Maria Fairfax's marriage; she, like her ancestress Isabella, will abandon innocence for experience, acknowledging that paradise must be lost if it is to be regained. Time, as well as nature, is redeemed at Nunappleton because the Fairfaxes, submitting to the design of Providence, "make their *Destiny* their *Choice*" (l. 744). This submission is one of the conditions of living in a true paradise; the false paradise, on the other hand, is destroyed because the nuns work "against Fate" (l. 247), which means also against nature. History becomes romance to demonstrate the working of the divine artist; the scene recalls the destruction of those other sinister artifices, the Bower of Bliss and Busirane's castle.

> Thenceforth (as when th' Inchantment ends
> The Castle vanishes or rends)
> The wasting Cloister with the rest
> Was in one instant dispossest.
>
> (ll. 269–72)

Having demolished the dangerous structures of false art, Marvell explores and defines, in the central movements of the poem, the conditions of a true paradise. These conditions are founded upon delicate relationships between nature and imagination, model and imitation. Rosalie Colie's adjective for the poem, "shifty," is nowhere better illustrated than here, where tenors and vehicles, objects and their reflections, repeatedly change places. Critics have remarked upon Marvell's habit of literalizing his metaphors, but an even more complicated process is visible in the stanzas about Fairfax's garden, which is laid out "In the just Figure of a Fort" (l. 286). Stanzas 37–40 elaborate the figure, the flowers imitating metaphorically (but also in the actual design of the garden) the military activities of volleying, marching, bivouacking. "These five imaginary Forts" (l. 352) allude to, and are innocently modeled upon, their maker's vocation in the "real" world. But the game played by the lord general in his garden becomes something more serious under the pressure of the narrator's imagination. The pivotal stanza on the "fall" of England into civil war (41) is followed by a renewal of the metaphor of "sweet *Militia*" (l. 330), but now inflected so that we contemplate the meaning of innocence in the true original garden which was the model for this one. There, "all the Garrisons were Flowrs" (l. 332), and "The *Gardiner* had the *Souldiers* place" (l. 337). In Fairfax's figurative garden, flowers "are" garrisons; but originally garrisons "were" flowers. The shift in the direction of the correspondence registers the difference between a truly innocent world and a world of partly regained innocence which merely alludes to the true concept in the process of figuring its opposite.

In the final couplet of stanza 42, Marvell inflects the image once more:

> But War all this doth overgrow:
> We Ord'nance Plant and Powder sow.
> (ll. 343–44)

Whereas Fairfax now "shoots" only "fragrant Vollyes" (l. 298), he once "sowed" with artillery; the world is turned upside down along with the image, and England becomes a waste land, the overgrown garden described in Shakespeare's history plays, with reference to another war. Two aspects of "present" reality are defined in the two metaphors: the garden that is like a fort, the warfare that parodies gardening. Between them lies the original garden—whether unfallen England or unfallen Eden—where tulips *were* guards, because no other kind of guarding was known, or necessary. Reality had not yet split into tenors and vehicles; there are no metaphors in paradise.

In this triple-tiered exploration of the garden/warfare correspondence, Marvell defines the activities of the fallen imagination. It can, with Fairfax, attempt to create a mortal image expressing what the mind knows of innocence and virtue, though even here the created world will bear the marks of its fallen condition, as it does in the martial stance of flowers and bees. Imagination can also create diabolical parodies of its origins: the acts of destruction that terribly resemble those of creation—the "sowing" of ordinance. Finally, the human imagination can turn from the making of either earthly paradises or earthly hells, and assume the visionary power to represent the realm of eternal existence, what has been and one day may be again. Marvell touches only lightly this region, which is the home of Milton's imagination. But the historical and cosmological reach of "Upon Appleton House," from chaos to apocalypse, conveys indirectly the power of imagination to see what the eye cannot see, beyond the limits of space and time. This transcendence of limit is not presumption; it is, rather, the morality of imagination, corresponding to the virtue of Fairfax in regarding his house as a symbol of aspiration rather than a literalizing of heaven (the nuns, on the other hand, try to "draw *Heav'n* nearer" to themselves [l. 162]). There is an invisible perfection which provides the standard for man's incomplete perfections and fallings off. Marvell goes on, in a final inflection of the garden image, to describe another "planting," this time of a paradise within.

> For he did, with his utmost Skill
> *Ambition* weed, but *Conscience* till.
> *Conscience,* that Heaven-nursed Plant,
> Which most our Earthly Gardens want.
> A prickling leaf it bears, and such
> As that which shrinks at ev'ry touch;
> But Flowers eternal, and divine,
> That in the Crowns of Saints do shine.
>
> (ll. 353–60)

The stanza is framed allegorically to define a concept, and the peculiar allegorical relationship between the visible image and its invisible counterpart is strongly marked. What is metaphorical on earth—conscience feigned to be a plant—becomes literal in Heaven—a flower in the crown of a saint. Conscience, which has taken the saint to Heaven, is totally identified, at last, with the shining blossoms that crown the whole endeavor. But such identification can occur only "then" and "there"; in the here and now, we must make do with metaphors and a paradise within. Marvell's stanza bears witness to the power of the resolved soul, and of the virtuous imagination, to apprehend invisible reality and retire to a garden of the mind that is the only true anticipation of Heaven.

An analysis of the resources of figurative language and of imagination's legitimate and illegitimate powers, the garden stanzas of "Upon Appleton House" provide the poem with its structural and thematic center. In the next movement, perspective and tone alter. The narrator, up to now only a voice, becomes an "I" (l. 369), and with his entry into the action there is introduced the special ambiguous tone of self-inflation and self-mockery that Marvell reserves for his portraits of the artist. The self that is displayed here has a particularly crucial role. He is the contemplative, the visionary, the maker of sober or extravagant frames in poetry; he is the man of imagination, and insofar as he is celebrated, chastised, corrected, mocked, instructed, admired, so is imagination.

Although the design of "Appleton House" seems spontaneous and rambling, even haphazard, it is in fact a map of the contours of the imagining mind, and its parts do not follow one another at random. Having described imagination's powers in the course of perambulating the garden, Marvell turns to the world beyond it to seek for confirmation of the validity of imagining. The meadow section concerns metamorphosis, the central imaginative act; but these metamorphoses occur in nature, which thus reasserts its primacy as a model and source for human art, which must be rooted in "reality." The changes and doublings and identifications of a wonder-working imagination are here displayed before the innocently gazing observer, *in fact;* Nature has its fictions and its seemings too. Marvell at the outset asserts the congruence of nature and art in the cooperating lines of a couplet:

> No Scene that turns with Engines strange
> Does oftner then these Meadows change.
> (ll. 385–86)

Nature's above art; its changing scenes offer first the mock war of the mowers, then the mown field with its *"Pyramids* of Hay" in cocks, the "levell'd" space of the denuded meadow "polisht" into a pasture for the village cattle, and finally the "Sea" of the flooded river. Amid these changes, imagination plays its own descants, varying the angles from which we view reality, multiplying the mirrors in which vision catches what it regards.

Reality confirms these imaginings, sometimes disconcertingly. Stanza 50 begins with an apparently innocent, but ominously weighted, description of the mowers:

> With whistling Sithe, and Elbow strong,
> These Massacre the Grass along.
> (ll. 393–94)

The violent verb seems merely conventional in this couplet, invoking expectations of affinity between mowing and the death of all flesh. But the violence springs to life in the following lines, actualized in the unwitting but detestable murder of the rail:

> The Edge all bloody from its Breast
> He draws, and does his stroke detest;

> Fearing the Flesh untimely mow'd
> To him a Fate as black forebode.
>   (ll. 397–400)

Suddenly the blood is real, not metaphorical. The abrupt literalizing of images
is one of Marvell's characteristic devices, symptomatic of the self-consciousness of his art. Its effect here is even more complex than usual, almost too complex for the clumsy makeshift of explication.

Every reader of the poem has found himself puzzled by this stanza, and
its mock-heroic companion, stanza 53. The images function, as Rosalie Colie
has said, "to keep the notion of war trembling behind this landscape of bucolic
well-being." They carry our attention outward to the "real" world of events in
history, but the implications of this movement are metaphysical as well as
political. The stanza reminds us that language, and the transformations of
language in metaphor, have their roots in the way things are; their vitality
depends upon facts that are not linguistic or imagined. Marvell's dead metaphor
in *Massacre* is revived when the mower carves the rail, and the fancy that had
so casually used the verb is recalled to its responsibilities. There is a real shock
in this movement from the metaphorical to the actual, and the shock forces
us to consider the seriousness of imagination's contrivances. They are at once
more serious and less serious than we might be inclined to suppose. More
serious—because if we regard them merely as a game our art loses touch with
its models; but also less serious—because imagination has a tendency to press
its insights further than actuality will tolerate. This second truth about imagination emerges as the stanza ends, in a couplet that teeters on the edge of absurdity. "The Flesh untimely mow'd" derives its resonance from the unexpected
intrusion of fact into fiction, the bloody stroke actually observed. But the fact
will not bear the superstructure that imagination builds on it in the last line:
"To him a Fate as black forebode." In a way, of course, it merely asserts the truth:
the mower *will* suffer a fate as black, will himself be cut down—"For Death
thou art a Mower too." But talk of Fate and untimely death is a little too weighty
for this context, and the tone collapses, in the next stanza, into self-mockery,
as if to warn us that a self-absorbed imagination can err in the direction of por-
tentousness as well as frivolity.

The extraordinary intervention of "bloody *Thestylis*" into the poem's fabric
at this point has interested many critics. It is another shift of perspective, another
crowding of imagination by reality, another reminder of the limits of fiction,
and of its dependence upon an only partly controllable world of fact. But the
tone this time is remarkably genial, even hilarious. Murdered birds multiply
comically:

> When on another quick She lights,
> And cryes, he call'd us *Israelites;*
> But now, to make his saying true,
> Rails rain for Quails, for Manna Dew.
>
> (ll. 405–8)

"To make his saying true," reality once more presses upon the poet's innocent locutions and proves them less than innocent; he cannot call anyone an Israelite with impunity in this emblem-ridden world that constantly displays the artfulness of God. Thestylis "carries the poet's biblical metaphor to an area into which he had not planned to take it" [to use Colie's words], and once again the determination of reality to cooperate in his fancies makes the poet seem a little irresponsible, or at least a little careless of his own premises.

Perhaps determined to evade a charge of fanciful foolishness, Marvell assumes in the next stanza an air of laborious spelling out. His argument has the explicitness of a demonstration, in contrast to the glancing allusiveness in the stanza just preceding it. The analogy between this field and a field of battle is explained point by point.

> In whose new Traverse seemeth wrought
> A Camp of Battail newly fought:
> Where, as the Meads with Hay, the Plain
> Lyes quilted ore with Bodies slain:
> The Women that with forks it fling,
> Do represent the Pillaging.
>
> (ll. 419–24)

Seemeth, as nearly always in Marvell, is a warning to tread lightly. Then the *as . . . so* of the simile reinforces the cautious tone. Inflecting vehicle and tenor, Marvell suggests the two-way perspective on the nature/war comparison that was examined in the passage on the military garden. On the field of battle, the plain is "quilted" with bodies as a mown field is with bundles of hay. And this hayfield "seems" a battlefield. The rhetorical patterning of the lines insists upon the imagination's self-awareness. A simile makes us think about both similarities as differences in the terms; it holds them apart, analytically. The effect here is to make the speaker seem careful and responsible; the mowing of a field *is* like the mowing down of flesh on a battlefield, but at the same time it is reassuringly unlike. Its heroism is only mock, its innocence genuine. The stanza thus restores the balance in our view of the mowers; they are neither murderers nor heroes nor spoiled innocents, though their actions point in all these directions. Fiction and fact are firmly distinguished. The women making hay "Do *represent* the Pillaging," but they are not pillagers. The statement expresses an analogy, no more and no less; there is enactment, but no dangerous identification.

Imagination must learn to know its limits. On the other hand, it may be surprised to find its seemings echoed by reality, as in the massacre of the rail and the intervention of Thestylis. A third and climactic instance of counter-metaphorical transformation is the flood which concludes this section of the poem. The river, released from the floodgates,

> make the Meadow truly be
> (What it but seem'd before) a Sea.
> (ll. 467–68)

Thirty lines before, the smooth meadow was said to surround the rocklike or pyramidal haycocks, "Like a calm Sea" (l. 434); now that sea becomes literally visible, moving from the world of mind to the world without. The flood allows Marvell to play with notions of boats sailing overhead, in another sequence of topsy-turvy paradoxes. The disorientation produced by the flood appropriately rounds off this section, which is dominated by bewildering shifts of perspective (as from microscope to telescope in stanza 58), and by oscillations between literal and figurative description.

The flood stanzas match the two stanzas which introduce the section; together, they make a watery frame for the multiple reflecting glasses of the meadow. As the narrator moves into that wilderness of mirrors, he enters "the Abbyss . . . Of that unfathomable Grass" (ll. 369–70), a "sea" where men are lower than grasshoppers, as later they are lower than boats and fish. These dislocations are susceptible of many readings, and have kept many critics busy. In terms of the poem's major themes, the whole meadow passage represents, I think, Marvell's effort to describe the medium in which a rational amphibium must lead his life. We are amphibious not only between earth and heaven, but between the world within and the world without. Imagination unites the two, mediates between them; or, more accurately, imagination is the means whereby we perceive the continuity between world and mind. Elements from the two worlds can change places readily because these realms of being are congruent and interdependent, though we must resist the temptation to assimilate them completely to each other. "What we see is what we think": this title of a poem by Stevens perfectly catches the ambiguities where mirrors confront each other at the center of "Appleton House":

> Where all things gaze themselves, and doubt
> If they be in it or without.
>
> (ll. 637–38)

In a fine kinesthetic image, Marvell reminds us of how it feels to live in our element.

> To see Men through this Meadow Dive,
> We wonder how they rise alive.
> As, under Water, none does know
> Whether he fall through it or go.
>
> (ll. 377–80)

The swimmer sinking through seas profound cannot tell whether he moves as the result of his own efforts, or is merely passive in the hands of gravity. Do we "go" or "fall," control our environment or submit to it? And, of course, in this stanza the sea is not really a sea anyway, but a meadow; the very element is ambiguous. But Marvell will not allow priority to either side, so at the end the meadow is not "really" a meadow, but a sea.

"Upon Appleton House," beginning with a lecture on the misuse and abuse of imagination, proceeds, in its later stages, to its true subject, which is also Wordsworth's subject: the great consummation between mind and the world, in which perception and creation, mirror and lamp, are evenly balanced. The nuns lock themselves away from their world, expressly denying the amphibiousness of human nature.

> "These Walls restrain the World without,
> But hedge our Liberty about.
> These Bars inclose the wider Den
> Of those wild Creatures called Men."
>
> (ll. 99–102)

The human soul is split into an "interior" spiritual self, and a "wild" natural self. Breaking down bars and walls, the virtuous Fairfax reunites the two in his marriage to Isabella Thwaites. The decent order of Nunappleton, at once natural and artful, expresses this union. Though in other poems by Marvell the resolved soul confronts the creation as its antagonist, here there is a truce between them, uneasily maintained but satisfying to both.

The retreat of the poet to his "Sanctuary in the Wood" (l. 482) balances the episode of the nunnery. At first, there is admiration for the artfulness of nature's designs. A union of opposites, amicably interlocked, finds an *exemplum* in the marriage of Fairfax and Vere, and the wood itself:

> Dark all without it knits; within
> It opens passable and thin.
>
> (ll. 505–6)

In this passable world it is easy to be a philosopher. The tone of the passage suggests the spontaneity and ease of an imagination delighted by a wholly intelligible universe. What it sees and what it makes are indistinguishable; voice and echo vibrate to the same frequency. "And there I found myself more truly and more strange."

This is the subtlest of Marvell's paradises. The poet is restored to a state of innocence without losing his worldliness. The wisdom of the ages is condensed in the "light *Mosaick*" (l. 582); he wears this learning lightly. Like Adam, he speaks the "learned Original" (l. 570) that is the language of Nature itself. Stockdoves, heron, stork, woodpecker, "Traitor-worm"—these creatures delightfully instruct the poet in the manner of the emblem books of the day. They are, in fact, living emblems, offering a final example of Marvell's counter-metaphorical technique, the literalizing of the figurative. The pages of "*Natures mystick Book*" (l. 584) are animated before our eyes, as the poet turns their "Leaves." We are meant to notice also, of course, that the emblems almost all point a sad or sobering moral; this paradise remains postlapsarian, and the climactic emblem of the worm in the oak (stanza 70) speaks explicitly of our corrupt flesh.

We are, therefore, prepared for the denouement of this episode, and for its successor which will conclude the poem. The poet, ravished by his reunion with nature, revels in extravagant identifications.

> And little now to make me, wants
> Or of the *Fowles,* or of the *Plants.*
> Give me but Wings as they, and I
> Streight floating on the Air shall fly:
> Or turn me but, and you shall see
> I was but an inverted Tree.
> (ll. 563–68)

Embroidered with oak leaves, clasped by ivy, he can think of nothing more desirable than perpetual bondage in the arms of benevolent nature. Yet he is, after all, neither a fowl nor a plant; he has no wings, and he maintains, perforce, the upright posture of a man. The imagery of bondage in stanza 77, which has attracted critical notice for the violence of its tone, gives a clue to the wishes thus expressed:

> Bind me ye *Woodbines* in your 'twines,
> Curle me about ye gadding *Vines.*
> (ll. 609–10)

We may remember another kind of bondage, differently judged:

> Cease Tempter. None can chain a mind
> Whom this sweet Chordage cannot bind.
>> ("A Dialogue between the Resolved Soul,
>> and Created Pleasure," ll. 43–44)

The resolved soul, immune to the charms of music, cannot now submit to the ministrations of vegetable loves. The narrator of "Upon Appleton House" has found a refuge more salubrious than the artificial Eden of the nunnery, but he has pressed too far the idea of nature as a model, soberly recommended in the poem's opening stanzas. And he, like the nuns, thinks of his sanctuary as shutting out rather than encompassing.

> How safe, methinks, and strong, behind
> These Trees have I incamp'd my Mind.
>> (ll. 601–2)

But this is an illusion. The rail, too, had thought itself safe.

> Unhappy Birds! what does it boot
> To build below the Grasses Root;
> When Lowness is unsafe as Hight,
> And Chance o'retakes what scapeth spight?
>> (ll. 409–12)

Chance may sometimes display "better Wit" (l. 585); but it can just as easily work in this destructive way. Nature may be designed, but history is not, and history, "the World," is where we live. Against it, imagination must provide its own sanctuaries, temporary though they may be; nature cannot do this for us. Marvell's curious image for his isolation from "the World" may strike us as precarious:

> But I on it securely play,
> And gaul its Horsemen all the Day.
>> (ll. 607–8)

This is a dangerous sort of play; we remember the wanton troopers who, "riding by / Have shot my Faun and it will dye." The Nymph's paradise was invaded; this one may be too.

In fact, Marvell keeps it safe for the extent of this poem, but only by another metamorphosis, which entails the poet's breaking of nature's "Silken Bondage" and his submission to a new, more human enchantment. One of the games played in the final section is to pretend that Mary Fairfax is wiser than her tutor; he becomes a "trifling Youth," fumbling away his fishing gear before her "judicious Eyes" (ll. 652–53). She speaks all languages, the mistress of Babel. This complimentary conceit points more seriously, however, to the superiority of the ideal embodied in Maria over the return to Adamic innocence briefly indulged by the poet. The "vitrifi'd" nature contemplated in these stanzas (83–88) is outside time; it is described in the same visionary, nonmetaphorical mode as the flowers of conscience, "That in the Crowns of Saints do shine" (l. 360). The stillness of the presented moment, "betwixt the Day and Night" (l. 670), is not natural, but supernatural, an intermittence of the heart when imagination takes wing. We see, for a moment, a new earth, replacing the one that will be consumed in the flames of time; it is a world redeemed, and in it the redeemed soul takes its central place, reassuming its forsaken command over nature.

> 'Tis *She* that to these Gardens gave
> That wondrous Beauty which they have;
> *She* streightness on the Woods bestows;
> To *Her* the Meadow sweetness owes;
> Nothing could make the River be
> So Chrystal-pure but only *She*.
>
> (ll. 689–94)

Nature "recollects" itself around Maria. The human figure is now the model, Nature legitimately the mirror which gives man back his own image.

> And for a Glass the limpid Brook,
> Where *She* may all *her* Beautyes look.
>
> (ll. 701–2)

This paradise exists within the visionary imagination, though it is composed of elements visible to the physical eye. It is the paradigm for the poem's other paradises, but we are not allowed to contemplate it long. In the end we must reenter time and history; so Marvell looks ahead to the moment when fate will "translate" Maria to another role, where she can extend the family "Line." The Fairfaxes, like their "double Wood," measure the generations of time, make destiny their choice, and, marrying into the family of "starry *Vere*," incorporate fortune's emblem in their arms (l. 724). In three penultimate stanzas, Marvell returns to the actuality of Nunappleton and gives it a precise ontological location. He begins with one of his key terms: *Mean time.*

> Mean time ye Fields, Springs, Bushes, Flow'rs,
> Where yet She leads her studious Hours.
>
> (ll. 745–46)

It is like the pause in "Little T.C." before her entry into the arena of love: "Mean time, whilst every verdant thing / It self does at thy Beauty charm" (ll. 25–26). In a reverse process, in "The Garden" the mind withdraws through the portal of "Mean while" into its happiness. Human beings may enjoy interludes outside time when they can play at recreating paradise. Some historical examples of such interludes, evoked and dismissed in stanza 95, witness to mankind's enduring preoccupation with this *topos*. Nunappleton overgoes them all, but there is an implication that it too may someday become "obsolete." For it is, after all, not paradise but *Paradice's only Map*" (l. 768)—a chart for a journey whose real goal lies elsewhere. It is a place that can "entertain / Its *Lord* a while, but not remain."

In the concluding stanzas, Marvell achieves a delicate balance between art and nature, and between imagination's strength and its weakness. As in his shorter complimentary poem to Fairfax, "Upon the Hill and Grove at Bilbrough," so more subtly here, he approves the virtuous soul's impression of its stamp upon nature. For the natural world is fallen too, full of "excrescences"—"a rude heap together hurl'd" (l. 762).

> Your lesser *World* contains the same.
> But in more decent Order tame.
>
> (ll. 765–66)

Yet the decent order of Nunappleton, though it may endure in the mind, or in a poem, is transient, because our experience will not sustain any sort of permanence. It exists "mean time," a containing microcosm that can provide the ground for self-contemplation and self-transcendence. So nostalgia becomes the appropriate note for the poem's last movement: nostalgia for all the lost paradises, and for the world "as once it was" (l. 761). We are not surprised to find in the final stanza of "Upon Appleton House" a last version of pastoral, the mode devised by humanity to contain all its nostalgias.

Stanza 97 provides a series of contexts, spatial and temporal, for the gardens of Nunappleton in the macrocosm. *But now* does not arrest time; rather, it acknowledges time's flow, which concludes in the corresponding *now* eight lines later.

> But now the *Salmon-Fishers* moist
> Their *Leathern Boats* begin to hoist;
> And, like *Antipodes* in Shoes,
> Have shod their *Heads* in their *Canoos*.
> How *Tortoise* like, but not so slow,
> These rational *Amphibii* go?

> Let's in: for the dark *Hemisphere*
> Does now like one of them appear.
> (ll. 769–76)

The stanza moves in a tiny perfect arch from the observed detail of the salmon fishers, back to the earth at nightfall. At the center, imagination revels in analogies to make a paradoxical definition of man. He is an amphibium, an earthdweller whose imagination can outsoar its limits, can travel to the ends of the earth, and turn upside down the fixities of quotidian reality while preserving a decorum of "natural" forms. Though he may be *"Tortoise* like," he is "not so slow"; he can solve Zeno's paradox. At the end, as the hemisphere darkens, he returns to contemplate the multiplied concentricities cooperatively generated by nature and his own mind. The sky "does now like one of them appear"; one of what? The salmon fishers carrying their boats, the Antipodes in shoes, the rational amphibii in their tortoiselike dwellings? One of them or all of them: all happily consent to shape themselves in the same form. In this magical conclusion, expansion of vision is accompanied by an awareness of finitude; the sense that nothing is ever finished coincides with the sense of an ending, appropriate and inevitable and satisfying, to this poem. Sweetness and wit, which Donne once declared irreconcilable, here become natural partners.

Marvell's most profound poems are those in which he is reconciled to his own imagination, that human faculty so disposed to exaggeration and self-serving delusion. For him it is admirable only when it consents to work within limits, growing thereby more strong and heroic. In "To His Coy Mistress" it splendidly rises to the challenge of temporality, and at the end of "The Garden," having tried its wings, it willingly binds the zodiac of wit into a fragrant zodiac of flowers. Imagination gracefully capitulates to the conditions of mortality, and so transforms and makes beautiful those very conditions. Marvell's skill at ending poems is itself an honoring of the claims of limit. "Upon Appleton House" ends, like "Lycidas" and its forerunners, with the end of the day, acknowledging our submission to diurnal revolutions and the poet's acceptance of a traditional genre. The poem's limit is the sun's limit; the allusion to other pastoral cadences reminds us of the union of art and nature that characterizes this mode. We are invited to reenter the sober frame that is Nunappleton and "Upon Appleton House": "Let's in."

MICHAEL SEIDEL

A House Divided: Marvell's "Last Instructions" and Dryden

At one point in his panegyric "To Sir Godfrey Kneller," John Dryden asks pardon for inserting what appears to be an insulting reference to the origin of Kneller's art, painting. Dryden traces the artist's craft to Eve "making-up" in the garden. He doesn't really mean it, after all, "But Satire will have room, where e're I write" (l. 94). The growth of the satiric spirit—what Swift called the "Satyrical Itch"—is in a way endemic for the seventeenth century. Dryden was the first practitioner and theorist to understand the full transforming potential of satiric action. He recognized the ranging power of satire in appropriating the strategies of other modes and genres while changing the perspective from which those modes and genres reflect material. In his *Discourse concerning the Original and Progress of Satire*, Dryden writes of satire as variously manifest, from the negative reflections (*médisance*) of invective to the sublimities of heroic mockery. In essence, "Why shou'd we offer to confine free Spirits to one Form, when we cannot so much as confine our Bodies to one Fashion of Apparel?"

In one of the many attacks on Dryden at the time of the Exclusion Crisis, his arch enemy, Elkanah Settle, wrote in frustration of what Dryden had refined as a satiric strategy: "you have got a damnable trick of turning the Perspective upon occasion, and magnifying or diminishing at pleasure." Settle is onto the counterfeit. At least in theory, Dryden knows that literary genre is a matter of separable parts. But in practice the satirist is mercurial. In his *Parallel of Poetry and Painting* Dryden writes: "In the character of an hero, as well as an inferior figure, there is a better or worse likeness to be taken: the better is panegyric, if it be not false, and the worse is libel." The idea is not new. Aristotle

From *Satiric Inheritance: Rabelais to Sterne.* © 1979 by Princeton University Press.

has a witty passage in the *Rhetoric* where he speaks of contraries and metaphoric values: "And if we wish to ornament our subject, we must derive our metaphor from the better species under the same genus; if to depreciate it, from the worse. Thus, to say (for you have two opposites belonging to the same genus) that the man who begs prays, or that the man who prays begs (for both are forms of asking) is an instance of doing this" (Loeb trans., 1405a). But what is new, or at least dominant, for Dryden's period is the urge to expand the paradigm from metaphor to mode—to scratch, as Swift put it, wherever satire itched.

What lies behind a good deal of Dryden's thinking on the cross-generic and cross-modal "room" for satire is expressed by Neander in the *Essay of Dramatick Poesie.* According to Neander, literary change accommodates the genius of an age. Thus modernity is the battle against anachronism, and modes, genres, and styles (what Claudio Guillén calls "literary systems") actually change their character as a matter of course. In the literature of his own age Dryden sees an essential flexibility in representation: modal and stylistic range counter generic rigidity. In the *Discourse concerning Satire,* he even goes so far as to challenge conventional Horatian wisdom on satiric "lowness":

> But how come Lowness of Style and the Familiarity of Words to be
> so much the Propriety of Satire, that without them, a Poet can be
> no more a Satirist, than without Risibility he can be a Man? . . .
> If *Horace* refus'd the pains of Numbers, and the loftiness of Figures,
> are they bound to follow so ill a Precedent? Let him walk a Foot,
> with his Pad in his Hand, for his own pleasure; but let not them
> be accounted no Poets, who choose to mount, and shew their
> Horsmanship.

Later in the *Discourse,* Dryden makes his famous observation on Boileau's *Le Lutrin,* pointing out that, when well-executed, heroic counterfeits are but a species of the higher forms of heroic poetry. Although he is the most elegant theorist of satire in the century, some of Dryden's better ideas had been anticipated and put into practice by others. In 1666 Dryden wrote *Annus Mirabilis,* an heroic-historical poem on the great fire of London and a victory at sea over the Dutch. A year later, when the English lost a famous sea battle, Andrew Marvell turned Dryden's perspective. In his "Last Instructions to a Painter," he forged a replacement not only for Dryden's *Annus Mirabilis* but for the historical subgenre or "instructions to a painter" poems intended as Stuart panegyric. Marvell's "Last Instructions" are *last* in two senses: latest, hence the most recent accommodation of contingent event to historical narrative; and last, hence final, as befits a satirically revealed scene of fraud and folly. Satire is the last word in heroic fashion.

In his "Last Instructions" Marvell included a panel from a semiserious poem, "The Loyall Scot," in which he portrayed the heroism of Lord Douglas in defending his ship against the 1667 incursion up the Thames by the Dutch Admiral De Ruyter. Marvell notices the double response to contingent events and the implied modal crossover in recording them. He writes of "Worth Heroick or Heroick Crimes" (l. 241). The chiasmus is strategic—in all Marvell's major political poems, both heroism and heroic enormity are matters of timing. Worth can sometimes sanction criminality, but the untimely abrogation of heroic power is as bad as its excessive tyrannic abuse. Heroism is circumstance. Isolated from appropriate expression, it can look absurd. And it is a subtle satiric mind that sees a kind of criminal barbarity in heroic absurdity. In *The Growth of Popery and Arbitrary Government,* Marvell writes of the misappropriation of power: "For by how much a thing is more false and unreasonable, it requires more cruelty to establish it: and to introduce that which is absurd, there must be somewhat that is barbarous."

Marvell's "Last Instructions" reviews a state conspiracy in crimes of greed, collective guilt, paranoia, lust, improperly allocated monies and taxes, poor defense planning, and shameful bureaucratic scapegoating. The important scenes of the poem, the Excise debates in Parliament and the naval invasion up the Thames, are separated by months in actual historical sequence, but they conveniently overlap as satiric "instructions." Marvell reserves his mock-epic machinery for a parody of the parliamentary debates over the funding of an impossible land war on the Continent while he presents the invasion by sea as a pastoral epithalamion, the absurd marriage of violated rivers, the Thames and Medway. The debates have the trappings of battle; the battle has the trappings of parody. The chicanery of Parliament is glorified by the heroic; the necessarily heroic resembles a regatta on the Thames. Admiral De Ruyter meets little resistance, so he participates in the only action available to him: he sports with water nymphs. The violator ceremoniously takes his pleasure.

> *Ruyter* the while, that had our Ocean curb'd,
> Sail'd now among our Rivers undisturb'd:
> Survey'd their Crystal Streams, and Banks so green,
> And Beauties e're this never naked seen.
> Through the vain sedge the bashful *Nymphs* he ey'd
> Bosomes, and all which from themselves they hide.
> The Sun much brighter, and the Skies more clear,
> He finds the Air, and all things, sweeter here.

> The sudden change, and such a tempting sight,
> Swells his old Veins with fresh Blood, fresh Delight.
> Like am'rous Victors he begins to shave,
> And his new Face looks in the *English* Wave.
> His sporting Navy all about him swim,
> And witness their complaisance in their trim.
>
> (ll. 523–34)

De Ruyter's ravishment of England's spaces defines not so much the intent of the perpetrator as the willingness of the perpetrated. The absence of one force defines the presence of another. The first sound of Dutch gunfire sends the English viewers from the shore, running back to the safety of the court and town, running out on the heroic action. That De Ruyter ravishes the land is not so important as the fact that he can do whatever he pleases. And he can do so because England is heroically (and financially) spent, her body (land, water, defenses, commercial lifelines) raped, her inheritance as a naval power diminished.

Marvell leads up to the generic condition of the poem by beginning with a series of court portraits. His strategy is to represent the decaying body of heroic lineaments, and he opens with the King's ambassador to France, Henry Jermyn, Earl of St. Albans. The Earl has inherited a title from Francis Bacon, but he has debased Bacon's interests: "Well he the Title of St. *Albans* bore, / For never *Bacon* study'd Nature more" (ll. 35–36). A more telling portrait is reserved for Anne Hyde, the King's sister-in-law and the daughter of his recently dismissed first minister. Anne is of Diana's ilk, a perverse pastoral nymph who "after Childbirth" can "renew a Maid" (l. 54). Like England, she "hides" her condition. What's in a name? In the portrait of Lady Castlemaine, Charles's aging mistress, the sexually profligate network continues and touches yet closer to the King. Like one of Pope's veteran "Sex of Queens," Lady Castlemaine finds herself sexually used up, passed from Charles to Jermyn to her footman. When Charles finally appears later in the poem, we are primed for his behavior. The virgin and naked image of *"England* or the *Peace"* comes to him (and he to it) in a Pharsalian vision, and in the most absurd gesture of all Charles exercises his libido as a function of state (or a function of *his* state). If De Ruyter rapes a spent victim and enemy, Charles attempts to possess his own body ("the Country is the *King"*), thus adding a kind of incest to lust.

> There, as in the calm horrour all alone,
> He wakes and Muses of th' uneasie Throne:
> Raise up a sudden Shape with Virgins Face,
> Though ill agree her Posture, Hour, or Place:

Naked as born, and her round Arms behind,
With her own Tresses interwove and twin'd:
Her mouth lockt up, a blind before her Eyes,
Yet from beneath the Veil her blushes rise;
And silent tears her secret anguish speak,
Her heart throbs, and with very shame would break.
The Object strange in him no Terrour mov'd:
He wonder'd first, then pity'd, then he lov'd:
And with kind hand he does the coy Vision press,
Whose Beauty greater seem'd by her distress;
But soon shrunk back, chill'd with her touch so cold,
And th'airy Picture vanisht from his hold.
In his deep thoughts the wonder did increase,
And he Divin'd 'twas *England* or the *Peace.*

(ll. 889–906)

In the "Last Instructions", the satiric perspective implies so lost an order of things that even the elegiac is subject to parody. Only one stylized figure remains as a kind of vestige from a previous world. He is a lone and somewhat hapless Scotsman, Lord Douglas. And in the separate poem, "The Loyall Scot" (part of which Marvell inserted in the "Last Instructions"), we see all too clearly the curious relation of satire to discarded systems. Marvell requests that the dead satirist John Cleveland step forward to praise Douglas. Although Cleveland's soul has been purged of satire in the Elysian Fields, his praise of Douglas, as mimicked by Marvell, begins with a reference to satiric impulses: "Abruptly he began disguising art, / As of his Satyr this had been a part" (ll. 13–14). Marvell suggests that all praise is given over to satire. Heroic action in the Douglas poem or the Douglas interval becomes at best part of a memorable code—its fate is elegiac because it exists to no real effect. As a youth, Douglas sports with nymphs and virgins who are to reappear somewhat less innocently for De Ruyter and Charles II. Marvell depicts the scene in "Last Instructions."

Among the Reeds, to be espy'd by him,
The *Nymphs* would rustle; he would forward swim.
They sigh'd and said, Fond Boy, why so untame,
That fly'st Love Fires, reserv'd for other Flame?

(ll. 657–60)

Marvell's language is almost painfully mannered because Douglas, even as a youth, was something of a "burnt-out" case. The flame of love is the

Virgilian flame of destruction, and of course in heroic death the warrior or lover
either goes out like a house of fire or swoons in a sort of post battle *tristesse*.

> And, as on Angels Heads their Glories shine,
> His burning Locks adorn his Face Divine.
> But, when in his immortal Mind he felt
> His alt'ring Form, and soder'd Limbs to melt;
> Down on the Deck he laid himself, and dy'd,
> With his dear Sword reposing by his Side.
> And, on the flaming Plank, so rests his Head,
> As one that's warm'd himself and gone to Bed.
>
> (ll. 683–90)

The very archaism of the Douglas interlude forces a revaluation of the later
seventeenth-century heroic "scene." In one sense, the Douglas sequence barely
manages to skirt bathos (or modal burlesque); in another, it allows Marvell
to work a legitimate hero into a poem and world that is generically insufficient
for his literary image. Douglas is a dying swan, and Marvell knows that his
loss, although regrettable, does not answer to what is a greater loss in the contingent world of the poem—the loss of England's commercial and military fleet.
If Douglas appears ridiculous in his heroism, Marvell directs his subversive wit
less at his absurdity than at his uselessness. In the later seventeenth century,
satiric narrative adapts its strategies for a changing historical order, and, reflex-
ively, the changing historical order forces the modal adaptation of the literary
structures chosen to represent it.

CLEANTH BROOKS

Andrew Marvell: Puritan Austerity with Classical Grace

Andrew Marvell's "The Garden" and "To His Coy Mistress" are, by common consent, two of the finest lyric poems in English. Yet the clash between the world views they involve, though calculated to bring up the ever-thorny question of the poet's sincerity, has been little discussed. "To His Coy Mistress" carries so much conviction that it is difficult to dismiss it as simply an exercise. On the other hand, Marvell's known Puritan leanings suggest to many readers that such poems as "The Garden" must surely represent his real convictions. What I shall be concerned with here, therefore, is what gives both poems that sense of conviction and their seeming inevitability as dramatic "statement."

For all their apparent oppositions and contradictions, the two poems have much in common. They share several themes, one of which, I believe, has received in the past less attention than it deserves: the theme of time in relation to eternity.

I suggest that we try to imagine the lover of "To His Coy Mistress" to be the same man who steps into "The Garden" and savors its cool delights. Let's imagine that he has been unable to persuade his coy mistress to yield. Now, after having run through his "Passion's heat," he has indeed found in this delightful place "Love['s] . . . best retreat." Nature, no coy mistress, offers her innocent pleasures wholeheartedly. Would he, in this situation and this state of mind, find the "lovely green" of nature more "am'rous" than the "white" and "red" of his mistress? An hour before, let us suppose, he has used the phrase "vegetable Love" to dismiss rather contemptuously a love affair that had little

From *Poetic Traditions of the English Renaissance*, edited by Maynard Mack and George deForest Lord. © 1982 by Yale University. Yale University Press, 1982.

to recommend it except the longevity and slow growth characteristic of plant life. But if the "Fair Trees" of the garden are indeed more amorously attractive than any woman, would not their love be also a despised "vegetable Love"? These questions help us see, I think, how much each poem depends on a given dramatic situation, on the mood of the character speaking the poem, and on the tone in which he makes his various utterances.

Let me begin with time and mortality. The lover of the coy mistress never relaxes his concern with the swift rush of time. His account is studded with references to events in the far-off past, such as Noah's flood, or to events that are to occur only in some very remote future, such as the conversion of the Jews.

All this witty hyperbole is meant, of course, to render preposterous so slow-paced a courtship and to prepare for the sudden speed-up of time found in the middle third of the poem—a rush that will soon take the lovers out of life altogether and strand their bodies in "Desarts of vast Eternity." The strategy, of course, is to present with laconic irony a bleak reality that exposes the earlier fantasy of timelessness for the posturing that it is. Having done so, the lover is ready to urge his conclusion: the only course is to beat time at his own game, to live with such breathless speed as to make the sun lag behind them.

Though a reference to speed—that of the lovers' outracing the sun—occupies the final couplet, the dominant image of the closing lines of the poem is one of eating. The lovers are to devour their pleasures greedily. Far from being the love birds of tradition, they are "am'rous birds of prey"—snatching and tearing at the flesh of their kill. Like them, time also is a devourer, but with jaws ponderous and slow as he gradually masticates all that is mortal.

It is not a pretty picture, this scene of ravenous gluttony: the lovers tear their pleasure with "rough strife through The Iron Gates of Life." Nobody seems to know what this refers to. (Someone has even taken the gates to be the lips of the vagina, in which case "iron" seems an oddity.) For me, the image that comes to mind is simply that of feeding time for a pair of hawks mewed up in an iron cage. They will not wait for their keeper to finish poking through the bars the meat he brings. They snatch at it and pull it through themselves. What seems obvious, at any rate, is a sense of creatures savage and violent; and the violence suits the poem, for the poem is realistic and even desperate.

Such images indicate one way in which "To His Coy Mistress" differs from most of the carpe diem poems of this period. Another instance of grim insistence on the physical and realistic is the allusion to the rotting corpse and the grave-worm. True, the worm here is not the never-dying worm of the Scriptures, cited by generations of hell-fire preachers. This worm is a quite matter-of-fact worm, doing what he may be expected to do to every all-too-mortal carcass. Yet, if one is to look for Marvell's Puritanism, I think a trace of it may be found here.

The note of horror sets up a reverberation that is deeper and more powerful than is to be heard in any other carpe diem poem that I can think of. Compare it with the Anglican Herrick's masterpiece, "Corinna's Going a-Maying." Marvell's poem is not necessarily "better," but it is of another order.

For most readers, the voice heard in this poem cannot be that of a Puritan but has to be that of a libertine—someone, say, like the Earl of Rochester. Yet Puritan and libertine were more closely allied than we are in the habit of supposing. The libertine of Marvell's day was not a pagan suckled in a creed outworn. He had almost certainly been brought up on the Ten Commandments and the Apostle's Creed. In short, he was typically a lapsed Christian, whether now cynical, indifferent to, or defiant of, his heritage. Yet it would be difficult for him to expunge completely what he had been brought up to believe and that to which his society still gave more than lip-service.

As I have already suggested, the general tone of Marvell's poem is not precisely classical. When Catullus reminds his Lesbia that both will eventually have to descend into everlasting night, the note sounded is different. *Nox est perpetua una dormienda* is sufficiently somber to give urgency to his plea that Lesbia give him her love while she may. But Catullus' description of that perpetual night as one in which one must sleep forever mitigates much of its horror. He does not mention the grave-worm nor the lady's "virginity" being "tried" by it.

In sum, the lover in "To His Coy Mistress," in spite of his brilliant rhetoric, highflown compliment, urbanity and grace, impresses me, I repeat, as a desperate man, though his desperation is held under firm control.

II

Time pervades "The Garden" as well as "To His Coy Mistress." The man whose thoughts constitute the poem is very much conscious of time, even though in this poem he is stepping out of its hurrying blast.

The poem begins on a note of surprise, happy surprise at what the speaker has just discovered when he enters the garden precincts: quiet and innocence. Clearly he has heretofore failed to find them in the "busie Companies of Men" or, as stanzas 3 and 4 indicate, in the society of women and the attendant disappointments in love. His discovery of quiet and innocence is as surprising to him as it is welcome. How else account for the tone of "Fair quiet, have I found thee here, / And innocence thy sister dear!" The note is one of almost shocked relief.

To assess correctly the dramatic situation out of which the garden meditation arises—whether or not we indulge the fancy that the man speaking is the lover of "To His Coy Mistress"—allows us to take in the proper spirit the teasing of the ladies that occupies stanzas 3 and 4. A literal reading would make the speaker a misogynist or at least a very sour Puritan. Though he is here sardonic about romantic love, this disillusioned lover is not a man with a settled dislike for women.

Praise of the beauty of trees and plants to the disparagement of woman's beauty brings up once more the subject of "vegetable Love." Some commentators on "To His Coy Mistress" have been apprehensive that "vegetable Love" might make the modern reader envisage a cabbage—Gilbert and Sullivan's Bunthorne, one remembers, pretends to a "passion of a vegetable fashion" and meditates on a dalliance with a "not too French French bean." They therefore take pains to point out that Marvell refers only to the "vegetative soul," the vital principle of the plant world. The next highest was the "animal soul," the animating principle of animal life. Man alone possessed the highest in the hierarchy, a "rational soul."

This is all true enough, but the concession hardly diminishes the disparagement contained in "vegetable Love." Things animated by no more than a vegetative soul constitute the very lowest rung of animate nature. The lover speaking to his coy mistress is properly contemptuous of a love that, like a plant, even a centuries-old yew or redwood, can do little more than keep growing and propagating itself. He asks for a love that has fire and passion.

What, then, does one make of the love for trees, fruit, and flowers professed in "The Garden"? How seriously—even setting aside the mocking reference in "To His Coy Mistress"—can we accept the assertion?

If we indulge a little further the supposition that the person speaking to his coy mistress is the person now admiring the garden, we may say that after having failed to convince his mistress, he is now venting his pique. In any case, his ironic assessment of the conventional tributes to female beauty plainly does not come from indifference or inexperience. This complainer against women has been very likely one of the "Fond Lovers" at whose folly he now smiles.

Still, there is more to his mood in the garden than mere revulsion from an unrequited love. It springs from genuine joy. To this man Nature is not only delightful in itself but points to delights beyond itself. It hints of a peace and innocence that transcends the mortal world. The lusts of the animal soul, of the "am'rous birds of prey," are here replaced by the contemplations of the rational soul, the bird with "silver wings" that in "The Garden" prepares itself "for longer flight."

In "The Garden" the speaker's attitude thus shifts from amused reflections on the folly and self-deception of men to happy surprise and glad relief at discovering—almost accidentally?—the true abode of quiet and innocence. Then his delight moves him toward a witty and high-spirited praise of plants and trees and to mockery of the conventional claims for female beauty. With a learned mock-seriousness, he brazens out his case with proofs fabricated by a reinterpretation of two classical myths.

With stanza 5, he gives himself up to the fruits and flowers of the garden's little paradise. He compares his "wondrous Life" to that led by an as yet sinless and solitary Adam during the first hours of his existence in an Eveless Eden. A brave new world, indeed, then made its impact on the first man's unjaded senses. It was a world to be raptly explored, devoid of distraction from anything—even the distraction provided by an Eve. Nature is regarded here as a completely yielding mistress. Her fruits and flowers offer themselves to him without hesitation or reservation. The vines press their grape clusters into his mouth. The melons before his feet seem to wish to make him stumble, and the very flowers ensnare him and pull him down upon the earth.

"Stumble," "ensnare," and "fall" are loaded terms in the Christian vocabulary. The words suggest seduction to sensual pleasures and a fall from grace; and indeed, the speaker soon becomes, like Adam, a fallen man. But Nature's embrace is innocent. There are no broken vows, jealousies, or aftermaths of remorse. (In stanza 8 the poet will develop this hint of the Eden story into an explicit reference.)

Yet, though Marvell has deliberately invoked sexual overtones in describing the reception that Nature affords this grateful recipient of its peace, he never relaxes his grasp upon common sense and reality. The man in the garden has given himself up wholly to the garden's cool shade because it offers a blessed respite from the burden and heat of a day within a too-busy life. But we may be sure that he will not try to overstay his hour or so of bliss. The poem is no manifesto for primitivism. The man whose experience it describes has not resolved to live for the rest of his life in solitude as a hermit in some wilderness. He does not even suggest an anticipation of Wordsworth.

The conception of nature implied in "The Garden" seems to me thoroughly orthodox. Nature is innocent. In this poem it is not Plato's lower and grosser element on which the divine forms can only imperfectly make their imprint. It is certainly not the Manichaean's actively evil force at war with good. The natural world has been created good by a good Creator. It has not brought about man's fall. Man has only himself to blame for that. Having in mind the possible influence of his Puritanism on his poetry, we can say that on this particular issue Marvell is as orthodox as that other great Puritan, his friend, the John Milton of *Paradise Lost*. Neither holds nature in contempt.

Marvell does indeed regard the felicities that nature offers as lower than those available to the soul. A number of his poems confirm this, among them "A Dialogue between the Resolved Soul, and Created Pleasure," "On a Drop of Dew," "Clorinda and Damon," "Thyrsis and Dorinda," and "A Dialogue between the Soul and Body." Yet one notices that in this last-named poem the poet allows the body to make a good case for itself, even allows the body the final word—and what a telling word it is. The body argues that it is not the body that corrupts the soul, but the soul the body:

> What but a Soul could have the wit
> To build me up for Sin so fit.
> So Architects do square and hew
> Green Trees that in the Forest grew.

The body, like the trees praised in "The Garden" for their "lovely green," would, if left to itself, fulfill its own possibilities instinctively and innocently. It is the "Tyrannic Soul" that frustrates and tortures it.

One learns to respect the solid intellectual and theological base that undergirds such poems. That the poems are so based has much to do with their structural coherence and furnishes the grounding for the pointed applications of Marvell's serious wit. One might observe that even "To His Coy Mistress" can be fitted to this same theological base. For if one puts the highest valuation on the pleasures of the body, then one had indeed better seize the day and enjoy those pleasures now. They perish with the perishing of the body. One would be foolish to expect them in an afterlife, for the Scriptures are very specific on this point: in the Christian heaven there is no more marriage or giving in marriage. If one does not believe in an afterlife or, even if he does, sets highest value on the fulfillment of bodily desires, then the argument made to the coy mistress is sound.

The best evidence that the speaker of "The Garden" regards the pleasures of nature as in themselves innocent is to be found in stanza 6, where the body's delight in nature does not distract the rational soul from its higher pleasure. Indeed, it is when the body is appeased and innocently happy that the mind can "[Withdraw] into its happiness" (stanza 6). This pleasure peculiar to the rational soul points toward a transcendence that is fully developed in the final stanzas of the poem. The garden's quiet joys allow the contemplative man to become for a moment a disembodied soul and to gain some sense of what the joyful freedom of pure spirit is.

Yet how carefully Marvell manages the tone. Instead of the high spirits and hyperbole of some of the earlier stanzas or the ironic teasing in others, in stanza 7 he is precise, restrained, careful not to overstate. The Soul, like an uncaged bird, flies only a little way from the body—goes no further than a nearby bough, where "it sits, and sings, / Then Whets, and combs its silver Wings." The image is beautifully apt: it catches the soul's timidity at being outside its familiar habitation, the joy that makes it sing, and its almost childlike pleasure in the discovery that it has silver wings, wings now preened in a sort of innocent vanity.

Stanza 7 provides a nice example of Marvell's classic restraint. Even at this high point of the experience, the metaphor used makes very moderate claims. The soul is allowed no more than a glimpse of its future bliss. It dares not presume on its spiritual powers. The poet is even very practical in justifying its actions in spreading its wings. Now is the time to prepare for the "longer flight" that some day, permanently separated from the body, it must take. When Marvell is thoroughly serious, his assertions are invariably moderate and credible.

The next stanza (8) resumes the banter we have heard earlier. In stanza 6 the speaker has perversely inverted the classic myths of Apollo's pursuit of Daphne and Pan's pursuit of Syrinx; now in stanza 8 he turns upside down the Biblical account of Eve's creation. God gave Eve to Adam not because he needed a suitable helpmeet, but because God thought his delicious solitude entirely too good for a mere mortal to enjoy (as if Marvell were unaware that Adam became mortal only *after* the creation of Eve and the breaking of God's express command, the act that brought death into the world and all our woe). But Marvell is quite cheerful in his irreverence. He can hardly be trying to delude his readers, saturated as they were in the Scriptures. His case for the delights of solitude is transparently specious.

In the next and final stanza of the poem, however, classic moderation again asserts itself. If he is playful in proposing that " 'twas beyond a Mortal's share" to live alone in the earthly paradise, he is very properly serious in implying, as the poem closes, that it is indeed beyond any mortal's share to live continually in the full light of eternity. If one could do that, he would have ceased to be mortal.

Our meditator on the garden's delights has by now clearly reentered the world of time. How do we know this? From, among other things, the reference to the sundial in the final stanza. The numerals of this dial consist of artfully shaped beds of flowers. Such a chonometer is, of course, thoroughly appropriate to the garden. Nevertheless, it is a timepiece, and it reminds us that time has never stopped its motion even during an experience which has seeemed a blessed respite from it.

The "industrious" bee, it is claimed, consults the clock for the time of day, and the sun duly moves through his twelve signs ("fragrant Zodiak") of the dial just as he moves through the heavenly zodiac in the course that makes up the year. Thus, the fact of time—winged chariot or no—is acknowledged. Mortal man escapes time only in brief blessed intervals, and even those escapes are finally illusory except as they possibly point to some future state. But to the contemplative man depicted in "The Garden," time is not terrifying, for *his* time does not eventually lose itself in vast deserts of eternity. For him there waits beyond time an eternity in a realm of joy that no earthly garden can do more than suggest.

III

"To His Coy Mistress" and "The Garden" are remarkable poems, but it is not remarkable that one and the same poet could write them. They reflect, to be sure, differing views of time and eternity, but they have much in common in the ideas they touch upon. In any case, they are not declarations of faith but presentations of two differing world-views, dramatizations made by a poet who, though suffused with the Christian sense of mortality and the ethic it implies, also knew his classics well and had evidently read them with sympathy.

Like a great many men of his age, Marvell was concerned to incorporate into the Christian scheme as much as possible of classical wisdom. When he chose, he could also treat with understanding and dramatic sympathy the great classical literary forms, not only as frames of reference, but as representing time-honored classical attitudes toward life and death. He makes such a presentation in "To His Coy Mistress." But as I have suggested earlier, even this pagan-classical poem bears more than a trace of Christian and even Puritan feeling, particularly in the references to death. Marvell had never lived in that happy pagan time when, as Théophile Gautier conceived it, the skeleton was unseen. Like John Webster, even in a love poem Marvell "saw the skull beneath the skin." The Christian alloy hardens the classical metal with a touch of medieval horror. It adds force to the poem's argument and gives it a sharper edge.

On the evidence of the two poems we have been comparing, Marvell was not a man who was unable to make up his mind or a waverer between commitments or a trimmer. The poems tell quite another story: they reveal a fair-mindedness, an awareness of alternatives, a sensitivity to the complexity of issues. Marvell's mind is a mind of the late Renaissance at its best. He is learned, thoroughly at home with the earlier literature of the West. He is familiar with classical philosophy as well as Christian theology. He regards both as constituting a valuable inheritance. His aim is to assimilate their lore and to develop, as far as is possible, a synthesis that will take the whole of human experience—animal and rational, active and contemplative, playful and sober, hawk and singing bird—into account.

KENNETH GROSS

"Pardon Me, Mighty Poet": Versions of the Bard in Marvell's "On Mr. Milton's Paradise Lost"

*If one wants to have a friend one must also want to wage war
for him: and to wage war, one must be capable of being an enemy.
In a friend one should still honor the enemy. Can you go
close to your friend without going over to him?
In a friend one should have one's best enemy. You should be
closest to him with your heart when you resist him.*
—NIETZSCHE

*In the prison of his days
Teach the free man how to praise.*
—AUDEN

Andrew Marvell's dedicatory verses to the second edition of *Paradise Lost* (1675) stage an encounter between two poets and two friends: the one a Puritan revolutionary, author of iconoclastic, Ciceronian prose tracts, two biblical epics, and a hybrid tragedy; the other a canny liberal member of Parliament, a defender of religious toleration, a brilliant satirist, a strange and serious lyrist. Responding to the "evil days" and "evil tongues" of the Restoration, the poem's first aim is public: it defends the career of a man condemned for his politics and religion, accused of sacrilege in his writings, and even mocked for his blindness, which his enemies insisted was a punishment from God for his service to the regicides. As a study in the rhetoric of reputation, the verses speak very much to their historical moment and complement Marvell's quite different

From *Milton Studies* 16 (1982). © 1982 by the University of Pittsburgh Press.

vindication of Milton in the second part of *The Rehearsal Transpros'd* (1673).
But for all the richness of their topical allusions, Marvell's lines map out a truly
inward critique of the epic and may introduce the reader of *Paradise Lost* to
a subtler knowledge of its complexities than is evident on a first reading. For
in questioning, praising, and defending his author, Marvell continually adapts
dramatic stances, metaphors, key words (not to mention the larger systems of
value which these imply), many of which derive from that author's major poetry.
One might say that Marvell examines and cross-examines Milton by speaking
to him in his own voice, paints him in his own colors, disguises and reveals him
with his own masks. This he does with great sympathy and respect; yet at the
same time he is always striving to put his subject in perspective and to maintain the integrity of his own poetic mode, if only because it is his individual
liberty of vision, rather than his skill at imitation, that is the truest measure
of his admiration. The poem may in fact be read as a quiet agon between
Marvell's desire to offer knowing praise to the poet who awes him, and his equal
desire for freedom, self-definition, and self-esteem. To commend and echo
Milton as he does, and yet keep imaginative space open for himself, is a task
which requires all of Marvell's resources of humor and faith.

Marvell unfolds his initial thoughts on *Paradise Lost* in the dramatic and
visionary scene of reading which occupies the first two verse paragraphs. Quite
simply, he fears the poet and his poem. And although he utters his fears in a
tentative, hypothetical manner, he undoubtedly means us to recall many of the
particular criticisms leveled at Milton by contemporaries like Richard Leigh,
who attacked Milton's obscurity of diction and his willful distortions of
religious truth, or Samuel Parker, who in *A Reproof to* The Rehearsal
Transpros'd revived the old claims about Milton's blindness. These and other
slurs have been discussed in an important article on Marvell's poem by Joseph
Anthony Wittreich, Jr. [published in *Approaches to Marvell,* edited by C. A.
Patrides]; but while they provide us with a useful historical analogue, the fact
is that none of the writers Wittreich cites ever reimagines his own anxieties in
so broad, balanced, and shrewdly dialectical a fashion as Marvell. Nor do they
show anything like his insight into the moral and imaginative challenge which
the epic thrusts upon its readers. I therefore want to risk abstracting the argument of the first sixteen lines of the verses, as much as possible in their own
terms, after which I can comment in more detail on the matter of Marvell's debt
to the poetics of Milton:

> When I beheld the Poet blind, yet bold,
> In slender Book, his vast Design unfold,
> *Messiah* Crown'd, *Gods* Reconcil'd Decree,

Rebelling *Angels,* the Forbidden Tree,
Heav'n, Hell, Earth, Chaos, All; the Argument
Held me a while, misdoubting his Intent,
That he would ruine (for I saw him strong)
The sacred Truths to Fable and old Song,
(So *Sampson* groap'd the Temples Posts in spight)
The World o'rewhelming to revenge his Sight.
   Yet as I read, soon growing less severe,
I lik'd his Project, the success did fear;
Through that wide Field how he his way should find
O're which lame Faith leads Understanding blind;
Lest he perplext the things he would explain,
And what was easie he should render vain.

Here Marvell tries to distinguish two "technical" problems facing the author of a biblical epic, and thus two ways of violating the sacred materials adapted in such a poem. First, although Milton is able to encompass with such grand eloquence and epic style all that the Bible presents in a difficult array of books, parables, histories, and prophecies—sometimes lucid, sometimes gnomic—is it not possible that such literary enrichment, such poetic rather than religious power, might trivialize or gloss over the austere text of Scripture, so much more sublime than any romance? By the sheer mastery of its fiction, might not Milton's poem suggest that the Bible's literal history is merely moral fable, or even worse, matter only for secular "old Song"? Milton's epic architecture, his competitive strength of poetic design, might then "ruine" rather than "justify" the revelation which ought to sustain it (as if his were a prophetic voice which, in the words of Jeremiah 1:10, could only "pluck up and break down" and not "build and plant" as well).

A second, contrasting difficulty is set forth in the next verse paragraph. If *Paradise Lost* avoids reducing Scripture either to entertainment or allegory, it might go to the other extreme by superadding complications to those truths which Scripture presents with great simplicity. As a result, Milton might not only confuse the understanding of his readers, but block the message of those "simple" dicta, proverbs, and eloquent structures of parable which allow shaky human faith to survive. By moving so easily through the field of Scripture, by so effortlessly compassing its theological complexities, Milton might overawe the already uneasy mutuality of "lame Faith" and "understanding blind" by which man seeks a path to his God. Marvell apparently fears that Milton's ponderous learning and strong imagination might enchain even a faithful reader's liberty to confront Scripture in its own terms, to believe according to the dictates of his own conscience—a freedom for which both men had long fought.

Marvell's defense *of* Milton begins, then, as a defense *against* Milton. The poet of *Paradise Lost* is ultimately absolved of both crimes suggested above. But the opening lines remind us that in that time of tense religious controversy, when even prophecy was seen as predominantly a matter of inspired interpretation (not God's voice, but its written echo), the crucial test of such a work was not simply the integrity of the poet's imaginative myth, but its relation to the authority and influence of the revealed Word. Marvell's *The Rehearsal Transpros'd* (part 1, 1671; part 2, 1673) employs exactly the criteria of reverence and violation that are implicit in the first verse paragraph to prove the writings of Archdeacon Parker as vile as those of Milton are praiseworthy:

> I thought his profanation of the Scripture intolerable; For though he alledges that 'tis only in order to shew how it was misapplyed by the Fanaticks, he might have done that too, and yet preserved the Dignity and Reverence of those Sacred Writings, which he hath not done; but on the contrary, he hath in what is properly his own, taken the most of all his Ornaments, and Imbellishments thence in a scurrilous and sacrilegious stile. . . . Methought I never saw a more bold and wicked attempt than that of reducing *Grace,* and making it meer *Fable,* of which he gives us *the Moral.*

Milton, by contrast, treats of divine things "in such state / as them preserves, and Thee, inviolate." In fact, the poet's chaste treatment of Scripture eventually raises in Marvell a further concern about the reverence which others, Marvell included, must rightfully accord to *Paradise Lost.* Marvell's uncertainty regarding the fitness of his own evaluation and praise is again paralleled by comments at the very end of *The Rehearsal Transpros'd,* part 1: "And now I have done," he says, feeling a need for some sort of self-absolution, "And shall think myself largely recompensed for this trouble, if any one that hath been formerly of another mind, shall learn by this Example, that it is not impossible to be merry and angry as long time as I have been writing, without profaning and violating those things which are and ought to be most sacred."

In his concern over the possible violation of both his own and others' virtue and integrity, Marvell recalls certain figures from his lyric poetry—the retiring, tree-loving speaker of "The Garden," the inward-turning, fragile, yet religious soul in "On a Drop of Dew," and perhaps even the erotically wounded "Nymph Complaining," who mourns for and yet transfigures her slain faun. The opening of the poem on *Paradise Lost* curiously mirrors the first stanza of "Upon Appleton House," with its picture of the devastating work of the

"Forrain Architect," "Who of his great Design in pain / Did for a Model vault his Brain"; its depiction of Milton also recalls the antipastoral violence of Cromwell in "An Horatian Ode."

Without tracing any of these likenesses in detail, one can still see a quite characteristic Marvellian drama being set up in the opening of the poem on *Paradise Lost*. But one of the devices which gives Marvell's anxieties such a surprising and powerful shape is the Miltonic ventriloquism that emerges here and works more or less throughout the piece. Most of the poem's critics have noted something of this; Rosalie Colie, for instance, observes that in the first ten lines "Marvell pays Milton the tribute of approximating his 'Number, Weight and Measure,' and in the poem as a whole the greater compliment of not daring to dispense with his own support, the rhymes." She is referring primarily to Marvell's rather fine use of long, enjambed sentences and a periodic, Virgilian syntax, but the influence of *Paradise Lost* goes far beyond matters of style. In fact, despite their tone of reticence and respect, the verses become a testing ground for some of the most radical metaphors and religious claims of Milton's poetry.

For example, the very drama of amazement in the opening lines seems to reflect Milton's interest in the dilemmas of the witness, in the moral imperative of beholding all phases of spiritual good and evil. Compare to Marvell's "When I beheld" the following passage from the close of book 1 of *Paradise Lost:*

> Behold a wonder! they but now who seemd
> In bigness to surpass Earths Giant-Sons
> Now less than smallest Dwarfs, in narrow room
> Throng numberless, like that Pigmean Race
> Beyond the *Indian* Mount; or Faerie Elves,
> Whose midnight Revels, by a Forrest side
> Or Fountain, some belated Peasant sees,
> Or dreams he sees, while over head the Moon
> Sits Arbitress, and nearer to the Earth
> Wheels her pale course: they on thir mirth and dance
> Intent, with jocond Music charm his ear;
> At once with joy and fear his heart rebounds.
>
> (ll. 777–88)

Marvell, another belated watcher, likewise witnesses a vision of tremendous spiritual and phenomenological ambiguity, a vision which tests his powers of recognition, resistance, and choice, suspending him in doubt about both his object and himself. In the lines from *Paradise Lost,* the Virgilian *mirabile dictu,* with its self-reflexive indication of the poet's own rhetorical difficulties, gives way to the more urgent optative of "Behold a wonder!" Milton actually posits two witnesses, an earthly and a celestial one, and juxtaposes the ambiguous motions of the devils in Pandemonium with those of more benign, Shakespearean daimons. For both the reader and the peasant there is no single, fully adequate perspective for judgment; the impression shifts, quite as it does in Marvell's poem, among surprise, fear, sedate wonder, and even a sense of the ridiculous. Marvell's attention to the contrast between the "slender book" and its "vast Design" does recall the paradoxes of scale so lovingly described in lyrics like "A Drop of Dew" and "Upon Appleton House." But in the poem on *Paradise Lost,* as in the lines quoted above from book 1, references to such curious perspectives and ambiguities of dimension convey a more pressing sense of imaginative danger, the moral threat of chaos and enchantment.

The religious burden placed on such a witness is difficult to define. It entails a self-consciousness rather different from that involved in the schematic, highly visual, and often dramatic strategies of formal meditation which, as Louis Martz has shown [in *The Poetry of Meditation*], so appealed to the metaphysical poets. For Marvell is not struggling to recall or visualize a critical scriptural topos (indeed, his eye can hardly fix itself within the flux of "places") and so question, cure, or humble his conscience. On the other hand, there is something more than a feeling of sheer, untrammeled awe. The stance of the witness is more likely derived from prophetic and apocalyptic literature, where the alienated reader and speaker are set to watch the conflict between the false visions of history and the true, providential design of God. Book 1 of *Paradise Lost* again provides an example, a severe one, in the lines which foretell the earthly career of the demon Thammuz as the god of a mystery cult that will seduce the "daughters of *Sion,*"

> Whose wanton passions in the sacred Porch
> *Ezekiel* saw, when by the Vision led
> His eye survayd the dark Idolatries
> Of alienated *Judah.*

> (ll. 454–57)

Marvell, too, stations himself at the threshold of what should be a sacred house, not knowing whether he beholds true religion or abomination. He lacks the inspired certainty of truth and falsehood which he later seems to gain, and for the moment we remain unsure as to who is idolater and who is prophet. In the text to which Milton alludes (Ezek. 8:3–15), the prophet stands at a gate of the Temple "where was the seat of the image of jealousy," a pagan idol whose name yet ironically points to the jealousy of the One God and of the seer who defends him. It is a feeling which Marvell will show only in the third verse paragraph, when he grows jealous of those who would violate a poem which he begins to recognize as sacred.

There is no question that Marvell might have adapted the prophetic or apocalyptic stances which I have noted from sources other than Milton, that is, from the Bible and contemporary religious writing. Yet such stances have little place in Marvell's other poetic work and on the whole seem rather alien to his own more introverted, hermetic mode. This circumstance, as well as the poem's very curious way of setting the prophetic elements in perspective, suggests that, whatever their ultimate source, Marvell's use of them in the poem was formally and thematically controlled by this particular encounter with Milton's work.

As I have suggested, the important point is that Marvell first sees the blind poet and his work through one of that poet's own dramatic models of ambivalent or alienated vision. Though primarily a figure for the relation of the reader Marvell to the writer Milton, the fact that Marvell himself is writing about another poet's reading of the Bible puts all easy distinctions between writing and reading into question. The very opening line of the poem, in fact, suggests a visionary symbiosis between Marvell and Milton by means of the alliteration which links Marvell's "I beheld" to the adjectives "blind" and "bold," which describe the object of the beholding. Still, we must see that Marvell does not allow his perspectivizing imitation of his subject to collapse into blind identification; nor does he turn into an unwitting idolater under the mask of a critic. Marvell is not simply aping a Miltonic form of encounter; rather, he shrewdly reshapes the details of that poem whose unfolding he witnesses. His list of the epic's main topics, for instance—"*Messiah* Crown'd, *Gods* Reconcil'd Decree, / Rebelling *Angels,* the Forbidden Tree, / Heav'n, Hell, Earth, Chaos, All; the Argument"—pointedly alters their real sequence, both as they are summarized in the invocation to book 1, which runs from "Man's first disobedience" to the recovery of "one Greater Man," the Messiah, and as they occur in the epic as a whole, which opens with the fallen legions of Satan. Marvell's lines tend to suppress the connections between the various events, realms, and persons of the poem. He traces a descending path from the Messiah to the forbidden tree (leaving out all mention of "Man," which holds together Milton's opening lines), moves from Heaven to Hell, back to earth, then to Chaos, as if undoing the entire sequence of creation. "Chaos," the penultimate item in the list, seems a not unironic glance backward over the whole work just surveyed. And it is difficult to determine whether Marvell's "All" refers to the actual universe or to the book which aspires to contain it.

"All" is one of Milton's favorite words, as William Empson pointed out some time ago, and Marvell manages to give it much of the resonance it possesses in *Paradise Lost.* As Empson tells us [in *The Structure of Complex Words*], the word "seems to be suited to the all-or-none man. All else is unimportant beside one thing, he is continually deciding. . . . The generosity of the proud man also requires the word; when he gives, he gives all. It is as suited to absolute love and self-sacrifice as to insane self-assertion. The self-centered man, in his turn, is not much interested in the variety of the world, and readily lumps it all together as 'all.' " Milton is blind, yet boldly claims to see all the truth there is to see. The problem is that in Marvell any discrete design or argument dissolves into the equally confusing alternatives of "All" or "Chaos." The hurried survey of the epic suggests not plenitude or generosity, but a world in ruins; Milton's poem becomes a false apocalypse, not a revelation of a new world, but simply the overwhelming of the old by the poet's own catastrophic phantasmagoria.

The undoing of creation is a design of Satan's, yet rather than explicitly compare the poet's work to that of his archvillain, Marvell choses another, equally problematic destroyer:

> That he would ruine (for I saw him strong)
> The sacred Truths to Fable and old Song,
> (So *Sampson* groap'd the Temples Posts in spight)
> The World o'rewhelming to revenge his Sight.

Samson Agonistes had appeared five years before these lines, and the analogy which Marvell suggests here may not have been terribly surprising. What is astonishing is the picture of Samson's act as willfully destructive, rather than redemptive. The scandal or stumbling-block for most readers of the dedicatory poem is that while Milton's tragedy suggests that the hero's pulling down of the Philistine temple represents "a good purgation of hatred" and "a regained public consciousness of covenantal power and destiny," Marvell attaches to the act a purely selfish motive [William Kerrigan in *The Prophetic Milton* and Sanford Budick in *The Poetry of Civilization*]. In the article already mentioned, Wittreich even goes so far as to suggest that the Samson/Milton analogy must be read as a palpably ironic relation and that the lines point to a strong contrast between the self-slain Samson and the providentially preserved poet. Wittreich quite justly takes to task those critics who have willfully misconstrued the plain meaning of "spight" in order to give the text a gentler, more orthodox sense. Yet it seems to me no less plain that Marvell is asserting a real likeness between the two men of power. The syntax of the couplet actually helps to confuse the two, for while Marvell's reference to Samson is, strictly speaking, confined to a one-line parenthesis, the clause which describes him seems continuous with the line following (as might be expected in the case of a couplet), so that the possessive pronoun in the phrase "his Sight" may refer to Samson or to Milton.

I had at one point thought that this ambiguous allusion might begin to make poetic sense if we were to assume that Marvell is speaking through a persona. His error, if it is that, would then be quite consistent with the poet's intention to represent his experience of *Paradise Lost* in its earliest, most uncertain stages. Such a misprision of Samson's motivations—not unlike that of Manoa or the chorus in the play itself—would show that Marvell's speaker has his own blindness to overcome. He is tested by the very Miltonic masks which he is himself testing. While he sees an authentic analogy between Milton and Samson, he has not yet comprehended the full dialectic by which self-destruction can become, if not creation, then heroic and divine self-fulfillment.

Such an interpretation may still prove serviceable, but it requires at least two qualifications. First, as I shall argue below, even in the later portions of the poem Marvell evades any confrontation with the difficult moral and redemptive ironies of the tragedy. He wants somehow to supersede the prior images of ruin, rather than directly to reject or reinstate them; the chaotic opening vision is never truly opposed or displaced (though it is an open question whether Marvell deceives himself that it has been). Second, it is important to see that in misrepresenting Milton's play, Marvell has at the same time more accurately represented the starker picture of Samson in Milton's biblical source: "And Samson called unto the Lord, and said, O Lord God, remember me, I pray thee, and strengthen me . . . that I may be at once avenged of the Philistines for my two eyes" (Judg. 16:28). It is not simply a question of Marvell's exposing Milton's misappropriation of this text, for Marvell's reductive return to such fundamental violence also serves as the basis for his own surprising extension of the original narrative. In the context of a poem defending the integrity of sacred Scripture, Marvell's reference to "the Temple" suggests that Samson tore down a Hebrew, rather than a Philistine, place of worship, just as the following line suggests that this act of violence encompasses not one enemy race, but the entire world.

In lines 11–16, Marvell's fear of a chaos wrought by a sacrilegious poetic strength yields to the contrasting suspicion that the theologian in Milton is erecting a labyrinth, a temple that is overbuilt and overcomplicated. Instead of trivializing Scripture, the blind poet may overwhelm his readers' "Understanding blind" (Marvell's repetition of "blind" here forcing us to wonder whether the literally sightless Milton shares the metaphorical affliction as well and, in general, to consider how the tropes of seeing relate to sight's realities). The problems created by Milton's intellectual obscurity are real, but as if to demonstrate the poetic uses of learning, Marvell goes on to attempt a very

Miltonic sort of Latinate punning. Line 15, "Lest he perplext the things he would explain," which states the speaker's fear most succinctly, deploys the opposed words "perplext" and "explain" so that their etymological meanings ("tangle together" and "smooth out") reinforce the figurative representation of thought and faith in terms of travel and topography, as in Milton's "on th'*Aleian* Field I fall, / *Erroneous* there to wander and forlorne" (*Paradise Lost,* 7.19–20; emphasis mine).

Lines 17–22 shift from anxious hypothesis to prophetic satire

> Or, if a Work so infinite he spann'd
> Jealous I was that some less skilful hand
> (Such as disquiet alwayes what is well,
> And by ill imitating would excell)
> Might hence presume the whole Creations day
> To change in Scenes, and show it in a Play.

Such a decreation of the Creation would at least be certain of obeying the unity of time. Marvell is presumably mocking John Dryden's project for making a rhymed "opera" of *Paradise Lost* (*The State of Innocence and the Fall of Man*), although the lines may also allude to Davenant's praise of epic drama in the "Preface to *Gondibert.*" Of more immediate interest, however, is that Marvell's attack on what seems to him literary parasitism continues to employ terms of evaluation uncannily like those in Milton. Taken in isolation, the lines about writers "Such as disquiet alwayes what is well, / And by ill imitating would excell," refer as aptly to the political program of Satan, his aim being "out of good still to find means of evil" (1. 165). No form of the verb "to imitate" occurs anywhere else in Marvell's poetry, and although it may recall classical notions of literary mimesis or *imitatio,* equally important is the fact that Milton always applies the word to forms of demonic mimicry. There are a number of examples of this in *Paradise Lost,* (2.270, 511; 5. 111), but Marvell's phrasing recalls more precisely Christ's rebuke to Satan in *Paradise Regained:*

> Our Hebrew Songs and Harps in *Babylon,*
> That pleas'd so well our Victors ear, declare
> That rather *Greece* from us these Arts deriv'd;
> *Ill imitated,* while they loudest sing
> The vices of thir Deities, and thir own
> In Fable, Hymn, or Song, so personating
> Thir Gods ridiculous, and themselves past shame.
>   (4.336–42; emphasis mine)

By an allusive stroke worthy of William Blake, Marvell aligns Dryden's presumptuous, neoclassical dramaturgy with the temptations of a debased Hellenism
which Satan offers the Son. Without anticipating too much, it would also be
useful to compare Marvell's later scorn of false and alluring rhyme (lines 45–50)
to the verses in *Paradise Regained* which immediately follow those quoted
above:

> Remove thir swelling Epithetes thick laid
> As varnish on a Harlots cheek, the rest,
> Thin sown with aught of profit or delight,
> Will farr be found unworthy to compare
> With *Sions* songs, to all true tasts excelling,
> Where God is prais'd aright, and Godlike men,
> The Holiest of Holies, and his Saints.
>
> (ll. 343–49)

Marvell's poem, though it imitates Milton, also seeks to praise aright that
God-like man. Still, he does not directly address the epic poet until the beginning of the fourth verse paragraph, just about the midpoint of the poem: "Pardon me, *mighty Poet,* nor despise / My causeless, yet not impious, surmise."
This sudden recognition of the poet as a presence of authority and regard is
the major turn of the poem. It is also the moment when Marvell remembers
and comments upon his own words, for he specifically asks the poet to pardon
his "surmise," that is, the satirical prediction of his previous verse paragraph.
The force of the turn is that Marvell has suddenly been enabled to set aside
the religious anxieties which had so distanced him from Milton in the earlier
verses, and can speak to him with such confidence. Marvell later returns to the
question of Milton's reverence for Scripture and vindicates the poet of sacrilege.
But his conviction is not won through any reasoned demonstration within the
poem itself; in fact, his later words of praise tend to beg the questions he had
before so urgently posed to himself and Milton. Marvell's vindication of Milton
seems to depend on a more hidden moment of recognition, one in which he
realizes the power of his own "surmise." For his apology to Milton makes it suddenly clear both to reader and speaker that in the act of imagining other writers'
"ill imitating," the earlier anxieties about Milton's relation to Scripture have
been turned around and directed toward Milton's text itself. That is to say, the
poem has begun to regard *Paradise Lost* as a scriptural or sacred work in its
own right—at least insofar as such a work can be defined by the claims it makes
on its readers and interpreters. Milton's poem turns out to be equally susceptible to violation by sacrilegious writers, so much so that even the author who
defends it must guard against seeming "impious."

The poet's crucial coincidence with his subject on the question of a surmise may owe something to a similar turn in Milton's "Lycidas." There too, the speaker emerges from the uncertainties of grief at the point where he begins to think about both the consolations and the limitations of his fictions about another poet: "For so to interpose a little ease, / Let our frail thoughts dally with false surmise." Even Marvell's way of entering into his causeless, satirical, if not completely false surmise shows something of Miltonic character. The third verse paragraph ("Or if a Work so infinite he spann'd") opens with that very subtle "or" which, as Leslie Brisman has argued in detail [in *Milton's Poetry of Choice*], so characterizes Milton's poetry. Rather than merely contrast two different terms, this conjunction sets up an urgent moment of choice between certain real or fictive alternatives, the matter of selection and rejection becoming a continual part of the process of self-denial, self-revision, and self-election by which the poet orients himself toward a higher vision. Likewise, Marvell's sudden access to a stance of unqualified regard emerges from the negative act of rejecting his surmise, rather than from any more rational process of argument. The turn is quite literally a conversion, a leap out of the flux of literary and religious opinion into the certainty of faith.

To map such discontinuities in the progress or argument of a poem is difficult without recourse to some falsifying, genetic logic. What can be said, however, is that the second half of the poem must be judged for its renewed rhetorical assurance, rather than as a direct, reasonable answer to the questions raised in the first half. The paradox of this section is that while Milton's poetry has now begun to be accepted at its authentic value, the presence and pressure of the Miltonic *voice* are considerably lessened. One is more conscious of Marvellian urbanity keeping oratory in control. The anxious, unstable stances of the opening, the images of disorder, perplexity, and discontinuity—all of these disappear, and while Milton's poetry is still figured through images of power and sublimity, these are generally subdued, even domesticated. Lines 25–30, for instance, praise Milton's vast design for its exacting fitness and plenitude, rather than as a chaotic flood of vision:

> But now I am convinc'd, and none will dare
> Within thy Labours to pretend a Share.
> Thou hast not miss'd one thought that could be fit,
> And all that was improper dost omit:
> So that no room is here for Writers left,
> But to detect their Ignorance or Theft.

Lines 29 and 30 are in some ways the most astonishing of the poem. They can be read as an uncanny prediction of the anxiety felt by many eighteenth- and nineteenth-century poets that any attempt at writing a sublime poem after Milton could find a place within the imaginative space he had usurped only if it could violate, in retrospect, or willfully forget the greater poet's priority. The historical fulfillment of this prophecy (studied in different ways by Walter Jackson Bate and Harold Bloom) is not within the scope of this essay. But Marvell's own relation to his pronouncement is, and what militates against any simplistic acceptance of his hyperboles is that Marvell himself has all along pretended a share in the labors of his poet. This local irony points to a broader problem in the poem. One might justify Marvell's half-truth by saying that his bold theft of some of *Paradise Lost*'s ample store of tropes aims only at achieving a subtler critical perspective. Yet no such chrestomathy of echoes and imitations as this poem can really escape some subversion of its source, and it only enlarges the dialectical ironies of the poem to say that Marvell also subverts his own idealizings of that source.

Our awareness of this carefully balanced undermining of the praiser and the praised must qualify, although it does not in any way disqualify, the further hyperboles of the next four lines. These, in their subtly opposed images of sacred and secular power, claim for Milton both the integrity and the inviolability which had previously seemed so uncertain:

> That Majesty which through thy Work doth Reign
> Draws the Devout, deterring the Profane;
> And things divine thou treatst of in such state
> As them preserves, and Thee, inviolate.

Marvell's use of "Majesty" may seem a rather good joke, Christopher Hill remarks, coming as it does in verses dedicated to a former servant of the regicides. But Marvell is not only joking here. His deeper point is that, even with the Restoration, true kingship could not be realized as a political fact, but only as an internalized poetic preeminence, as if majesty survived the Puritan revolution only within the realm of trope. As Hill himself goes on to say, such majesty ensures rather than challenges the inviolability of "things divine," since it represents the majesty of God, to whom the poet dedicates his career. The poet, too, remains inviolate, set apart from danger like those Marvellian figures mentioned above, although the lines from the commendatory verses do not fully convey Milton's acute awareness of both prophetic election and Orphic vulnerability.

Lines 35 and 36 continue to revise the speaker's initial impressions of Milton, substituting for his violent shifts between fascination and fear the assertion that "At once delight and horrour on us seize, / Thou singst with so much gravity and ease" (although this still recalls the ambivalences of the belated watcher in book 1: "At once with joy and fear his heart rebounds"). The chiastic arrangement of the four nouns in this couplet has the surprising effect of letting delight parallel gravity, horror ease. Painful and gentle feelings thus not only relieve but transform each other, so that the idea of poetic "ease" no longer resembles the innocent "easie" of line 16 or that playful, meditative easiness one finds in "Upon Appleton House." Instead, Marvell evokes something closer to the intense, visionary condition which Milton describes when he calls on his "Celestial Patroness,"

> who deignes
> Her nightly visitation unimplor'd
> And dictates to me slumbring, or inspires
> *Easie,* my unpremeditated Verse.
> *(Paradise Lost,* 9.21–24; emphasis mine)

The next couplet echoes two other invocations from *Paradise Lost,* those in books 1 and 7, particularly the images of the poet pursuing "things unattempted yet in Prose or Rhyme" (1. 16) and soaring "Above the flight of *Pegasean* wing" (7. 4) to describe the great war in Heaven. Marvell's lines, however, match their initial suggestion of transcendence with a controlled decrescendo, a leveling out of such flight: "And above humane flight dost soar aloft / With Plume so strong, so equal, and so soft." Miltonic sublimity is identified with a force more genial, sweet, and controlled than either sheer rising or destructiveness; the epithet "strong," which earlier described the temple-breaking Samson, here refers to a strength of continuity and elevation. Lines 39 and 40 take this process of subduing the Miltonic sublime even further. They compare the poet's flight not to the presumptuous ascent of Pegasus, but to that of the ever-flying but more terrestrial bird of paradise, bound to the atmosphere if not to the surface of the world. Yet lest he be accused of distortion, Marvell slyly places on Milton himself the responsibility for this not terribly sublime simile, referring to the bird as one "named from the Paradise *you* sing."

This vision of a mild, almost Spenserian Milton, a poet of earthly continuities rather than prophetic discontinuities, is not in itself entirely false, as critics like Geoffrey Hartman [in *Beyond Formalism*] have taught us. But the next verse paragraph, a scant four lines, makes a sudden leap toward a more obviously sublime conception, both more severe and less catastrophic than Marvell's opening vision. In lines 41 and 42, Marvell reassesses the confusing array of spatial tropes by which he had earlier characterized Milton's poem—worlds, skies, plains, chaos—and localizes its power within a wholly inward space: "Where couldst thou Words of such a compass find? / Whence furnish such a vast expense of Mind?" It is words which inhabit and measure the poet's world. Taking advantage of the ambiguities of seventeenth-century orthography, Marvell makes of the poet's mind both the source of that heroic outpouring, that *expense,* of intelligence and the near infinite *expanse* which that intelligence fills. This remarkable couplet may remind us that Marvell was a contemporary of Descartes. Yet, lest this suggestion of imaginative autonomy collapse into the Satanic claim that "the mind is its own place," Marvell suddenly displaces the power he describes to somewhat remoter origins and answers what might have seemed purely rhetorical questions with a sudden assertion of Milton's prophetic calling.

The comparison of Milton to the Greek seer Tiresias is worth looking at carefully, not only because it again possesses Milton's authority (see *Paradise Lost,* 3.36). but because it explicitly parallels the earlier comparison of the poet to Samson. The greater assurance of the later simile marks the distance the speaker has traveled from his fearful, ambivalent representations to glorification of Milton's mythic and poetic identity:

> (So *Sampson* groap'd the Temples Posts in spight)
> The World o'rewhelming to revenge his Sight.

> Just Heav'n thee, like *Tiresias,* to requite,
> Rewards with *Prophesie* thy loss of sight.

Milton's power is justified as God's reward, rather than as a man's revenge, the energy of his spiteful selfhood. The design of *Paradise Lost* thus coincides with the design of the revealed Word because they are equally productions of prophetic speech. To suggest, as I think Wittreich does, that Marvell is betraying the truly revolutionary nature of Milton's poetic enterprise and reconciling him with orthodox theology is not quite fair. This powerful act of evasion and elevation sets aside the specific question of doctrinal reverence. The prophetic voice granted to Milton obviates any lesser questions of his fidelity to textual authority. Marvell may be qualifying his extreme claim by comparing Milton to a classical rather than an Hebraic prophet, but he means quite precisely what he says: here is a man of divine vision. Thus Marvell's own stance has altered; he is no longer only a defender or a giver of praise. To announce another's divine powers is to become, like John the Baptist, oneself a prophet.

In the coda of this poem, secure for the moment in his sense of Milton's worth, Marvell returns with new enthusiasm to more strictly literary matters, particularly to the question of rhyme. He takes Milton's part in scorning those who, lacking any purer and more severe inspiration, take refuge in the seductive, fashionable music of tagged lines. Milton's poetic *virtù* is measured in the end by the stand he takes against rhyme, and the poem quickly drops its harsh, satirical voice for what seems to be praise even higher than that already offered:

> I, too, transported by the *Mode* offend,
> And while I meant to *Praise* thee, must Commend.
> Thy verse created like thy *Theme* sublime,
> In Number, Weight, and Measure, needs not *Rhime.*

The final verse echoes Wisdom 11:21, "Thou hast ordered all things in measure, number and weight," but Marvell's slight reshuffling of this passage subtly signals his reappropriation of the scriptural text for his peculiar poetic needs. The allusion raises Milton's achievement above prophecy by intimating that he possesses a creative power like that of the deity. This ideal is admittedly something of a commonplace for artists in the Renaissance, but the distinctive wit of Marvell's lines lies in their discovery of a divine creativity embedded in the most immediate, technical facts of prosody. Number, measure, and weight refer literally to a poem's meter as well as figuratively to its mythopoesis or power of world making (an implicit warning to any critics or theologians who, on the authority of the verses from Wisdom, would foist elaborate numerological allegories on sacred texts, rather than follow the Protestant rule that one must read them with strict attention to an integrated, literal sense). Such curious word play, at once arch and profound, is more Marvellian than Miltonic; yet these lines still point forward to the great moral and symbolic significance with which Milton will invest his choice of meter in his note on "The Verse," which directly follows Marvell's poem in the edition of 1674. Marvell's coda in fact warns the reader that Milton's stern talk about "ancient liberty" and "the troublesome and modern bondage of Riming" is of an order of seriousness far beyond the witty, paradoxical criticism of rhyme's "fetters" and "false weight" in a poem like Ben Jonson's "A Fit of Rime against Rime."

Yet Marvell cannot help but write as an ally of the unhappy party— whether God's or the Devil's—of rhyme, and he knows it well. Still drawing on key words and ironies derived from Milton's poems, his apology for his own tagged lines continues to show an archness which calls the easy self-deprecation into question. The hyperbolic "transported" in line 51 recalls God's mocking use of the word in book 3 of *Paradise Lost,* at line 81, to describe the angry but impotent Satan's excursion through Chaos—as if Marvell the rhymer would now take on himself the demonic guise he cast before on Milton and Dryden. But the irony in the poet's account of himself may not be so simple; Adam too uses the word, and with a triumphant wonder, to describe his newly discovered capacity for sexual delight: "transported I behold / Transported touch" (7. 529–30). Marvell even implies that the bondage for which he mocks himself, the need to find a rhyme for "offend," is the real reason that he can redeem his offense by rising from mere praise to the increased confidence and responsibility entailed in the act of commendation.

The final charm and marvel of the poem is, in fact, that while it allows Milton the highest possible justification for his choice of blank verse, the poet refuses to concede his own God-given right to rhyme. As tags and jingling bells, as "bushy-points" on the modish coats of poetasters, rhymes may be absurd. But they are crucial instruments for this most pointed of versifiers. The last words of the poem simultaneously declare Milton's liberty—he "needs not" match line ends—and show the necessity which holds Marvell—he "must" match "offend" to "Commend," "sublime" to "Rhime." The last rhyme, however, is neither a simple admission of fatality nor a subtle mockery of Miltonic sublimity—the poetry of rhymelessness being chained to its enemy by an unbreakable likeness of sound. The effect is rather more like a smiling, noble, liberating bow to subjectivity. Without directly challenging his ideas, Marvell implies that Milton's vatic castigation of rhyme is more private than public. The prophetic poet has set forth an antithetical law which makes imaginative sense and possesses imaginative authority within one particular poem, *Paradise Lost*, a world for which his verse was "created," as earth for man or Hell for the fallen angels. Marvell's distinction at once helps to invest Milton's choice of blank verse with greater tropological force and places the literal circumstances and conventions of Restoration rhyming effectively beyond the reach of his prosodic strictures. One might easily bring out the defensiveness which glimmers through this half-humorous gesture of self-limitation. Even if it could be said that Marvell wholeheartedly embraces his own position as a minor author facing the major Milton, the gesture still depends on Marvell's contrasting himself with a slightly distorted version of the latter, a version on the whole less effective than the darker, almost parodic vision of the poet offered in Marvell's opening lines. The main burden of the ending, however, is to allow rhyme and the sublime to stand independent of one another, each with its own proper work. This much at least the poet achieves. In the closing couplet, Marvell's elusive and allusive wit fixes a boundary to his own imaginative endeavors, but it is a boundary which allows him freedom, admiration, and something very like truth.

WARREN CHERNAIK

The Search for Form in
Marvell's Satires:
The Rehearsal Transpros'd

Marvell's historical position as a satirist is in no way comparable to his place in the history of the Renaissance lyric; rather than being an assured master building on the example of his predecessors, Marvell the satirist has an uncertain touch, and his satires represent an uneasy marriage between the metaphysical and the Augustan. Their most striking quality allies them to earlier Renaissance poetry, especially the metaphysical line in the seventeenth century: a proliferating wit, throwing off unexpected comparisons which, at times grotesquely, take on an independent life:

> He gathring fury still made sign to draw;
> But himself there clos'd in a Scabbard saw
> As narrow as his Sword's; and I, that was
> Delightful, said there can no Body pass
> Except by penetration hither, where
> Two make a crowd, nor can three Persons here
> Consist but in one substance.
>> ("Fleckno, an English Priest in Rome,"
>> ll. 95–101)

> *Excise,* a Monster worse than e're before
> Frighted the Midwife, and the Mother tore,
> A thousand Hands she has and thousand Eyes,
> Breaks into Shops, and into Cellars prys.

From *The Poet's Time: Politics and Religion in the Work of Andrew Marvell.* © 1983 by Cambridge University Press.

With hundred rows of Teeth the Shark exceeds,
And on all Trade like *Casawar* she feeds:
Chops off the piece where e're she close the Jaw,
Else swallows all down her indented maw.
She stalks all day in Streets conceal'd from sight,
And flies like Batts with leathern Wings by Night.
                              ("Last Instructions," ll. 131–40)

His shape exact, which the bright flames infold,
Like the Sun's Statue stands of burnish'd Gold.
Round the transparent Fire about him glows,
As the clear Amber on the Bee does close:
And, as on Angels Heads their Glories shine,
His burning Locks adorn his Face Divine.
But, when in his immortal Mind he felt
His alt'ring Form, and soder'd Limbs to melt;
Down on the Deck he laid himself, and dy'd,
With his dear Sword reposing by his Side.
And, on the flaming Plank, so rests his Head,
As one that's warm'd himself and gone to Bed.
                              (ll. 679–90)

What ethic river is this wondrous Tweed,
Whose one bank vertue, other vice does breed?
Or what new perpendicular does rise
Up from her stream, continued to the skies,
That between us the common air should bar
And split the influence of every star?
                              ("The Loyal Scot," ll. 85–90)

But a market, they say, does suit the king well,
Who the Parliament buys and revenues does sell,
And others to make the similitude hold
Say his Majesty himself is bought too and sold.
                              ("The Statue in Stocks-Market," ll. 21–24)

These passages differ greatly in style and tone (and of course in context), but
they share certain characteristics. They are all strings of conceits, examples of

the quickness and fertility of invention which Dryden emphasizes in his definition of wit:

> Wit in the poet, or wit writing . . . is no other than the faculty of imagination in the writer which, like a nimble spaniel, beats over and ranges through the field of memory, till it springs the quarry it hunted after; or, without metaphor, which searches over all the memory for the species or ideas of those things which it designs to represent.

It is doubtful that Dryden or any other neoclassical critic would cite these passages by Marvell to illustrate the complementary quality of judgment, "accuracy," or aptness, by which, according to neoclassical canons of taste, the fancy needs to be bounded and circumscribed; by these standards, they are typical of the "wild and lawless" nature of wit which threatens to "outrun the judgment."

In all of them, heterogeneous materials are yoked by violence together: with the exception of the last passage, which uses a popular style and homely comparisons, all employ metaphors which are learned, self-conscious, and *outré*, and the comparisons in the last example are no less incongruous and shocking, both in their violation of social decorum and in the revaluation forced on the reader. Yet on reflection, each of them turns out to be surprisingly "accurate" and appropriate to its circumstances. Each seeks "to make the similitude hold," to illuminate reality by the unexpected comparisons, showing that royalty and the marketplace have more in common than one would think, that the divisions of custom and prejudice have neither celestial nor terrestrial basis, and that a quarrel on a staircase can illustrate both the laws of physics and the doctrine of the Trinity. By metaphorical analogy, the universe is made coherent. Metaphysical wit can be defined as lies in the service of truth: rhetorical distortions, logical sleight-of-hand, argument by "Metaphors and Allegories" (which as [Samuel] Parker says, literally considered "is nothing else but to sport and trifle with empty words, because these Schems do not express the Natures of Things, but only their Similitudes and Resemblances"), which light up the contours of reality like a lightning-flash, reveal the truth hidden under the veil of custom.

Each of the passages follows a different poetic model; Marvell has not a single style, but a whole armoury of styles varying according to the individual context and the different genres in which he works. The passages quoted show the variety of approaches possible within the single broad genre of satire. The first is the manner of Donne's satires, imitating their abrupt movement, involved syntax, avoidance of end-stopped lines, and recondite imagery. In the second, the models are different and so, in consequence, are the versification, syntax, and type of imagery: here Marvell is writing mock-epic verse in closed heroic couplets, and draws on the tradition of epic and romance, with particular echoes of Spenser and Milton. The allegorical imagery is pictorial and expansive in the Spenserian manner. As with *The Faerie Queene,* the reader is simultaneously aware of the literal narrative and of the moral and historical allegory. The wit lies in the full and precise detail with which the allegory is carried out: each phrase of epic description not only calls up the image of a properly fearsome monster, but dramatizes the effects of the tax bill Marvell is attacking and, in terms of the general moral allegory, demonstrates the dangers of arbitrary power, the greed with which governments, unless they are checked, can swallow up the property of defenceless citizens. The third passage is again heroic, and again draws on Renaissance models—in this case, the Renaissance epyllion, the Ovidian mythological narrative. Here the strained imagery seeks to depict the exact moment of metamorphosis, the interpretation of the earthly and the spiritual; this is Marvell at his most baroque and fantastic, and one can cite equivalents in baroque painting and sculpture, such as Bernini. The fourth passage begins with relatively straightforward statement, in a couplet phrased with typical Augustan balance, but then proceeds to two further couplets whose imagery is more complex and learned, in the metaphysical style. There is a strong element of the grotesque in the lines, and an implicit appeal to common sense; though there is a less specific model here than in the other passages, the example of Cleveland underlies the poem, as Marvell wittily seeks to refute Cleveland's "The Rebel Scot" in more or less Clevelandesque terms. The last passage finds its models in popular poetry and its practical, down-to-earth analogies are suitable to its intended audience. It is the only one of the passages outside the tradition of learned wit and the only one which does not declare its allegiance to "European, that is to say Latin, culture," illustrating that aspect of Marvell which Eliot and, after him, such critics as Leishman, Colie, and Kermode have emphasized; the figures of Horace, Virgil, and Ovid are present behind the first three passages. In all five of the passages, abstractions are visualized, and the unexpected literalness with which the ideas are rendered into images creates a sense of shock: the soldered limbs, the split stellar influence, the stalking monster with her indented maw, the two bodies striving to occupy a single space, are of a piece with the vegetable love, the brain vaulted as a model, the soul deaf with the drumming of an ear, and the unfortunate lover braving the tempest.

The metaphysical conceit can be a unifying device when linked with a firm structure of argument. But in a succession of couplets or quatrains united only by a common origin, an assigned topic on which they can display a series of dazzling variations, the effect of freely proliferating wit is more likely to be centrifugal than centripetal. There are various strategies by which Marvell seeks to give overall form to his satires: the close following of a model, the direct refutation of an adversary by using the adversary's own words, particular attention to the decorum of occasion and genre. But none of these is sufficient in itself to hold a long poem together; they may suggest a general direction for the poem, but do not provide a principle governing the articulation and disposition of parts. The problem is compounded when, as with the court and university wits of Marvell's day, a poem is conceived as "a Tissue of Epigrams," loosely stitched together [as Joseph Addison puts it in the *Spectator*]. Leishman has shown how common it was for a poet-courtier in the seventeenth century to use an occasion as an excuse for a display of virtuosity. Such titles as "A forsaken Lady to her false Servant," "A Black patch on Lucasta's Face," "My Mistris commanding me to returne her letters," "A Flye that flew into my Mistris her eye," "Upon Master W. Mountague his returne from travell," suggest the tendency in occasional poems written within an enclosed society to become merely counters in a game, instruments of social intercourse. When a poem not only follows the general pattern of an epistle or an epigram, but in fact serves the function of a letter or a ready commentary on any situation that might arise in a courtier's life, then its form is likely to be rudimentary, unless it can draw on the aid of stanzaic pattern or structure of argument, or unless it can find a rhetorical and thematic scheme of organization suitable to a long discursive poem.

It is precisely the combination of freely flowing wit and loose, occasional structure which makes Marvell's satires often seem invertebrate. The structural difficulties here are not limited to satire as a genre, but are characteristic of all poetry with a strong topical element. The principles of organization in such poems as "Upon Appleton House" and "The First Anniversary" are no easier to discern than those in "Last Instructions" and "The Loyal Scot." Legouis has characterized "Last Instructions" and "The First Anniversary" as essentially "rimed chronicle," a series of observations tied to a chronological progression of concrete historical details. The method of "Upon Appleton House" is that of "occasional meditation," in which the imagination expatiates freely upon natural particulars. The difference between "Last Instructions" and "Upon Appleton House" is less in method than in the object of the poet's meditations: one deals primarily with the political and one with the natural world, though both show these two realms as intertwined. Yet if occasional meditation provides a general method of procedure in the two poems, a series of miscellaneous reflections chosen at random from "the infinite multitude of objects" will not in itself give a poem a coherent form. "Upon Appleton House" is more than a ramble round Fairfax's estate, with appropriate meditations on what the poet observes, and "Last Instructions" is more than a ramble through recent history. "Upon Appleton House" suggests one way of organizing a long discursive poem: its structure is essentially thematic. The poem is a meditation in time of civil war, in which the infinite variety of "Scene" gives rise repeatedly to the same questions: can one regain "*Paradice's only Map*," find a secure refuge from the destructiveness of war and the painful consciousness of loss? In his satires, Marvell seeks similarly to give thematic unity to his disparate topical materials. He also tries other devices which might impose form on the flux of events: rhetorical patterning, control of point of view, dramatization of ideas, attention to decorum of speaker, language, and situation, the creation of fictional personae and plots. If Marvell is less successful in finding an appropriate form for his satires than his near-contemporaries Rochester and Dryden or the major satirists of the next century, the fault in part lies in his reliance on the occasional method and the conceit, characteristic devices of an earlier age. Though his experiments as a satirist are not always successful and his command of overall form is inconsistent and uncertain, the brilliance of his individual effects and the alert poetic intelligence displayed throughout makes even his failures attractive.

From one point of view, *The Rehearsal Transpros'd* is the most successful of Marvell's satires, since contemporary comment indicates that Marvell triumphed easily over his adversary Parker. As Anthony à Wood, whose political and religious sympathies lay more on Parker's side, conceded:

> It was generally thought, nay even by many of those who were otherwise favourers of Parker's cause, that he (Parker) thro' a too loose and unwary handling of the debate . . . laid himself too open to the severe strokes of his snearing adversary, and that the odds and victory lay on Marvell's side . . . Tho' Marvell in a second part replied upon our author's reproof, yet he judged it more prudent rather to lay down the cudgels than to enter the lists again.

Here Marvell seems to have succeeded triumphantly in validating his standards; as with Dryden's re-creation of Shadwell as the son of Flecknoe, the historical Parker, even in his lifetime, disappeared into the image of "pert *Bayes,* with Importance comfortable" about whom Rochester remarks dismissively in "Tunbridge-Wells" (1674–75), "*Marvell* has enough expos'd his Folly." Swift writes in *A Tale of a Tub:* "We still read *Marvel's* Answer to *Parker* with Pleasure, tho' the Book it answers be sunk long ago."

The success of *The Rehearsal Transpros'd* is largely due to Marvell's choice of persuasive strategy. In combining jest and earnest, Marvell is directing his arguments at two distinct audiences: those who were sympathetic toward the doctrines he espoused and those who, initially indifferent to these doctrines, could be brought to sympathize by an implicit appeal to common sense, geniality, and membership in a community of wits. Rhetorically, such an approach is effective because, as Ian Watt points out [in *Focus: Swift,* edited by C. J. Rawson], it flatters the reader, appealing to a shared identity of attitude among all men of wit and judgment, who would not wish to associate with such fools as Parker.

> The ironic posture, in fact, was both a formal expression of the qualitative division in the reading public, and a flattering reinforcement of the sense of superiority which animated one part of it.

The distinction on which the ironic code depends is not primarily social, but intellectual and, in Marvell's view, moral. Though we need not take literally Marvell's claim that the general "acceptance" of *The Rehearsal Transpros'd* was due to the cause he was defending rather than any abilities of his own, the moral sanctions he invokes clearly play a role in bringing about the reader's assent to an attack on "unspeakable arrogance . . . a Vice so generally odious, that to repress it is no less grateful . . . there being scarce any spectacle more pleasing to God and Man than to see the proud humbled." Still, much of the appeal of witty satire like *The Rehearsal Transpros'd* is aesthetic, and its persuasiveness is in large part a function of the method of raillery which Marvell has chosen to use.

The urbanity of Marvell's approach to prose controversy, looking forward to "a more Augustan method of handling disputation" [M. C. Bradbrook and M. G. Lloyd Thomas's phrase], has often been pointed out. Marvell anticipates Swift in preferring ironic insinuation to direct, bludgeoning assault, masking his indignation in a controlled, conversational tone. The effectiveness of "fine raillery" comes in part from the illusion of unconcern: raillery is both a social and a stylistic ideal, associated with aristocratic nonchalance, and the rise of this new mode reflects a concern with form, in art as in social intercourse, characteristic of the Restoration and early eighteenth century. Dryden's remarks on his own practice in raillery, his desire to "make a malefactor die sweetly," are full of the craftsman's pride in exercising his art. A similar quality is apparent in *The Rehearsal Transpros'd.*

> This is the mystery of that noble trade, which yet no master can teach to his apprentice: he may give the rules, but the scholar is never the nearer in his practise.

The wit of *The Rehearsal Transpros'd,* like that of *Absalom and Achitophel* and *A Tale of a Tub,* though it is prompted by its occasion and never loses sight of its polemical end, nevertheless transcends its circumstances. But where in the greatest Augustan satires the central metaphors provide an organizing myth around which details can cohere, in *The Rehearsal Transpros'd* the element of fictionality is intermittent. This structural weakness is a serious flaw in the work, though individual episodes are brilliant displays of wit turned to satiric purposes.

The structural difficulties of *The Rehearsal Transpros'd* are in part the legacy of characteristic methods of disputation in the seventeenth century. In both *The Rehearsal Transpros'd* and *Mr. Smirke* (the subtitles of which are "Animadversions Upon a late Book. . ." and "Certain Annotations, upon the Animadversions on the naked Truth"), the work's form is determined by what "the nature of *Animadversions* requires": both are detailed, point-by-point refutations of an opponent, quoting the words of the adversary as they fall, with appropriate satiric comment. Marvell's remark, "I will take a walk in the Garden and gather some of Mr. *Bayes* his Flowers," suggests the potential for satire in such an approach at the same time as it reveals its essential formlessness. There is no more effective way of convicting a man of folly than by turning his own words against him.

> But therefore it was that I have before so particularly quoted and bound him up with his own Words as fast as such a *Proteus* could be pinion'd . . . Every change of Posture does either alter his opinion or vary the expression by which we should judg of it: and sitting he is of one mind, and standing of another.

Milton, who employs a similar method in *Animadversions upon the Remonstrants Defence against Smectymnuus* and *An Apology against a Pamphlet,* like Marvell, justifies "this close and succinct manner of coping with the Adversary" for its polemical effectiveness in the war of truth against sophistry "in the detecting, and convincing of any notorious enemie to truth and his Countries peace, especially that is conceited to have a voluble and smart fluence of tongue." Milton's *Animadversions* observe the conventions of debate scrupulously: the pamphlet is set out in the form of statement and response, labelled "Remonstrant" and "Answer," and is divided into sections corresponding to those in the work it is answering. Some of the "Answers" are brief explosions of scorn ("Ha, ha, ha," "O pestilent imprecation!," or, their equivalents in Marvell, "here is indeed material intellectual Puff-past"; "you foam again as in the Falling-Sickness"), others argue a contrary case in detail, and still others use the words of the Remonstrant as occasion for rhetorical displays. The subtler touches of "fine raillery" have no place in Milton's conception of the proper language of satire: his "vehement vein throwing out indignation" is conceived in religious terms as "a sanctified bitternesse against the enemies of truth." The precedents he cites for his practice are not the standard classical authors, but the words of Christ and the Old Testament prophets: "Christ himselfe speaking of unsavory traditions, scruples not to name the Dunghill and the Jakes." Wit and indirection are not part of his arsenal; instead, he speaks out, casting "derision and scorne upon perverse and fraudulent seducers," using such phrases as "beggarly, and brutish," "a sot, an ideot," "insatiate avarice, & ambition," "the very garbage that draws together all the fowles of prey and ravin in the land to come, and gorge upon the Church." But if the style is different, the form is the same, and this quotation-and-comment method can be found in much of the controversial writing of the century—e.g., in the exchanges of the rival Civil War newsletters, *Mercurius Aulicus* and *Mercurius Britanicus*.

Marvell's comments on the method of animadversions suggest that he felt a certain uneasiness about the form. However brilliant the local effects may be, the author of animadversions can only respond to what his opponent has said:

> Therefore I shall look to it as well as I can, that mine Arrows be well pointed, and of mine own whetting; but for the Feathers, I must borrow them out of his Wing.

The metaphor of pursuit, which Marvell employs in several passages, presents the hunting down of a malefactor as both a pleasure and a duty:

> Yet I will not decline the pursuit, but plod on after him in his own way, thorow thick and thin, hill or dale, over hedge or ditch wherever he leads; till I have laid hand on him, and deliver'd him bound either to Reason or Laughter, to Justice or Pity.

A secondary implication of the hunt metaphor is that the satirist, as well as the quarry, is bound: where one goes, the other must follow, whether he wants to or not. The satirist, by reason of his greater self-knowledge and skill, is the master of the situation, controls the chase; May thus in "Tom May's Death" is "only Master of these Revels" when he provides the entertainment unwittingly by his own discomfiture, ending in a masque-like disappearance "in a Cloud of pitch" (ll. 98–99). But "I will not decline the pursuit" implies "I cannot decline the pursuit." It is odd how often Marvell uses phrases suggesting that he himself is constrained by the rules of the game and has become a victim of necessity, if not a prisoner of his opponent's folly: "Yet though I must follow his track now I am in, I hope I shall not write after his Copy." To say as he does at one point, "I have not committed any fault of stile, nor even this tediousness, but in his imitation," seems a curious abdication of artistic responsibility. "Imitation" is not normally incompatible with an artist's shaping control, but here Marvell argues, quite fallaciously, that the corrective end of satire requires that the model to be scrutinized ("it being so necessary to represent him in his own likeness") must be followed exactly, even at the cost of "tediousness." When he comes to write *Mr. Smirke,* his impatience with the method of animadversion is plainly evident: it is a "new Game" after the manner of academic disputation, redolent of "the *Schools* and *Pew*" and suitable for pedants and ambitious "Divines in Mode" who seek reputation by being "received into the band of Answerers." After almost fifty pages, he abandons the method entirely (with comments on the folly of "endless disputing to no purpose") and turns instead to *A Short Historical Essay,* a clearly organized historical narrative and an entirely independent work. Here he no longer need submit to "The Rules of . . . Play" whereby "he always that hath writ the last Book" in a series establishes the terms of debate and awaits his turn "until the other has done replying":

> For I had intended to have gone Chapter by Chapter, affixing a distinct Title, as he does to every one of them . . . But in good earnest, after having consider'd this last Chapter, so Brutal whether as to Force or Reason, I have changed my resolution. For he argues so despicably in the rest, that even I, who am none of the best *Disputers of this World,* have conceiv'd an utter contempt for him. He is a meer Kitchin-plunderer, and attacks but the Baggage. . . .
>
> But the Printer calls: the Press is in danger. I am weary of such stuffe, both mine own and his. I will rather give him the following Essay of mine own to busie him, and let him take his turn of being the *Popilius.*
>
> (*Mr. Smirke, or the Divine in Mode*)

The most effective (and most characteristically Marvellian) passages in *The Rehearsal Transpros'd* are those in which he manages to break free of the constraints of the animadversion form. Even in quoting Parker and holding him to his own words, Marvell typically proceeds less by logical examination than by the free play of wit upon the materials Parker has inadvertently supplied. Parker is imprudent enough to apologize for any inadequacies in his book with the excuse that "it must be ravish'd out of his hands before his thoughts can possibly be cool enough to review or correct the Indecencies either of its stile or contrivance." The ineptness with which Parker uses a conventional apologetic formula provides Marvell an opening for a criticism both intellectual and moral, in which faults of language are shown to be faults of character: Parker can be convicted out of his own mouth of "writing without thinking," the distinguishing mark of a fool.

> Some Man that has less right to be fastidious and confident, would, before he exposed himself in publick, both have cool'd his Thoughts, and corrected his Indecencies: or would have consider'd whether it were necessary or wholesom that he should write at all . . . But there was no holding him. Thus it must be, and no better, when a man's Phancy is up, and his Breeches are down; when the Mind and the Body make contrary assignations, and he hath both a Bookseller at once and a Mistris to satisfie: Like *Archimedes,* into the Street he runs out naked with his Invention.

In the course of the passage, debate modulates into fiction: the historical Parker is melted down in an alembic and transformed into the comic character Bayes.

Marvell finds precedents for his method of dramatization in earlier English prose satire. As several recent critics have shown, the most effective satiric device employed in the Marprelate tracts is the transformation of "Martin's" opponent John Bridges into a stage figure of a "worshipful jester . . . whose writings and sermons tend to no other ende then to make men laugh." By assuming the persona of a clever and bumptious country clown, creating miniature dramatic confrontations in which his opponents are addressed as though they were in the room with him ("But now alas brother Bridges I had forgotten you all this while. My brother London and I were so busie that wee scarce thought of you. Why coulde you not put me in minde that you staid al the whyle?"), Martin Marprelate gains the reader's approbation with his energy and inventiveness, while at the same time diminishing the authority of his opponents, defenders of the Anglican establishment who like Parker made much of their dignity. But the quality of ironic detachment so characteristic of Marvell's verse and prose is absent from the Marprelate tracts, as it is from the prose polemic of the Civil War period. The element of fictionality is subordinate to the element of debate—indeed, of intense hand-to-hand combat. Pamphlet wars reflected literal wars, in which lives were at stake: "Martin Marprelate" was hunted down mercilessly by the state, the press on which the tracts were printed was destroyed, and the probable author was hanged, while the editors of *Mercurius Aulicus* and *Mercurius Britanicus,* the royalist and parliamentary journals, treated their verbal exchanges as extensions by other means of the battles they wrote about. The humour of the Marprelate tracts and of the Civil War newsletters tends to be broad, aimed at inflicting pain on an adversary, and its primary modes are invective and burlesque. *Mercurius Aulicus* and *Mercurius Britanicus,* especially the latter, have moments of lively, entertaining writing (together with

a good deal of crude caricature and name-calling), but the prose has none of
Marvell's urbanity. The most vigorous passages are in the manner of medieval
and Elizabethan flyting, the joy of insult:

> But harke ye, thou mathematicall liar, that framest lies of all dimen-
> sions, long, broad and profound lies, and then playest the botcher,
> the quibling pricklouse every weeke in tacking and sticking them
> together; I tell thee (Berkenhead) thou art a knowne notorious
> odious forger: and though I will not say thou art (in thine owne
> language) the sonne of an Egyptian whore, yet all the world knowes
> thou art an underling pimpe to the whore of Babylon, and thy con-
> science an arrant prostitute for the base ends. This is truth, not
> railing.
>
> *(Mercurius Britanicus)*

Marvell's prose in *The Rehearsal Transpros'd,* on the other hand, has been
accurately described [by Bradbrook and Lloyd Thomas] as "the prose version
of the 'metaphysical' style." As in his poems, a metaphor can provide a sudden
illumination, remind us both of the variety of experience and of its unexpected
connections. Marvell's wit can express itself in an aphorism, using homely allusions to point the lessons of common sense: "A Prince that goes to the Top of
his Power is like him that shall go to the Bottom of his Treasure." Or, as in
metaphysical poetry, conceits can be extended to a great length in a dazzling
pyrotechnical display. Several conceits in the prose have close parallels in the
poems, using geometrical, architectural, and scientific imagery in a manner
reminiscent of such poems as "The Definition of Love," "A Dialogue between
the Soul and Body," and "Upon Appleton House."

> *Bayes* had at first built up such a stupendious Magistrate, as never
> was of God's making. He had put all Princes upon the Rack to
> stretch them to his dimension. And, as a streight line continued
> grows a Circle, he had given them so infinite a Power that it was
> extended unto Impotency.
>
> And you would do well and wisely not to stretch, Gold-beat, and
> Wyerdrawe Humane Laws thus to Heaven: least they grow thereby
> too slender to hold, and lose in strength what they gain by exten-
> sion and rarefaction.

Each of the metaphors, by a *reductio ad absurdum,* points out the buried implications of Parker's position, evoking an ideal of order by presenting grotesque
and comic images of disorder. The wit here is an effective means of validation,

since the reader, as he works out the conceit, tacitly allies himself with the author against Parker, who dreams of power and ends in "Impotency." One of Marvell's characteristic methods is a sudden and unexpected literalizing of a metaphor—seen, for example, in the following passage, in the course of which the conventional trope of the royal shepherd and his flock comes alive as a terrified herd of animals charging across the page:

> The wealth of a Shepheard depends upon the multitude of his flock, the goodness of their Pasture, and the Quietness of their feeding: the Princes, whose dominion over mankind resembles in some measure that of man over other creatures, cannot expect any considerable increase to themselves, if by continual terrour they amaze, shatter, and hare their People, driving them into Woods, & running them upon Precipices.

Rosalie Colie has described this technique in Marvell's poems as "unfiguring" and "refiguring," where the poet, alert to the implications of language, seeks to revitalize traditions, "cleans them of their conventional metaphorical associations to begin anew." A similar literalizing of a metaphor occurs in Marvell's attack on Parker's claim that all earthly laws carry the obligation of Divine Law, to be obeyed at the peril of damnation:

> Take heed of hooking things up to Heaven in this manner; for, though you look for some advantage from it, you may chance to raise them above your reach, and if you do not fasten and rivet them very well when you have them there, they will come down again with such a swinge, that if you stand not out of the way, they may bear you down further then you thought of.

The irony in the last of these passages is typical of Marvell's conduct of his attack on Parker. Irony often involves *faux naiveté*: the pretence of offering friendly and wholesome advice, the patient, literal exposition of the logical consequences of a position which entirely undermines that position, allowing the reader to draw the necessary conclusions. An extended comic episode at the beginning of part 2 of *The Rehearsal Transpros'd* builds a satiric fiction out of a few ill-chosen words by Parker: "a dull and lazy distemper" which, Parker tells the readers of *A Reproof to* The Rehearsal Transpros'd (1673), prevented him from answering Marvell sooner. Marvell seizes on the phrase and mercilessly develops its full implications, until his opponent is reduced to a state of helplessness. For a dozen brilliant pages of sustained irony, he speculates on the nature, causes, and cure of Bayes's illness:

I am sorry if that should occasion a distemper, which I order'd as
Physick; the *Rehearsal Transpros'd* being too only a particular
prescription in his case, and not to be applyed to others without
special direction. But some curious persons would be licking at it,
and most Men finding it not distastful to the Palate, it grew in a short
time to be of common use in the Shops.

His method here once again is to literalize the terms of the metaphor unex-
pectedly, giving the common terms "taste" and "marketplace" a direct physical
reality. Metaphor becomes allegory, as he simultaneously makes the hapless
Bayes appear a more and more ludicrous figure and, on another level, presents
a defence of satire as a genre:

> But it hath brought up such ulcerous stuff as never was seen; and
> whereas I intended it only for a *Diaphoretick* to cast him into a
> breathing sweat, it hath had upon him all the effects of a Vomit.
> Turnep-tops, Frogs, rotten Eggs, Brass-coppers, Grashoppers, Pins,
> Mushrooms &c. wrapt up together in such balls of Slime and
> Choler, that they would have burst the Dragon, and in good earnest
> seem to have something supernatural . . . But it is possible that after
> so notorious an evacuation he may do better for the future; and it
> is more then visible that either his Disease or his Nature cannot hold
> out much longer.

In "The Character of Holland" passages using comparable materials rarely rise
above name-calling; here the materials have undergone imaginative transformation from polemic into fiction. The humour of the passage conveys a dual
"ethical argument" in the characterization of Bayes and the implied characterization of the satirist as scrupulous, impersonal anatomist, who knows that it is
more important to lay open and diagnose the illness he has observed than to
tell the patient what he wants to hear. His strong language, he suggests, is
justified by its educative purpose: the foul matter released by purging the patient
may be an object of revulsion, but it is far more harmful when festering within
a diseased body than when it is evacuated.

A comparable passage in part 1 is the extended character sketch of Bayes
the mad priest. Here again the persuasive ends are achieved less through explicit
argument than through the creation of an imaginary world. The episode
resembles Swift in its inventiveness and effective use of irony, as in the central
assumption on which it is predicated—that the most damaging of diseases is
self-delusion: "Never Man certainly was so unacquainted with himself."

With pretended sympathy, Marvell traces the course of the affliction by which Bayes, "a man in the flower of his age, and the vigor of his studies," has fallen "into such a distraction, That his head runs upon nothing but Romane Empire and Ecclesiastical Policy." The illness, he tells us, began with Bayes's early reading of *Don Quixote* and the Bible, which in combination "have made such a medly in his brain-pan" that he became incurably mad. The description of Bayes's arrival in London after leaving university uses another of the mathematical conceits so characteristic of Marvell's poems; one is reminded of the attack on architectural ambition and scholarly folly in "Upon Appleton House" ("Let others vainly strive t'immure / *The Circle* in the *Quadrature!*" ll. 46–46).

> But coming out of the confinement of the Square-cap and the Quadrangle into the open Air, the World began to turn round with him: which he imagined, though it were his own giddiness, to be nothing less then the *Quadrature* of the *Circle*. This accident concurring so happily to increase the good opinion which he naturally had of himself, he thenceforward apply'd to gain a-like reputation with others.

But his first severe attack, Marvell continues, came with his first wordly success. In the passage that follows, the ironic application of mechanistic terms to human behaviour resembles Swift's association of madness, pretended inspiration, and Cartesian mechanism in sections 8 and 9 of *A Tale of a Tub*. The wit lies partly in the surprisingly apposite details ("Precipice of his Stature," recalling "mine own Precipice I go" in "A Dialogue between the Soul and Body"), partly in the scientific neutrality with which the symptoms are narrated:

> The thing alone [the praise he received] elevated him exceedingly in his own conceit, and raised his *Hypocondria* into the Region of the Brain: that his head swell'd like any Bladder with wind and vapour. But after he was stretch'd to such an height in his own fancy, that he could not look down from top to toe but his Eyes dazled at the Precipice of his Stature; there fell out, or in, another natural chance which push'd him headlong.

Though he has a highly practical side, an eye for "the main chance," any worldly achievements only serve as fuel for Bayes's madness; he may bask in the approbation of others, especially women, but his universe is essentially solipsistic. The conceit, familiar in Donne, of the lover's face reflected in the eye, emblematic of the shared universe the lovers inhabit, is here converted to satiric effect, suggesting Parker's grotesque, blind self-regard: "For all this Courtship had no other operation than to make him stil more in love with himself: and if he frequented their company, it was only to speculate his own Baby in their Eyes."

Throughout this extensive character portrait, the implicit standards of judgment are clear. The distorting mirrors of vanity and self-love are contrasted with the mirror of truth, madness with rationality. The ambitious, unprincipled man who frames his actions with regard only to what he believes "would take," who sees in others only what use he can make of them, violates nature in repudiating his common bond with all men. For a man to assume that he makes the world turn round, that he has, fulfilling Archimedes' prophecy, found a place outside common humanity from which "he could now move and govern the whole Earth with the same facility," is simple madness. Such an affliction can only grow worse, since any accident the patient may meet with is likely to cause further deterioration:

> He was transported now with the Sanctity of his Office, even to extasy: and like the Bishop over *Maudlin Colledge* Altar, or like *Maudlin de la Croix,* he was seen in his Prayers to be lifted up sometimes in the Air, and once particularly so high that he crack'd his Scul against the Chappel Ceiling . . . But being thus, without Competitor or Rival, the Darling of both Sexes in the Family and his own Minion; he grew beyond all measure elated, and that crack of his Scull, as in broken Looking-Glasses, multipli'd him in self-conceit and imagination.

Once more the implicit metaphorical content of familiar phrases (rising in the world, the love of self, reflections seen in a mirror) is revitalized. The rhetorical technique in the narrative is akin to that in such poems as "Mourning" or the meadow and forest sections of "Upon Appleton House," where the writer presents phenomena and speculates on their possible cause: the ironist withholds his "silent Judgment" ("Mourning," l. 33), yet it is implied in the ordering of his materials. So the account remorselessly continues, describing the later stages of Bayes's illness, his rapid decline into total lunacy. Bayes decides "he must be a madman in print" and the strain of writing causes new symptoms. When his book has been published and he can envision himself as a famous author, "the Vain-Glory of this totally confounded him. He lost all the little remains of his understanding, and his Cerebellum was so dryed up that there was more brains in a Walnut and both their Shells were alike thin and brittle." His further writings, "all . . . howling, yelling, and barking," are proof of total, irremediable insanity.

And so in conclusion his Madness hath formed it self into a perfect *Lycanthropy.* He doth so verily believe himself to be a Wolf, that his speech is all turn'd into howling, yelling, and barking: and if there were any Sheep here, you should see him pull out their throats and suck the blood. Alas, that a sweet Gentleman, and so hopeful, should miscarry!

The account of Bayes's madness, extending over several pages, is an example of the ironic dismantling of the pretensions of an opponent which in rhetorical skill, suavity, and an eye for the telling detail rivals Swift. Yet it is characteristic of *The Rehearsal Transpros'd* that the passage is an isolated episode rather than part of an integrated whole.

MICHAEL McKEON

Andrew Marvell and the Problem of Mediation

In the following essay I will argue that Andrew Marvell's poetic career has a consistency that belies a venerable assumption regarding both the man and his epoch. To understand either, it has been assumed, we must see them as internally divided: we must sharply distinguish the lyric poet from the satirist, the "poet" from the "propagandist," the "metaphysical" from the "neoclassical," the revolution from the restoration. Of course the immediate political evidence of such a division is obvious enough. To appreciate the more profound element of continuity, for both Marvell and his age, requires a more unified perspective on seventeenth-century literature and history. This perspective is provided by what I will call "the problem of mediation." The utility of this term lies in its relevance to diverse human pursuits that we, unlike Marvell and his contemporaries, are inclined to isolate from one another: religious belief, political theory, historiography, the "new philosophy" of scientific method, and the ongoing experimentation with literary form. To see Marvell's career as a perpetual engagement with diverse reformulations of the problem of mediation permits us to understand it as a complex unity.

"Imperialism" has a double status within this unity. First, much of Marvell's poetry, whether political or pastoral, amatory or devotional, is concerned with the imperialistic and deeply problematic relation between unequal entities: dominant and subordinate nation-states, absolute sovereigns and aspiring subjects, improving landlords and exploited tenants, artful technology and natural rusticity, imperious loves and argumentative lovers, diffident souls and

From *The Yearbook of English Studies* 13 (1983). © 1983 by the Modern Humanities Research Association.

disingenuous pleasures. These varied contests, and the particular problems of mediation which they entail, are bound together by the seventeenth-century notion and language of empire. But I also will suggest that the theory of empire itself is in process of transformation during this period. By this means the topic of imperialism will lead us to the more broadly epistemological and historical terrain of the seventeenth-century crisis of secularization.

This crisis is the enabling precondition for Marvell's most compelling poetic activities, and it too must be understood in the paradoxical terms of the problem of mediation. The idea of secularization may imply a faithful accommodation or translation of the sacred to a profane world, of the past to the present, whereby an essential matter is understood to be preserved within an altered form. But to secularize also may be a process of mistranslation in which reformation amounts to deformation, purification to corruption—in which to know and experience the given now amounts to a crudely "imperialistic" act of comprehension, a swallowing up of sacred truth by a secular reduction of it. As the capacity to be moved by this crucial distinction slowly diminishes, secularization attains the status of a relatively unquestioned good and the crisis itself begins a gradual but inexorable process of evaporation. The early modern rise of secularizing modes of knowledge and action coincided historically with the emergence of the modern theory and practice of imperialism because the connexion is more than an adventitious metaphor. What is presupposed by both developments is that mediation has ceased to be a problem, that the innate authority and consequence of realms apart from our own, suffused with the power of an ideal otherness but for that very reason infinitely difficult of access, no longer carries conviction.

I

The modest and traditional pastoral dialogues with which Marvell is thought to have begun his poetic life encapsulate, in miniature, the characteristic preoccupations of the career that would follow. They are tentatively Christian pastorals: the central contest between human simplicity and sophistication has already been absorbed within the complicating challenge of Nature by Grace. Innocent shepherds struggle to express their rudimentary sense of another world in words that will be comprehensible to this one, and still more innocent shepherdesses persist in comprehending more than they ought. Thus Thyrsis locates their future Heaven at "the centre of the soul," but Dorinda prods him into adding details that will naturalize the intuition as a concretely rustic utopia of *otium* and social levelling. "Oh sweet! Oh sweet!" she says,

> How I my future state
> By silent thinking antedate:
> I prithee let us spend our time to come
> In talking of Elysium.
> ("A Dialogue between Thyrsis and
> Dorinda," l. 27)

Can eternity be anticipated in this temporal fashion? Thyrsis's hopeful translation ("There always is a rising sun, / And day is ever but begun" [l. 35]) only persuades Dorinda to the decidedly unChristian resolve that the prophecy must be not mentally antedated, but actively fulfilled through a pact of suicide. The Damon of another poem is more cautious. He does not so much decline Clorinda's concretely carnal invitations as suggest their spiritual signification, but with such persistent obliquity that she soon gives up and ingenuously inquires, "What is't you mean?" ("Clorinda and Damon," l. 16). Damon can offer no more than that he has changed; that "The other day / Pan met me"; that Pan spoke "Words that transcend poor shepherds' skill" but fill his thoughts and inspire all of nature (ll. 19, 21). To sing Pan's praises is a project that Clorinda can understand, but for that very reason we must be left in some doubt as to just what has changed, what new truths have been communicated.

What is Pan to Christ? What is Nature to Grace? What is the letter to the spirit? What is Art to Nature? The problem entailed in the condition that we are able to know what is unknown only by comprehending it within the terms of the known is a venerable one that Christian thought only served to enrich. The delicacy of Marvell's early dialogues, written probably in the 1640s, consists in their capacity to dramatize this central paradox of Christian pedagogy in such a way that the likely failure to accommodate Christ's truth, within these fictions, only serves to accommodate the paradox itself to other realms of human thought and activity.

Marvell's most brilliantly concise access to the paradox of Christian knowledge is "The Coronet," a palinode whose consummate circuity seems only to replace in form what it retracts in substance. This is not the case in his best-known religious dialogue, for example, where the Resolved Soul is successsful in employing the language of martial and material combat, like St. Paul, to spiritual ends. Created Pleasure's counter-strategy there is to clothe the fallen delights of Nature with the deceptive language of Grace:

> Lay aside that warlike crest,
> And of Nature's banquet share:
> Where the souls of fruits and flowers

> Stand prepared to heighten yours.
> ("A Dialogue between the
> Resolved Soul and Created
> Pleasure," l. 13)

The Soul easily resists these pastoral snares, however, by recognizing the spiritual figure as no more than that, and only then proceeding to translate its sensuous materiality into a figure for truly spiritual nourishment:

> I sup above, and cannot stay
> To bait so long upon the way.
> (l. 17)

But in "The Coronet" this resort to translation has become problematic largely because the general strategy upon which it depends, the artful medium of figurative language, now constitutes the principal target under attack. The ostensible aim of retraction assumes the possibility of an artless devotional style, or of an art whose concrete figures accommodate us, like the Resolved Soul's martial habit, to immaterial truths. Yet Marvell's pastoral poems, once embraced as a natural alternative to artifice, must now appear an artful avoidance of Christian humility. However much it is renounced, moreover, pastoral art provides the self-regarding motive and the rhetorical flowers ("my fruits are only flowers" l. 6) from which the putatively sacred alternative will be fashioned. This very recognition Marvell incorporates explicitly within his poem, and it is confirmed both by the unavoidable positing of pastoral matter here even if only to the end of its own negation, and by the tangled syntactical growth which snares the poet and belies the false humility of a paradoxically "natural art." Here the act of translation, the use of corrupt language and motives to purify themselves, appears doomed to failure. By calling upon the mediator Christ to disentangle or to destroy his labour, the poet in the end regretfully renounces his own capacity not simply to mediate the gulf between matter and spirit, but even to assign a significance to the present poem, to tell whether it is pastoral or anti-pastoral.

At this point, of course, as the power to discriminate is allowed to be Christ's alone and the poet lapses into silence, Marvell may be said at last to enact that genuine renunciation which escaped him so long as the poem's mediating creativity challenged the authority of divine creation. One is tempted to see "The Coronet" not simply as a Christian but as a Puritan poem, for its exquisite sensitivity to the way human figuration conveys us to error under the guise of truth goes beyond the general paradox of Christian knowledge to what might be seeen as a more particularly Puritan problem of mediation. The seventeenth-century attack upon Roman Catholic and Anglican institutions, ceremonies, and images was fuelled by an iconoclastic animus against what Puritans took to be the careless and complacent ease of the orthodox translation from sin to salvation, from works to grace. For episcopal and priestly mediation, Lutheran Puritanism substituted the immediate and personal priesthood of all believers and Scripture readers. For the personal efficacy of good works, Calvinist Puritanism substituted justification by faith: the belief that salvation is to be neither earned nor won by the sinner's own worldly exertions, but can only be received as a gift of Christ's imputed righteousness. Here we must be reminded of the dilemma of "The Coronet." The repudiation of all mediators but Christ himself promises to preclude the reduction of spirit to the corrupt standards of material approximations; but who then is authorized to know Christ's will, as it were, immediately? The abolition of intervening steps only leaves the single great step, from divine to human knowledge, untaken. In Puritan teachings this gap was filled to a large degree by the system of discipline in the calling, whereby "good works" (devotional poetry?) may return not as the means by which grace is won but as the visible signifier that grace (the prior and unearned signified) has indeed been given. The reading of individual experience, like the interpretation of the Bible, has become an exercise in the discovery of preordained but personally significant meaning. In other words, it is not so much that dependence on fallible human mediators has been obviated, as that the power and burden of mediation have passed from the political authority of the church hierarchy to the community of believers and to the individual Puritan conscience.

As Max Weber's famous and controversial thesis suggests, the historical proximity of Puritan discipline and capitalist industry may lead us to infer the treacherous ease with which signifiers can be transformed into signifieds, material success into the very substance of spiritual fulfilment. To find a professing Puritan willing to subscribe to this thoroughly secularizing transformation is another matter, for it only recapitulates, with greater finality, the orthodox error of human sufficiency against which the iconoclastic impulse of Puritanism was originally directed. As evidence that Puritanism leads to capitalism "The Coronet" is of no utility. But Marvell's poem vindicates the more general and tentative concerns of Weber's thesis as it reveals Protestant casuistry to be a singularly ambiguous protest against the secularizing tendencies of modern orthodoxy. For in its single-minded devotion to reform—to rationalize and personalize—religious authority, conscientious introspection aggravates the old and deadly desire to become, as if by default, one's own mediator, and elevates the threat of secularization to a more volatile level of consciousness and debate.

The precariousness of things in "The Coronet" is reflected in the indeterminacy not only of the poet's spiritual status but also of the poem's generic identity. Several related questions are raised. Can the pastoral contest of Art and Nature usefully accommodate to us the Christian one of Nature and Grace, or does the former amount to no more than a skirmish over territory which, from the perspective of the latter confrontation, has long since fallen to the enemy? Does the heuristic adequation of Pan to Christ lead us to Christian truth or confirm us in pagan error? What are we to make of an anti-pastoral whose (pastoral, poetic, linguistic) flowers, invoked only to be renounced, so thrive and luxuriate in the pruning as to be indispensable to the life of the sober structure whose purpose is to kill them off?

Although specifically religious in nature, these questions also suggest more general problems of the meaning and persistence of human forms and institutions over time. By exploiting the conjunction of Puritan historiography with the allegorical resonances of the pastoral mode, Marvell developed that highly characteristic style whereby his subjects are saturated with the suggestive aura and immanence of English politics and sacred history. This is less a "poetic technique" than a delicately provisional world view. Like Clorinda, modern critics tend to ask of these poems, "What is't you mean?", surely the necessary question so long as it does not seem to require as a response a definitive and irreversible translation from signifier to signified. Marvell's turn to a more explicit engagement with politics in the 1650s only expands the territory within which the problem of mediation may continue to be addressed. And as before, the central questions concern the workings of what is now conceived as a specifically historical process of translation. What precedents may be available for authenticating the apparently unprecedented events of the English revolution? How amenable are those events to the traditional rhetorical figure of the *translatio imperii*?

II

In 1650 Marvell composed the "Horatian Ode" on Cromwell and entered the service of Thomas Fairfax, newly retired Commander in Chief of the republican forces. Cromwell now leads the New Model Army, which he had been so instrumental in modelling upon the principles not of feudal and chivalric service, but of Puritan discipline and the career open to talents. His success is announced in a Roman ode that is replete with the modern statecraft of that most enthusiastic admirer of Roman exempla, Machiavelli, and pointed everywhere to suggest (but not to prophesy) the imminent transformation of the English republic into a renovated Roman Empire. But Cromwell's Vulcanian valour is a decidedly innovative capacity

> To ruin the great work of time,
> And cast the kingdoms old
> Into another mould.
>
> (l. 34)

And the poet's obligatory song of "ancient rights" therefore must be equivocal:

> Though justice against fate complain,
> And plead the ancient rights in vain:
> But those do hold or break
> As men are strong or weak.
>
> (l. 37)

The boldness of Marvell's ode may of course be appreciated on many levels. During these critical years, English revolutionaries of diverse political and religious hues were concerned to validate their acquired power through the common lawyers' language of ancient rights and fundamental law even as they also sought a theory of sovereignty (the universal rights of man?) that would not be tied so severely to the argument from precedent or to the monarchal past. Marvell's tacit Roman *translatio* thus counters the *realpolitik* of the last-quoted lines, but the theory of sovereignty with which he flirts depends less on the vision of the Levellers than on that of the Puritan God, who on occasion will enter directly the drama of human history in order to achieve his ends. The equilibrium of Marvell's perspective here seems to be expressed in the alternation between "heaven" and "fate," a movement which defines what might be called the political dimension of the problem of mediation. Hebraic thought bequeathed to Puritanism this notion of a God who mediates heaven to earth not just through the epochal Coming of his son, but through the perpetual intrusions of the divine will into the course of history. Cromwell's promise, still muted for Marvell in 1650, is that of one whose talent, formerly lodged with him in pastoral privacy, God now summons into irresistible activity. But as in "The Coronet," the danger is that the enticingly material means of mediation deform and corrupt its spiritual ends, that to fight and kill for the Prince of Peace is really to fight for Satan.

The balance (or "detachment," or "ambivalence," or "irony") which all readers recognize in the "Horatian Ode" thus appears to express an extension of the epistemological problem of mediation to the sphere of politics and history. And here, as so often, Marvell uses the pastoral choice (contemplation *vs.* action, privacy *vs.* publicity) to weight the balance evenly. In life and in art, the choice now becomes personalized as "Fairfax *vs.* Cromwell," and Marvell spends the next few years first as tutor of the former's daughter, then as tutor of the latter's ward. Yet his deep commitment to both men renders the choice, thus personalized, an untenable one. In retirement at Nun Appleton, Fairfax encloses the great world within his microcosm, and the civil wars themselves are internalized through Marvell's enchanted figures of fort-like gardens, soldierly gardeners, drummer bees, flowery artillery, and starry patrols ("Upon Appleton House," ll. 281–344). The enchantment is not to be dismissed as an illusion. The little world here recreated is closer to our first world (the Garden of Eden, the garden of prelapsarian England) than is Cromwell's revolutionary England, where death and its instruments have unhappily acquired an autonomous significance:

> Unhappy! shall we never more
> That sweet militia restore,
> When gardens only had their towers,
> And all the garrisons were flowers,
> When roses only arms might bear,
> And men did rosy garlands wear?
>
> (l. 329)

Before the Fall, Marvell seems to suggest, the martial arts of death were no more than metaphorical expressions for various aspects of what was in fact eternal life; the Fall has transformed these signifiers into signifieds. Yet this is surely a perverse way to characterize an existence distinguished by the very *absence* of figuration, doubling, and division, by the unitary reference of human language; and it is a likely irony on Marvell's part that the only way he can express his subject here is by a duplicity of language that accommodates the garden to us by attributing to it precisely what it lacks. Fairfax's private *imperium* now flourishes as England's empire might have done under his martial horticulture (stanza 44), and the metaphor asserts both similarity and difference.

For the talent of Fairfax has been to "ambition weed, but conscience till" (l. 354), an act of Puritan casuistry quite compatible with public effort, but formulated here so as to define an individual rather than a collective discipline and to evoke Fairfax's private doubts about the spiritual efficacy of "thorough reformation" and regicide. From this perspective, the ends may be corrupted by the means, and so Fairfax's enchanted garden restores warfare to the figurative role that it has exceeded in the public world of contemporary England. Cromwell's equally plausible alternative, chronicled in the three poems of 1650, 1655, and 1658, begins from the assumption that the things of this world may conduct us, through the grace of God, to the next. Already in the "Horatian Ode," both the promise and the liabilities of the Cromwellian strategy are raised pointedly through the topic of empire. Cromwell has just returned from the brutal suppression of the rebellious Irish, who now "can affirm his praises best" ("An Horatian Ode," l. 77). The temptation to irony depends upon a perceived assimilation of ends to means, of right to might. But for this reason Marvell follows it immediately with the figure of the falcon and with the argument that here and in imperial acquisitions to come, Cromwell is himself only the instrument of a higher authority that is implicitly divine and explicitly republican:

> He to the Commons' feet presents
> A kingdom, for his first year's rents.
>
> (l. 85)

In traditional schemes of sovereignty, magistrates have had exclusive access to the *arcana imperii,* "reasons" or "mysteries of state" which transcend the interests and understanding of the individual subject. The experience of the English revolution contributed to the modern discovery that the public interest was not so much a sempiternal and transcendent mystery, administered by a succession of monarchal interpreters, as the pragmatic sum and interaction of all private interests within a given political and geographical arena. Some of the problems explicitly associated with the traditional model of sovereignty are already familiar to us as problems of mediation, between timeless and time-bound institutions, between the "political" body of monarchy and its successive, "natural" incarnations. Modern political theory might be said to begin when sovereignty is understood not as a relationship of "mediation" (of sacred authority to profane vessels, of precedent authority to present institutions) but as one of pragmatic, of democratic or despotic, "representation." This is also one precondition for the modern transformation of "empire" from a synonym for far-flung "sovereignty" to a technical term denoting the socioeconomic world-system of colonialism. The change may be seen as well in the outdating of the traditional figure of the *translatio imperii.* The *translatio* conceives of "empire" as "sovereignty," as a static and integral entity that is translated westward from realm to realm and from culture to culture. The great question here is whether each new vessel of empire is truly fit to accommodate it: whether the succession in fact entails a degeneration from a Golden to an Iron Age, a deformation of empire by an attempted comprehension of it within a stunted frame.

As empire is slowly brought down to earth and to the immediate contexts of social interaction, it begins to dissolve as a suprahistorical entity, and the argument of its "translation" loses not only its force but its very meaning. One result is that henceforth the easy justification of power by reference to invisibles will be viewed with increasing scepticism. A less benign result is that imperialism has lost the most powerful, because transcendental, constraint upon it: the humility attendant upon the belief that all human knowledge and action is profoundly vulnerable because merely creatural, suffered by an indulgent Creator through whose will alone the miraculous mediation of authority may be accomplished. This leap, from traditional to modern imperialism, is evidently related to the putative transformation from the "Protestant ethic" to the "spirit of capitalism," for both entail the comprehensive internalization of authority which, however problematic, has been acknowledged to rest until now with a transcendent power. But what I am calling here the "leap" taken by seventeenth-century thought may then be seen as the critical juncture at which the ongoing problem of secularization, primed by fundamental changes in material and social life, with a desperate grinding of gears shifts its terms and defines itself anew for the modern age. Henceforth human knowledge and power will be constrained only by the limits which self-conscious humanity, the signifier turned signified, itself undertakes to generate. For these reasons Cromwell's posture in the "Horatian Ode" has a compounded equilibrium. He is balanced not only between a faithful and a deforming mediation of sovereignty, but also between these traditional terms of the problem of mediation and the modern "Machiavellian" pragmatics of representation. In the later poems Marvell's hard-won trust of Cromwell will be registered by his legitimation according to the traditional scheme, as a successful secularizer of precedent and transcendent authority, while his enemies are invalidated either traditionally, as failed mediators, or as the thoroughly modern proponents of human autonomy and freedom.

III

During the 1650s the type of inimical modernity is the United Provinces of the Netherlands, nurse of economic and religious liberalism. In "The Character of Holland" (1653?), Marvell makes a complicated use of the *translatio* which seems to express, among other things, both an ease with the figure's traditionalism and regret and its shipwreck on the shoals of an alien world view:

> Sure when religion did itself embark,
> And from the East would Westward steer its ark,
> It struck, and splitting on this unknown ground,
> Each one thence pillaged the first piece he found:
> Hence Amsterdam, Turk—Christian—Pagan—Jew,

> Staple of sects and mint of schism grew,
> That bank of conscience, where not one so strange
> Opinion but finds credit, and exchange.
>
> (l. 67)

Like everyone else at this time, Marvell knows to associate freedom of trade and freedom of conscience. In both spheres, what has replaced the orderly translation of acknowledged authority is the capitalist system of commodity-exchange, wherein all things are confounded by being equalized on the market of abstract exchange-value. The profound problem of mediation (how to accommodate spirit to matter?) has been decisively secularized as the cheerful challenge of the marketplace (how to transform use-value into exchange-value?). When the *translatio* ceases to be steered by unchanging principle it becomes lawless and self-interested "pillage." In the traditional exchange of commodities, for example, the system of exchange is temporarily serviceable as a means of facilitating the end of acquiring and consuming goods (I trade with you because you have something I need). The attainment of the end coincides with the repudiation of the means. In its capitalist development, exchange becomes a permanent end in itself, and the homogenization of use-values as abstract exchange-value is guided not at all by the law of consumption, not by the determinate need for particular goods, but by the licence to generate endless profit.

It is this understanding, if not in these terms, that informs Marvell's economic figure for religious toleration in this passage. Thus, by the same token, a limited and thoughtful indulgence of tender consciences would seek to satisfy the particular institutional requirements of different sects to the great end of right worship and salvation. But in Dutch toleration the spiritual ends of indulgence have been replaced by the sheer will to indulge. If no faith is beyond credit then no faith may be credited: all are reduced (or abstracted) to the same equality, which depends strictly on an indifference to substantive spiritual considerations.

The medium of exchange with which Marvell and England are concerned in "The Character of Holland" is not only money but the seas themselves, for the commercial dominance of the Dutch in the early seventeenth century depended greatly on their adherence to the Grotian doctrine of *Mare liberum*, and to its insistence that nationalist doctrines of territorial sovereignty did not extend to the seas or hence to their mercantile exploitation by enterprising competitors. So it is nature itself that seemed to be expropriated from its "natural" and immemorial rulers, and in his attack on this enemy which impudently neglects even to salute English ships in their own waters, Marvell is content

to argue on traditionalistic grounds which at other times would seem to him
distinctly problematic:

> No, but all ancient rights and leagues must vail
> Rather than to the English strike their sail.
>
> (l. 107)

In short, no force restrains the unprincipled omnivorous imperialism of the
Dutch—except of course for Cromwell. Central to any enlightened defence of
Cromwell's foreign policy during the 1650s was the view that England's commercial success was inseparable from her championing of the international Protestant Cause against the imperialist aspirations of Roman Catholicism. Rivalry
with the Protestant Provinces interfered seriously with this claim, of course,
but Cromwell's policy might yet be seen as a successful reconciliation of
economic with religious interest, whereas the rapacious Dutch comprehension
of "spirit" within "matter" was clear (as we have seen) in her indiscriminate
toleration of all trading heterodoxy. To be sure, Cromwell's own policy of toleration (and in particular his campaign to readmit the Jews to England in 1655)
might be taken to close the gap between Dutch heterodoxy and English orthodoxy, but the return of the Jews at this time was seen by many sympathetic
Protestants to have not simply "spiritual" but millenarian and eschatological
import.

Marvell himself had become deeply receptive to the view that Cromwell's
imperial achievements were an act of Puritan discipline inscribed upon the
history of God's Chosen People. "The First Anniversary" (1655) situates
Cromwell at stage centre of international Protestant politics, uncomprehend-
ingly observed by an audience of dull and "heavy monarchs" (l. 15) whose
narrow *arcana imperii* ignore the imminence of the truly imperial eschatological
moment:

> How might they under such a captain raise
> The great designs kept for the latter days!
> But mad with reason (so miscalled) of state
> They know them not, and what they know not, hate.
> Hence still they sing hosanna to the whore,
> And her, whom they should massacre, adore.
>
> (l. 109)

The dangerous equilibrium of the Machiavellian prince now sounds more like
the ideal mediation of the Socratic philosopher king ("Hence oft I think if in
some happy hour / High grace should meet in one with highest power" [l. 131]),

but the model for this mediating power is not of course Platonic philosophy but Puritan messianism.

Throughout "The First Anniversary," Cromwell's sovereignty is confirmed not only by his translation of Roman *auctoritas,* but also by his typological fulfilment of Old Testament kingship, an act of successful "secularization" (the term now sounds paradoxical) that does not simply preserve what has been given but transvalues it from shadowy type to truth, from preparation to actuality. "If these the times, then this must be the man" (l. 144): Cromwell's messianic mediation of earthly means to heavenly ends distinguishes him not only from the self-absorbed "heavy monarchs" but also from his coreligionists (Fifth Monarchy Men, Quakers, Ranters, Anabaptists, Adamites) whom Marvell is willing now to see as taking the discipline of iconoclasm so far that it deforms the sacred truths which it was meant to purify:

> You who the scripture and the laws deface
> With the same liberty as points and lace;
> Oh race most hypocritically strict!
>
> (l. 315)

Now all Puritan sectarians may be homogenized into the same stew of error, joining with Dutch capitalists in the principled espousal of an antinomian "liberty" which, becoming unlimited, also becomes unprincipled. The poem concludes, in contrast, with that increasingly familiar vision of the later seventeenth century, the apocalyptic yet supremely worldly imperialism of the burgeoning mercantile state. In Marvell's version, the delicate balance of matter and spirit is substantiated by other evidences of Cromwell's mediating capacity, which recall the problematic formulations of the "Horatian Ode" even as they intimate that the problem of sovereignty has dissolved:

> He seems a king by long succession born,
> And yet the same to be a king does scorn.
> Abroad a king he seems, and something more,
> At home a subject on the equal floor.
>
> (l. 387)

The apotheosis of Cromwell's powers of mediation comes, for Marvell, only with the necessary recording of his death and the disconcerting acknowledgement of his uniqueness ("A Poem upon the Death of His Late Highness the Lord Protector" [1658]). What Fairfax attains in his private garden, Cromwell, obliged by "angry heaven" ("Horatian Ode," l. 26; "Upon the Death," l. 16) to forsake his own preferred retreat, has achieved in the public garden of the world:

What man was ever so in heaven obeyed
Since the commanded sun o'er Gibeon stayed?

Who planted England on the Flandric shore,
And stretched our frontier to the Indian ore

He first put arms into Religion's hand,
And timorous Conscience unto Courage manned.
                              (ll. 191–92, 173–74, 179–80)

Cromwell's life has been a unity, a successful materialization of spiritual ends in the treacherous media of space and time and human ambition, a comprehensible translation of transcendence into the fallen language of immanence. Now he "reigns" and "pitches" and "plunges" in heaven, Marvell fancifully tells us, like a frolicking falcon; now he may find and greet those Old Testament kings by whom he was prefigured (ll. 287–95). Through these self-conscious figures the poet freely confesses his own incapacity to attain that mastery of mediation which Cromwell's career achieved and of which his death deprives us:

And in those joys dost spend the endless day,
Which in expressing we ourselves betray.
    For we, since thou art gone, with heavy doom,
Wander like ghosts about thy lovèd tomb;
And lost in tears, have neither sight nor mind
To guide us upward through this region blind.
                              (l. 297)

On one other occasion, in praise of *Paradise Lost,* Marvell is moved to a similar gesture of profound humility, now in deference to the great Puritan poet of whose ambition to accommodate heaven to earth and "ruin the great work of time," like Cromwell's, Marvell had early misgivings:

                    the argument
Held me a while, misdoubting his intent
That he would ruin (for I saw him strong)
The sacred truths to fable and old song,

Lest he perplexed the things he would explain,
And what was easy he should render vain.
                    ("On Mr Milton's *Paradise Lost*" [1674],
                    ll. 5–8, 15–16)

Here, too, the early fears prove groundless: "And things divine thou treat'st of in such state / As them preserves, and thee, inviolate" (l. 33), a truth which simultaneously elevates Milton to the status of first of poets and raises the Cromwellian question of who shall follow in his footsteps. Thus Marvell's own tacit and tentative imitation of Miltonic periods in the first five lines of the poem is soon put in its place by the observation "that no room is here for writers left, / But to detect their ignorance or theft" (l. 29).

IV

The problem of empire and of imperialist comprehension, although raised explicitly by the achievements of Oliver Cromwell in the 1650s, is subtly implicated within Marvell's first experiments at pastoralism and the paradox of Christian knowledge. Created Pleasure tempts the Resolved Soul as if it were Eve in the Garden:

> Thou shalt know each hidden cause;
> And see the future time:
> Try what depth the centre draws;
> And then to heaven climb.
> ("A Dialogue," l. 69)

The Original Sin of curiosity, *libido sciendi,* undergoes its own secularization in the scientific revolution of the seventeenth century, and the profound ambiguity of this return (the Fall compounded or indemnified?) suffuses the movement from its inception. Francis Bacon is characteristically confident: "Only let the human race recover that right of nature which belongs to it by divine bequest, and let power be given it: the exercise thereof will be governed by sound reason and true religion." The Baconian promise is of a method of reading God's Nature as Cromwell reads his History. Both are energetically active modes of knowing God through his works, and of learning thereby how to manipulate material reality in simultaneous accord with divine will and practical human benefit. From this perspective the new philosophy is not an instance of, but a response to, the corruption of knowledge at the Fall, and it promises, like Puritanism, to liberate the tradition from the duplicity of false (Aristotelian, ecclesiastical) and deforming mediations.

When Marvell's enclosed gardens seem relatively successful in accommodating the divine plan to us, they may well suggest some of the disciplined but hearty sweat of Puritan industry and Baconian technology. Thus the "warlike studies" and elaborate martial figures of Fairfax, soldier-turned-gardener ("Upon Appleton House," ll. 281–88). Thus too the "skilful gardener" of "The Garden," whose mechanization of nature transforms it into its own sundial, the better to record the fruitful labours in which we and nature now

cheerfully participate: "And, as it works, the industrious bee / Computes its
time as well as we" (l. 69). The pun on "thyme," like the making of the garden
into a "dial new," seems in this context a quite harmless, if inevitable, duplicity. These gardens, though undeniably artful, are distinctly associated with
Eden and so enjoy the aura of God's art "now" recreated in the sempiternal
present of pastoral retirement. But when science and technology make a more
explicit appearance in the garden they transform it into a sewer of corruption,
the concrete and modern aggravation of our original Fall into human sufficiency. The central and extraordinary text here is, of course, "The Mower
against Gardens." Here gardening is an imperialist takeover: the artful mediation of nature succeeds not in accommodation but in rapacious seduction:

> Luxurious man, to bring his vice in use,
> Did after him the world seduce.
>
> (l. 1)

Technological experiments, agrarian "improvements," the opening up of new
markets, and the fabrication of new commodities—all these are part of the
rape of nature which consists simultaneously in the debasement of natural
ends to perverse human uses and in the transformation of use-values into
exchange-value:

> The tulip, white, did for complexion seek,
>   And learned to interline its cheek:
> Its onion root they then so high did hold,
>   That one was for a meadow sold.
> Another world was searched, through oceans new,
>   To find the *Marvel of Peru*.
>
> (l. 13)

Commodification, the subjugation of use to the universal standards of exchange, is here our central metaphor of human knowledge and action, the
reduction of all that is valued as an end in itself to the terms and standards of
that by which it is coveted. This confusion of values, of means and ends, of
signifiers and signifieds, is the primal confusion of our fall into moral, sexual,
and linguistic duplicity, now rejuvenated by the new science and capitalist
industry:

> The pink grew then as double as his mind;
> The nutriment did change the kind.
>
> And yet these rarities might be allowed
> To man, that sovereign thing and proud,

> Had he not dealt betwixt the bark and tree,
>   Forbidden mixtures there to see.
> No plant now knew the stock from which it came;
>   He grafts upon the wild the tame.
>
>   (ll. 9–10, 19–24)

Thus the hybrid creations of botanical science are like the parvenu creations of the royal sale of aristocratic honours, a usurpation of divine and natural creativity which confounds what should be distinguished and disrupts the authoritative order of genealogical succession. From the perspective of the Mower, then, the *hortus conclusus* is the product not of God's art but of a strictly human licence of enclosure, whose free enterprise consists in a freedom *from* external constraints and *to* expropriate and contain whatever lies in its path. The Baconian promise has become a pledge to engineer nature and society strictly acording to man's own depraved and insatiable desires.

As the Cromwell poems make clear, the search for "another world" does not always mean for Marvell an adventure in capitalist expropriation, but the "macro-pastoralism" of the voyages of discovery and settlement always entails for him the complex indeterminacy of pastoralism itself. A subtle case in point is "Bermudas" (1653?), the framed first-person narrative of a Puritan colonial party that has fled the sophisticated corruptions of Anglican prelacy to discover the *locus amoenus* of God's country in the Americas. Freedom of conscience, the dangerous concomitant of licentious market exchange in the United Provinces, may here be viewed sympathetically as the humble goal of godly pilgrims whose only desire is to be left in peace. Yet as we overhear them eagerly anticipating their solitude with God, we may be reminded of the pastoral Dorindas and Clorindas who innocently comprehend more than they ought. This is a related process of "exchange," the anthropomorphic accommodation of the spirit to the earnest but naïvely egocentric understandings of those who, like Bacon, would indulge the vision of themselves at the centre of a restored and oddly materialistic Eden:

> He gave us this eternal spring,
> Which here enamels everything,
>
> He hangs in shades the orange bright,
> Like golden lamps in a green night,
>
> He makes the figs our mouths to meet,
> And throws the melons at our feet,
> But apples plants of such a price,

No tree could ever bear them twice.
(ll. 13–14, 17–18, 21–24)

The paradisal topics are traditional enough; it is the delicately personalized tone of cheerful self-satisfaction that forces one to linger over the image of God as an improving landlord, to be valued for the "price" of his natural commodities. This is the religiosity (we might speculate uncomfortably) of which was born, in the very decades through which Marvell was living, the manifest destiny of modern imperialism.

V

The generic instability of much of Marvell's poetry, then, must be understood not only in terms of the putatively autonomous life-cycles of literary convention, nor simply as a reflection of the equivocal nature of his persistent and traditional themes, but also in relation to the instability of the social, political, and economic institutions of his times. A year after Cromwell's death and in the midst of the chaos that precipitated the restoration of Charles II, Marvell was elected to sit as Member of Parliament for Hull, a position he would retain until his death in 1678. In the public eye he slowly emerged, during these last decades, as the champion of toleration and parliamentary privilege, of religious and political freedom, whose writings prepared as much as any for the near-revolutionary politics of the Exclusion Crisis. This ideological sharpening of stance continues the movement of the Cromwellian period, and Marvell's own muted pastoral choice of public activism during that time is extended now, upon the hero's death, to an embrace of urban life in the metropolitan heart, punctuated by frequent letters home to the Hull Corporation in "the country" on matters of commercial and ecclesiastical policy. But the general effect of this movement is not (as some have thought) to sacrifice that characteristic eclectic equilibrium which I have discussed in terms of his habitual engagement with the problem of mediation.

After 1660 this continues to be Marvell's preoccupation, but with the death of the republic and its heroic "Protector," a subtle yet decisive modulation is required. If the years before the restoration are dominated by heroic panegyric leavened with satire, the succeeding period is marked by mock-heroic satire founded upon the perception of how things ought to be. And if "Upon Appleton House" (c. 1652) may be accounted Marvell's very singular "pastoral epic," "The Last Instructions to a Painter" (1667) is the pastoral mock-epic. In the earlier poem, the poet's ingenuous role as "surveyor" of the pastoral prospect is systematic (we move through house, garden, fields, woods and river) yet fundamentally passive. This is Marvell as Fairfax: only obliquely are we aware what the successive and dizzying artificializations of nature which are recorded in the poem owe to perspectival adjustments in the human camera from which our record proceeds. In "The Last Instructions," by contrast, poet and painter join in the strenuously active discipline of a satiric "reformation" of the prospect, a representation that is also explicitly an act of remaking:

> So thou and I, dear Painter, represent
> In quick effigy, others' faults, and feign
> By making them ridiculous, to restrain.
>
> (l. 390)

A large part of the difference lies in the prospect itself. As the minute particularity of Marvell's dissection encourages us to recognize, England's body politic has been overrun by a microscopic race of artful vermin bent upon stripping the living carcass to its skeleton. The Cromwellian arts of governmental mediation have failed, and England's leaders luxuriate in the corrupted arts of modern political management, of procurement, bribery, cheating, fraud, influence-peddling, acts of human depravity which Marvell finds it easy to associate with the dubious "experiments" of the new science and the newly instituted Royal Society. Yet if England's body is poisoned by these arts, it may be cured by others. In adopting now the traditional view of satire as the drastic but necessary antidote to moral and social ills, Marvell resists the chastened circumspection of "The Coronet" and embraces the power of human art to reform art, to mediate a path to an alternative. No longer afraid to attempt that "Which in expressing we ourselves betray," Marvell now takes on the role of poet as Cromwellian Hero, which he was soon to admire so greatly in his friend Milton. Thus one dominant mode of "The Last Instructions" is a confident mock-heroic procedure that consists in imitating his antagonists (as Milton imitates Satan) in the process of separating himself from them. Like the vermin, he indulges the fiction of their greatness, but to such heights that the praise reverses into degradation. Like them, he strips England naked, but it is this film of heroic folly and pretension whose very removal constitutes the cure. Like them he employs a "scientific" method, but now in the positive and Baconian sense of penetrating nature's laws to the end of reformation; thus the poet instructs the painter:

> With Hooke, then, through the microscope take aim,
> Where, like the new *Comptroller,* all men laugh
> To see a tall louse brandish the white staff.
>
> (l. 16)

The new poetry is allied to the new science through a shared confidence that human artifice, although it is the disease, may artfully achieve also the cure; that the end need not be comprehended and corrupted by the means of its attainment.

Yet there remains a crucial element of restraint in this hilarious but very angry poem. Throughout, Marvell is willing to take his satiric dissection of parasitic evil only as far as Charles's courtiers and counsellors; the king himself is spared. For Marvell, as for most others in 1667, the Lord Chancellor Clarendon is the great scapegoat, but most of the other ministers (not to mention scores of lesser functionaries), although they escaped Clarendon's actual punishment, are obliged to suffer Marvell's satiric one. In halting the indictment at this point Marvell no doubt responds to a number of poetic, political, and prudential considerations. The result is that he remains in nominal accord with that last vestige of *arcana imperii,* the doctrine that the king cannot err, however fallible his counsellors may be. These latter are to be repudiated unconditionally in the language of the Mower's satire against enclosure:

> Bold and accursed are they that all this while
> Have strove to isle our Monarch from his isle,
> And to improve themselves, on false pretence,
> About the Common-Prince have raised a fence;
> The kingdom from the crown distinct would see
> And peel the bark to burn at last the tree.
>
> (l. 967)

But Charles himself is reserved to play the more diverting and hopeful role of special audience and surrogate poet. The final section of the poem is an "Envoy" addressed to the king, frankly advising the extirpation of evil counsellors and immediately introduced by the suggestion that it is now time for the royal government to undertake that strenuous labour of reformation which thus far has proceeded by satiric means:

> But this great work is for our Monarch fit,
> And henceforth Charles only to Charles shall sit.
> His master-hand the ancients shall outdo,
> Himself the painter and the poet too.
> To the King
> So his bold tube, man to the sun applied
> And spots unknown to the bright star descried,

> Showed they obscure him, while too near they please
> And seem his courtiers, are but his disease.
>
> (l. 945)

Once again the magnifying powers of scientific technology are compared to those of satiric representation, but now also to the discernment of the king and to his potential capacity for a Cromwellian "thorough reformation" of the state. The invidious comparison of Charles with Cromwell has tacitly underlain much of this poem's outrage at England's present subjugation to Dutch naval and commercial power. How sincere are Marvell's hopes that Charles may exercise the discipline necessary to reform the political corruptions on which the English war effort has foundered? It is difficult to answer this question, but one hint is contained in Marvell's cynical account of attempts to blame the several miscarriages of the war on a relatively obscure commissioner of the navy, Peter Pett:

> Pett, the sea-architect, in making ships
> Was the first cause of all these naval slips:
> Had he not built, none of these faults had been;
> If no creation, there had been no sin.
>
> (l. 785)

In his unwillingness to be deceived by the scapegoat-fiction as it attaches to Pett, Marvell ominously (if silently) alludes to the arbitrariness of belief in the official Clarendonian version. In a corrupt body, disease spreads to every member. The distinction between the king's political and his natural capacity is an artificial one, not immune from the disease but a symptom of it.

This is not Marvell's or many people's public conclusion in 1667, partly because few wished to call up so soon the spectre of 1641. Yet the corruptions of the Second Anglo-Dutch War helped persuade him to see not Dutch liberalism but French absolutism, not licentious liberty but arbitrary monopoly, as the model of what was to be feared most at home. In three years, Charles was to sign the duplicitous Secret Treaty of Dover with the Catholic Louis XIV, and from this point on Marvell's progress into the role of parliamentarian patriot, champion of English freedoms, appears irreversible. When he died in 1678 on the eve of the Popish Plot he was being sought by the authorities for the recent publication of *An Account of the Growth of Popery, and Arbitrary Government in England,* a comprehensively inflammatory tract which nonetheless still forbears to indict Charles himself.

A great distance has been travelled, so far as public engagement is concerned, from the circumspect observer of 1650 to the Protestant patriot of 1678 and posterity. But Marvell's most central concerns have not altered, and in his gradual discovery of a fully public voice he has continued to meditate, in novel forms, upon the problems of human knowledge and action that preoccupy his entire career. Marvell's dedication to satiric and polemical reformation during the final decade of his life bespeaks a hard-won but permanent confidence in the powers of a "positive" secularization, in the efficacy of human inventiveness to achieve ethical and spiritual ends. If the seventeenth-century experience of secularization seems to us to have failed in the accommodation of the sacred to a profane world — if economic liberalism served only to licence individual acquisitiveness, if religious toleration of diverse faiths prefigured only secularism and the indifference to faith itself — these are the complex fruits of a historical process that exceptional men like Marvell were supremely gifted at reading and powerless, in the end, to direct.

Chronology

1621   Andrew Marvell born at Winestead-in-Holderness, Yorkshire, to the Reverend Andrew Marvell, a local vicar, and his wife, Anne Pease.

1624   Marvell's family moves to Hull, where he attends the Hull Grammar School.

1633   Marvell enters Trinity College, Cambridge.

1639   Receives his B.A. He converts for a brief time to Roman Catholicism.

1642   Writes "A Dialogue between Thyrsis and Dorinda," which William Lawes sets to music. Tours the Continent for four years, spending two years in Rome, where he writes "Flecknoe, an English Priest at Rome."

1650   Writes "An Horatian Ode upon Cromwell's Return from Ireland" and "Tom May's Death." Moves to Yorkshire, where he becomes the tutor of the daughter of Lord Fairfax, at Nun Appleton.

1653   Writes "The Character of Holland," "Bermudas," and "The First Anniversary of the Government under His Highness the Lord Protector," which is published anonymously in 1655.

1657   Appointed Latin Secretary to the Council of State.

1659   Elected the Member of Parliament for Hull.

1667   Writes "The Last Instructions to a Painter."

1672   Publishes *The Rehearsal Transpros'd* anonymously.

1678   Marvell dies of an ague.

1681   *Miscellaneous Poems* published.

Contributors

HAROLD BLOOM, Sterling Professor of the Humanities at Yale University, is the author of *The Anxiety of Influence, Poetry and Repression,* and many other volumes of literary criticism. His forthcoming study, *Freud: Transference and Authority,* attempts a full-scale reading of all of Freud's major writings. A MacArthur Prize Fellow, he is the general editor of five series of literary criticism published by Chelsea House. During 1987–88, he served as Charles Eliot Norton Professor of Poetry at Harvard University.

JOHN HOLLANDER is Professor of English at Yale University. He is the author of *The Untuning of the Sky: Ideas of Music in English Poetry, 1500–1700, Vision and Resonance, The Figure of Echo: Modes of Allusion in Milton and After,* and *Rhyme's Reason.* Hollander has also written several volumes of poetry, including *Spectral Emanations, Reflections on Espionage, Tales Told of the Fathers, The Night Mirror, Blue Wine,* and *Powers of Thirteen.*

RUTH NEVO is Professor of English at Hebrew University in Jerusalem. She is the author of *The Dial of Virtue: A Study of Poems on Affairs of State in the Seventeenth Century, Comic Transformations in Shakespeare,* and *Tragic Form in Shakespeare.* She has also translated into English the *Selected Poems* of Chaim Nachman Bialik.

GEOFFREY HARTMAN is Karl Young Professor of English and Comparative Literature at Yale. His books include *Wordsworth's Poetry* and *Saving the Text,* a study of Jacques Derrida.

LOUIS L. MARTZ, Sterling Professor Emeritus of English at Yale University, is the author of *The Poetry of Meditation, The Poem of the Mind, The Paradise Within,* and *The Wit of Love.*

DONALD M. FRIEDMAN is Professor of English at the University of California at Berkeley. He is the author of *Marvell's Pastoral Art* and several articles on Renaissance poetry.

ROSALIE COLIE was professor of English at Brown University until her death in 1972. She is the author of *Paradoxia Epidemica, The Resources of Kind, Shakespeare's Living Art,* and a book of poems, *Atlantic Wall and Other Poems.*

DAVID KALSTONE was Professor of English at Rutgers University. He published extensively on poets from Sir Philip Sidney to James Merrill and John Ashbery.

ISABEL G. MacCAFFREY was Professor of History and Literature at Harvard University. She published notable books on Milton and on Spenser and several essays on Wallace Stevens.

MICHAEL SEIDEL is Professor of English at Columbia University. He is the author of *Epic Geography: James Joyce's* Ulysses, and *Satiric Inheritance: Rabelais to Sterne,* as well as essays on Nabokov and Pynchon.

CLEANTH BROOKS is Gray Professor Emeritus of Rhetoric at Yale University. He is the author of several books of literary criticism, including *The Well Wrought Urn.*

KENNETH GROSS, author of *Spenserian Poetics,* teaches English at the University of Rochester.

WARREN CHERNAIK is Lecturer in English at the University of London. He has written many articles on Restoration satire as well as *The Poetry of Limitation: A Study of Edmund Waller.*

MICHAEL McKEON is Associate Professor of English at Boston University and the author of *Politics and Poetry in Restoration England: The Case of Dryden's* Annus Mirabilis.

Bibliography

Allen, D. C. *Image and Meaning: Metaphoric Traditions in Renaissance Poetry.* Baltimore: Johns Hopkins University Press, 1960.

Alpers, Paul. "Convening and Convention in Pastoral Poetry." *New Literary History* 14 (1983): 277–304.

Baruch, Elaine Hoffman. "Theme and Counterthemes in 'Damon the Mower.'" *Comparative Literature* 26 (1974): 242–59.

Bateson, F. W. "Marvell's Impossible Love: A Comment." *Essays in Criticism* 27 (1977): 109–11.

Berger, Harry. "Marvell's 'Garden': Still Another Interpretation." *Modern Language Quarterly* 28 (1967): 285–304.

————. "Marvell's 'Upon Appleton House': An Interpretation." *Southern Review* (Australia) 1 (1965): 7–32.

Berthoff, Ann E. *The Resolved Soul: A Study of Marvell's Major Poems.* Princeton: Princeton University Press, 1970.

Bradbrook, Frank W. "Marvell and the Line of Wit." In *The New Pelican Guide to English Literature, III: From Donne to Marvell.* Harmondsworth: Penguin, 1982.

Bradbrook, M. C., and M. G. Lloyd Thomas. *Andrew Marvell.* Cambridge: Cambridge University Press, 1940.

————. "Marvell and the Concept of Metamorphosis." *The Criterion* 18 (1938–39): 236–54.

Brett, R. L. "Andrew Marvell: The Voice of His Age." *Critical Quarterly* 20 (1978): 5–17.

————, ed. *Andrew Marvell: Essays on the Tercentenary of His Death.* Oxford: Oxford University Press, 1979.

Broadbent, John. "Marvell: Symbol, Structure, and Satire." In *The New Pelican Guide to English Literature, III: From Donne to Marvell.* Harmondsworth: Penguin, 1982.

Brooks, Cleanth. "Criticism and Literary History: Marvell's 'Horatian Ode.'" *The Sewanee Review* 60 (1952): 362–76.

————. "Literary Criticism." In *English Institute Essays, 1946.* New York: Columbia University Press, 1947.

————. "A Note on the Limits of 'History' and the Limits of 'Criticism.'" *The Sewanee Review* 61 (1953): 129–35.

Bush, Douglas. "Marvell's 'Horatian Ode.'" *The Sewanee Review* 60 (1952): 363–76.

Cherniak, Warren. *The Poet's Time: Politics and Religion in the Work of Andrew Marvell.* Cambridge: Cambridge University Press, 1983.

Colie, Rosalie. *"My Ecchoing Song": Andrew Marvell's Poetry of Criticism*. Princeton: Princeton University Press, 1970.

Collin, Dan S. *Andrew Marvell: A Reference Guide*. Boston: G. K. Hall, 1981.

Creaser, John. "Marvell's Effortless Superiority." *Essays in Criticism* 20 (1970): 403–23.

Cullen, Patrick. *Spenser, Marvell, and Renaissance Pastoral*. Cambridge, Mass.: Harvard University Press, 1970.

Davison, Dennis. *The Poetry of Andrew Marvell*. London: Edward Arnold, 1964.

Donno, Elizabeth Story. *Andrew Marvell: The Critical Heritage*. London: Routledge & Kegan Paul, 1978.

Duncan-Jones, E. E. "Marvell: A Great Master of Words." *Proceedings of the British Academy* 61 (1975): 267–90.

Eliot, T. S. "Andrew Marvell." In *Selected Essays*. New York: Harcourt, Brace, 1950.

Empson, William. *Some Versions of Pastoral*. London: Chatto & Windus, 1935.

———. *Using Biography*. London: Chatto & Windus, 1984.

Erickson, Lee. "Marvell's 'Upon Appleton House' and the Fairfax Family." *English Literary Renaissance* 9 (1979): 158–68.

Everett, Barbara. "Marvell's 'The Mower's Song.'" *Critical Quarterly* 4 (1962): 219–24.

Fisher, Alan S. "The Augustan Marvell: *The Last Instructions to a Painter*." *ELH* 38 (1971): 223–38.

Friedman, Donald M. *Marvell's Pastoral Art*. Berkeley: University of California Press, 1970.

Grove, Robin. "Poetry and Reader: Marvell's Triumphs of the Hay." *The Critical Review* 23 (1981): 34–48.

Guffey, George R. *A Concordance to the English Poems of Andrew Marvell*. Chapel Hill: University of North Carolina Press, 1974.

Guild, Nicholas. "The Contexts of Marvell's Early 'Royalist' Poems." *Studies in English Literature* 20 (1980): 125–36.

Hagstrum, Jean H. *The Sister Arts*. Chicago: University of Chicago Press, 1958.

Herz, Judith Scherer. "Milton and Marvell: The Poet as Fit Reader." *Modern Language Quarterly* 39 (1978): 239–63.

Hibbard, G. R. "The Country House Poem of the Seventeenth Century." *Journal of the Warburg and Courtauld Institutes* 19 (1956): 159–74.

Hill, Christopher. *The Experience of Defeat: Milton and Some Contemporaries*. New York: Viking Press, 1984.

———. "John Milton (1608–74) and Andrew Marvell (1621–78)." In *The Collected Essays of Christopher Hill, Volume One: Writing and Revolution in Seventeenth-Century England*. Amherst: University of Massachusetts Press, 1985.

———. *Puritanism and Revolution*. London: Martin Secker & Warburg, 1958.

Hodge, R. I. V. *Foreshortened Time: Andrew Marvell and Seventeenth-Century Revolutions*. Cambridge: D. S. Brewer, 1978.

Hunt, John Dixon. *Andrew Marvell: His Life and Writings*. Ithaca: Cornell University Press, 1978.

Hyman, Lawrence. *Andrew Marvell*. New York: Twayne, 1964.

———. "Marvell's 'Garden.'" *ELH* 25 (1958): 13–22.

Kelliher, Hilton. *Andrew Marvell: Poet and Politician, 1621-78*. Catalogue for an exhibition at the British Library. London, 1978.

Kermode, Frank. "The Argument of Marvell's 'Garden.' " *Essays in Criticism* 2 (1952): 225–41.

———. "Marvell Transprosed." *Encounter* 27, no. 5 (November 1966): 77–84.

———, ed. *Selected Poetry of Andrew Marvell.* New York: New American Library, 1967.

King, A. H. "Some Notes on Andrew Marvell's Garden." *English Studies* 20 (1938): 118–21.

Klause, John. *The Unfortunate Fall: Theodicy and the Moral Imagination of Andrew Marvell.* Hamden, Conn.: Archon, 1983.

Legouis, Pierre. *Andrew Marvell: Poet, Puritan, Patriot.* Oxford: Oxford University Press, 1965.

Leishman, J. B. *The Art of Marvell's Poetry.* London: Hutchinson, 1966.

Lerner, L. D. *The Uses of Nostalgia.* New York: Schocken, 1972.

Long, Michael. *Marvell, Nabokov: Childhood and Arcadia.* Oxford: Clarendon Press, 1984.

Lord, George deForest. *Andrew Marvell: A Collection of Critical Essays.* Englewood Cliffs, N. J.: Prentice-Hall, 1968.

Margoliouth, H. M., ed. *Poems and Letters by Andrew Marvell.* Oxford: Clarendon Press, 1927. Rev. ed. by Pierre Legouis and E. E. Duncan-Jones. Oxford: Clarendon Press, 1971.

Markel, Michael H. "Perception and Expression in Marvell's Cavalier Poetry." In *Classic and Cavalier: Essays on Jonson and the Sons of Ben,* edited by Claude J. Summers and Ted-Larry Pebworth, 243–53. Pittsburgh: University of Pittsburgh Press, 1982.

Meilander, Marion. "Marvell's Pastoral Poetry: Fulfillment of a Tradition." *Genre* 12 (1979): 181–201.

Miner, Earl. "The 'Poetic Picture, Painted Poetry' of *The Last Instructions to a Painter.*" *Modern Philology* 63 (1966): 288–94.

Moldenhauer, Joseph J. "The Voices of Seduction in 'To His Coy Mistress': A Rhetorical Analysis." *Texas Studies in Literature and Language* 10 (1968–69): 189–206.

Molesworth, Charles. "Marvell's 'Upon Appleton House': The Persona as Historian, Philosopher, and Priest." *Studies in English Literature* 13 (1973): 149–62.

Nevo, Ruth. *The Dial of Virtue: A Study of Poems on Affairs of State in the Seventeenth Century.* Princeton: Princeton University Press, 1963.

———. "Marvell's 'Songs of Innocence and Experience.' " *Studies in English Literature* 5 (1965): 1–21.

Newton, J. M. "What Do We Know about Andrew Marvell?" *The Cambridge Quarterly* 6 (1972–73): 125–43.

Osmond, Rosalie. "Body and Soul Dialogues in the Seventeenth Century." *English Literary Renaissance* 4 (1974): 364–403.

Patterson, Annabel. "*Bermudas* and *The Coronet*: Marvell's Protestant Poetics." *ELH* 44 (1977): 478–99.

———. *Marvell and the Civic Crown.* Princeton: Princeton University Press, 1978.

Patrides, C. A. *Approaches to Marvell: The York Tercentenary Lectures.* London: Routledge & Kegan Paul, 1978.

Poggioli, Renato. "The Pastoral of the Self." *Daedalus* 88 (1959): 686–99.

Polito, Robert. "His Affectless Gaze: Some Failures of Style in Marvell's Poetry." *Imagine* 1, no. 2 (1984): 162–85.

Press, John. *Andrew Marvell*. London: Longmans, 1958.

Rajan, Balachandra. "Andrew Marvell: The Aesthetics of Inconclusiveness." In *The Form of the Unfinished: English Poetics from Spenser to Pound*. Princeton: Princeton University Press, 1985.

Reedy, Gerard. "'An Horation Ode' and 'Tom May's Death.'" *Studies in English Literature* 20 (1980): 137–51.

Richards, Judith. "Literary Criticism and the Historian: Towards Reconstructing Marvell's Meaning in 'An Horatian Ode.'" *Literature and History* 7 (1981): 25–47.

Røstvig, Maren-Sophie. *The Happy Man: Studies in the Metamorphoses of a Classical Ideal*. 2 vols. Oxford: Basil Blackwell, 1954–58.

Roth, Frederic H. "Marvell's 'Upon Appleton House': A Study in Perspective." *Texas Studies in Literature and Language* 14 (1972): 269–81.

Sackville-West, Victoria. *Andrew Marvell*. London: Faber & Faber, 1929.

Scoular, Kitty. *Natural Magic*. Oxford: Clarendon Press, 1965.

Spinrad, Phoebe S. "Death, Loss, and Marvell's Nymph." *PMLA* 97 (1982): 50–59.

————. "Marvell's Gallery of Distorted Mirrors." *Interpretations* 15, no. 1 (Fall 1983): 1–12.

Spitzer, Leo. "Marvell's 'The Nymph Complaining for the Death of Her Faun': Sources versus Meaning." *Modern Language Quarterly* 19 (1958): 231–43.

Swan, Jim. "'Betwixt Two Labyrinths': Andrew Marvell's Rational Amphibian." *Texas Studies in Literature and Language* 17 (1975–76): 551–72.

Thomason, T. Katharine. "Marvell, His Bee-Like Cell: The Pastoral Hexagon of 'Upon Appleton House.'" *Genre* 16 (1983): 39–56.

————. "Marvell's Complaint against His Nymph." *Studies in English Literature* 18 (1978): 95–105.

————. "The Stoic Ground of Marvell's 'Garden.'" *Texas Studies in Literature and Language* 24 (1982): 222–41.

Toliver, Harold. "The Critical Reprocessing of Andrew Marvell." *ELH* 47 (1980): 180–203.

————. *Marvell's Ironic Vision*. New Haven: Yale University Press, 1965.

Wallace, John M. *Destiny His Choice: The Loyalism of Andrew Marvell*. Cambridge: Cambridge University Press, 1968.

Wallerstein, Ruth C. *Studies in Seventeenth-Century Poetic*. Madison: University of Wisconsin Press, 1950.

Warnke, Frank J. "Play and Metamorphosis in Marvell's Poetry." *Studies in English Literature* 5 (1965): 23–30.

Wilcher, Robert. *Andrew Marvell*. Cambridge: Cambridge University Press, 1985.

Wilding, Michael. "Marvell's 'An Horatian Ode upon Cromwell's Return from Ireland,' the Levellers, and the Junta." *The Modern Language Review* 82 (1987): 1–14.

————, ed. *Marvell: Modern Judgements*. London: Macmillan, 1969.

Wilson, A. J. N. "Andrew Marvell's 'The First Anniversary of the Government under Oliver Cromwell': The Poem and Its Frame of Reference." *The Modern Language Review* 69 (1974): 254–73.

Zwicker, Steven N. "Models of Governance in Marvell's 'The First Anniversary.'" *Criticism* 16 (1974): 1–12.

Acknowledgments

"Marvell's Commonwealth and the Empire of the Ear" by John Hollander from *The Untuning of the Sky* by John Hollander, © 1961 by John Hollander. Reprinted by permission.

" 'If these the Times, then this must be the Man' " by Ruth Nevo from *The Dial of Virtue: A Study of Poems on Affairs of State in the Seventeenth Century* by Ruth Nevo, © 1963 by Princeton University Press. Reprinted by permission of Princeton University Press.

" 'The Nymph Complaining for the Death of Her Faun' " by Geoffrey H. Hartman from *Essays in Criticism* 18, no. 2 (April 1968), © 1968 by Geoffrey H. Hartman. Reprinted by permission.

"Andrew Marvell: The Mind's Happiness" by Louis L. Martz from *The Wit of Love* by Louis L. Martz, © 1969 by the University of Notre Dame Press. Reprinted by permission.

"Knowledge and the World of Change: Marvell's 'The Garden' " (originally entitled "Knowledge and the World of Change") by Donald M. Friedman from *Marvell's Pastoral Art* by Donald M. Friedman, © 1980 by Donald M. Friedman. Reprinted by permission of Routledge & Kegan Paul Ltd.

"Visual Traditions behind 'Upon Appleton House' " (originally entitled "Visual Traditions") by Rosalie Colie from *"My Ecchoing Song": Andrew Marvell's Poetry of Criticism* by Rosalie Colie, © 1970 by Princeton University Press. Reprinted by permission of Princeton University Press.

"Marvell and the Fictions of Pastoral" by David Kalstone from *English Literary Renaissance* 4, no. 1 (Winter 1974), © 1974 by *English Literary Renaissance*. Reprinted by permission.

"The Scope of Imagination in 'Upon Appleton House' " by Isabel G. MacCaffrey from *Tercentenary Essays in Honor of Andrew Marvell*, edited by Kenneth Friedenreich, © 1977 by Kenneth Friedenreich. Reprinted by permission.

"A House Divided: Marvell's 'Last Instructions' and Dryden" (originally entitled "A House Divided: Marvell's 'Last Instructions' and Dryden's *Absalom and Achitophel*") by Michael Seidel from *Satiric Inheritance: Rabelais to Sterne* by Michael Seidel, © 1979 by Princeton University Press. Reprinted by permission of Princeton University Press.

"Andrew Marvell: Puritan Austerity with Classical Grace" by Cleanth Brooks from *Poetic Traditions of the English Renaissance,* edited by Maynard Mack and George deForest Lord © 1982 by Yale University. Reprinted by permission of Yale University Press.

" 'Pardon Me, Mighty Poet': Versions of the Bard in Marvell's 'On Mr. Milton's *Paradise Lost*' " by Kenneth Gross from *Milton Studies* 16 (1982), © 1982 by the University of Pittsburgh Press. Reprinted by permission of the publisher, the University of Pittsburgh Press.

"The Search for Form in Marvell's Satires: *The Rehearsal Transpros'd*" (originally entitled "Marvell's Satires: The Search for Form") by Warren Chernaik from *The Poet's Time: Politics and Religion in the Work of Andrew Marvell* by Warren L. Chernaik, © 1983 by Cambridge University Press. Reprinted by permission of Cambridge University Press.

Andrew Marvell and the Problem of Mediation" (originally entitled "Pastoralism, Puritanism, Imperialism, Scientism: Andrew Marvell and the Problem of Mediation") by Michael McKeon from *The Yearbook of English Studies* 13 (1983), © 1983 by the Modern Humanities Research Association. Reprinted by permission.

Index

237